Europe

Organizing
EUROPE

The institutions of integration

Second Edition

Clive Archer

Department of Politics and International
Relations, University of Aberdeen, Aberdeen, UK

Edward Arnold
A member of the Hodder Headline Group
LONDON   NEW YORK   MELBOURNE   AUCKLAND

© 1994 Clive Archer

First published in Great Britain 1990 as
Organizing Western Europe
Second edition 1994

Distributed in the USA by Routledge, Chapman and Hall, Inc.
29 West 35th Street, New York, NY 10001

British Library Cataloguing in Publication Data
Archer, Clive
  Organizing Europe: Institutions of Integration. — 2Rev.ed
  I. Title
  068.4

  ISBN 0-340-59039-4

Typeset in 10/11 pt Mallard by Colset Private Limited.
Printed and bound in Great Britain for Edward Arnold, a
division of Hodder Headline PLC, Mill Road, Dunton
Green, Sevenoaks, Kent TN13 2YA by Biddles Ltd
Guildford & King's Lynn.

Contents

Foreword

This book describes and analyses the major European international organizations established since the Second World War. In dealing with particular inter-state organizations in Europe, the text offers reasons for their establishment, outlines the major points in their founding treaties or documents, traces the main developments during their existence – their achievements and their failures – and evaluates their contributions to member states and the political system of Europe. The references at the end of each chapter also give the student guidance for further reading.

Chapter 1 gives a general appreciation of international organizations. It examines their membership, their aims and activities and their structure. It also looks at the roles and functions they can fulfil in the international political system. Chapter 2 provides a historical background to the creation and existence of international organizations in Europe. It traces the growth of these institutions in response to the economic and political needs of the member states. Chapters 3 to 12 cover particular international organizations that draw their membership – or most of it – from Europe. More space is devoted to the European Communities and the North Atlantic Treaty Organization because of their importance in the development of the economic and security policies of European countries. The OEEC (later OECD) and the Council of Europe are covered as early examples of organizations in Europe joined by many of the area's governments. The European Coal and Steel Community has importance as the precursor to the European Economic Community, as well as in its own right. Both the Nordic Council and the European Free Trade Association provide alternative models to that of the Communities. The Western European Union is included because of its historical importance and its potential for providing a forum for policy discussions on European security. The organizations established between East European

states, both before and after the collapse of communist governments there are covered, as is the pan-European Conference on
Security and Cooperation in Europe. A note should be appended
here about the Maastricht Treaty on European Union. At the time
of going to press there was still a legal challenge in the German
courts about the Treaty's ratification. However, I have assumed
that it will be ratified. It should be added that disruption of the
Exchange Rate Mechanism during the summer of 1993 made the
sections in the Treaty on Economic and Monetary Union even more
problematic than before.

In preparing this book I received particular assistance from
David Scrivener, for which I am very thankful. I am also indebted
to the following for their help: David Greenwood, David Hobbs,
Paul Laurent, Alasdair McLean, William Paterson, John Main,
Trevor Salmon and Lars Wedin. I am grateful to Lynn Gammie for
secretarial assistance with earlier drafts of the script. Finally,
any mistakes are my own and I would be beholden to readers who
point them out.

Clive Archer
September 1993

List of Abbreviations

ACP	African, Caribbean and Pacific states (EC)
ASEAN	Association of South East Asian Nations
Benelux	Belgium, Netherlands, Luxembourg (customs union)
BIS	Bank for International Settlement
BRITE	Basic Research in Industrial Technologies in Europe (EC)
CAP	Common Agricultural Policy (EC)
CEEC	Committee of European Economic Cooperation
CERM	Coordinated Emergency Response Measures
CET	Common External Tariff (EC)
CFE	Conventional Forces in Europe Treaty
CFP	Common Fisheries Policy (EC)
CFSP	Common Foreign and Security Policy
CINCHAN	Commander-in-Chief Channel (NATO)
CLRAE	Conference of Local and Regional Authorities
COMETT	Community in Education and Training for Technology (EC)
COPA	Committee of Professional Agricultural Organizations (EC)
COREPER	Committee of Permanent Representatives (EC)
CMEA/Comecon	Council for Mutual Economic Assistance
CSBM	Confidence- and Security-Building Measures
CSCE	Conference on Security and Cooperation in Europe
CSFR	Czech Slovak Federal Republic
DAC	Development Assistance Committee (OECD)
DG	Directorates General (EC)
EAEC	European Atomic Energy Community or Euratom (EC)
EAGGF	European Agricultural Guidance and Guarantee Fund or FEOGA (EC)
EBRD	European Bank for Reconstruction and Development
EC	European Communities
ECE	Economic Commission for Europe (UN)
ECHR	European Commission for Human Rights (of the Council of Europe)
ECSC	European Coal and Steel Community (EC)
ECU	European Currency Unit (EC)
EDC	European Defence Community
EDF	European Development Fund
EEA	European Economic Area
EEC	European Economic Community (EC)
EFTA	European Free Trade Association
EIB	European Investment Bank (EC)
EMS	European Monetary System (EC)
EMU	Economic and Monetary Union (EC)

END	European Nuclear Disarmament
EPC	European Political Cooperation or European Political Community
EPU	European Payments Union
ERDF	European Regional Development Fund (EC)
ESA	EFTA Surveillance Authority
ESC	Economic and Social Committee (EC)
ESCB	European System of Central Banks
ESF	European Social Fund (EC)
ESPRIT	European Strategic Programme of Research and Development in Information Technology (EC)
EUA	European Unit of Account (EC)
Euratom	European Atomic Energy Community (EC)
FEOGA	see EAGGF
GATT	General Agreement on Tariffs and Trade (UN)
IBRD	International Bank for Reconstruction and Development
IEA	International Energy Agency
IEP	International Energy Programme
IEPG	Independent European Programme Group
IGC	Intergovernmental Conferences
IGO	Intergovernmental organization
ILO	International Labour Organization (UN)
IMF	International Monetary Fund (UN)
INF	Intermediate-range Nuclear Forces
INGO	International non-governmental organization
IRA	International Ruhr Authority
ITU	International Telecommunications Union (formerly International Telegraph Union) (UN)
JET	Joint European Torus (EC)
MEP	Member of the European Parliament (EC)
MBFR	Mutual and Balanced Force Reductions
MCA	Monetary Compensatory Amounts (EC)
NACC	North Atlantic Cooperation Council (NATO)
NATO	North Atlantic Treaty Organization
NGO	Non-governmental organization
NPG	Nuclear Planning Group (NATO)
OCT	Overseas Countries and Territories (EC)
OECD	Organization for Economic Cooperation and Development
OEEC	Organization for European Economic Cooperation
OPEC	Organization of Petroleum Exporting Countries
QRs	Quantitative Restrictions
RACE	Research and Development in Advanced Communications Technology for Europe (EC)
SACEUR	Supreme Allied Commander Europe (NATO)
SACLANT	Supreme Allied Commander Atlantic (NATO)
SALT	Strategic Arms Limitation Treaty
SDI	Strategic Defense Initiative
SEA	Single European Act (EC)
SHAPE	Supreme Headquarters Allied Powers Europe (NATO)
TACs	Total Allowable Catches
UN	United Nations
UPU	Universal Postal Union (UN)
WEU	Western European Union
WTO	Warsaw Treaty Organization or Warsaw Pact

Europe in 1993

kilometres

0   1000

Europe before 1989

1

Introduction

This book will deal with the main international organizations of Europe.

First, a distinction should be made between international organization generally, international institutions and specific international organizations.

International organizations in Europe tend to be the most concrete form of international institutions (sometimes literally!). Though such an organization need not be physically apparent it will quite often have 'a formal technical and material organization: constitutions, local chapters, physical equipment, machines, emblems, letterhead stationery, a staff, an administrative hierarchy, and so forth' (Duverger, 1972, 68). International organizations are just one of the institutional frameworks (international law and diplomacy are two others) which adds 'stability, durability and cohesiveness' to relationships which otherwise might be 'sporadic, ephemeral and unstable' (Duverger, 1972, 68) in the organization of international activity in Europe. Inis Claude (1964, 4) claims 'International *organization* is a process: international *organizations* are representative aspects of the phase of that process which has been reached at a given time'. A further confusion of terms is sometimes introduced by reference to the 'institutions' of an international organization – its council, secretariat or assembly. This is a much more restricted use than can be seen in Duverger's definition but is one that will recur in this book.

International organizations have risen to prominence first in Europe in the nineteenth century, then more globally during the present century. Their existence therefore has to be placed in the context of the rise of the sovereign state (see Chapter 2), and it is possible that they may fade away should the current state system change substantially.

To sum up: the extension of international organization in Europe

1

has been partly achieved by the use of such international institutions (stable, durable and cohesive frameworks) as trade, diplomacy and international organizations. International organizations are made up of certain institutions, such as a council of ministers and an international secretariat. An international organization can be defined as 'a formal, continuous structure established by agreement between members (governmental and/or non-governmental) from two or more sovereign states with the aim of pursuing the common interest of the membership' (Archer, 1992, 37).

What sort of international organizations are there? Post-war Europe has experienced a wide range which may be classified by their membership, by their aims and activities and by their structure.

In distinguishing between international organizations with different sorts of *membership*, the most important dividing line is between the intergovernmental organizations (IGOs) and the international non-governmental organizations (INGOs). Intergovernmental organizations are those which are created by states' governments and in which governmental representatives play the dominant part. Clearly the Warsaw Treaty Organization, established as a security agreement between the countries of Eastern Europe, would be such an IGO. So would the Council of Europe, the European Free Trade Association and the European Communities (EC), though these four contain institutions with non-governmental representatives on them – some have parliamentary assemblies, some are advised by economic and social councils of experts or interest groups, and some even have independent courts. However all were established by agreements between governments and are in that sense 'intergovernmental'.

According to the United Nations Economic and Social Council 'Every international organization which is not created by means of intergovernmental agreements shall be considered as a non-governmental international organization' (Economic and Social Council, Resolution 288 (X) of 27 February 1950). This group of international organizations includes those between economic and social groupings such as the Committee of Professional Agricultural Organizations of the EC (COPA) and the Norden Association, and those established by political groups such as the European Liberal Democratic and Reformist Group consisting of the Liberal parties of the European Community states. Other groupings may be educational, cultural or recreational. All have in common that they bring together members from two or more European states in an agreement not originally established by governments to create an organization for the benefit of those members.

It should be noted that the line between IGOs and INGOs is not always hard and fast. The Nordic Council, often regarded as an intergovernmental organization, was not originally established by a treaty between the Nordic governments but by a common statute adopted by the Nordic parliaments. Many of the interest-group organizations established within the framework of the European Communities – such as the EC's farmers' organization (COPA) – are clearly non-governmental yet owe their existence to an organization established by the member governments of the EC. There are also certain international organizations which are hybrids containing some governmental representatives and some non-governmental ones and which are not the creation of just intergovernmental agreements – for example, the International Council of Scientific Unions (Judge, 1978, 57).

Another aspect of membership concerns its extent. Almost all of the European countries belong to the universalist IGOs such as the United Nations Organization and its specialized agencies like the World Health Organization and the Food and Agriculture Organization. At the other end of the scale some states belong to limited-member IGOs, for example the Benelux Customs Union with its three members, Belgium, Netherlands and Luxembourg. In between, there are organizations that cover all the continent (the Economic Commission for Europe of the United Nations), those with members from part of the continent together with a few out-side states (the Organization for Economic Cooperation and Development) and IGOs limited to states from one section of Europe – for example the European Communities with its 12 members in 1993.

International organizations in Europe thus span a wide range of membership – governmental, non-governmental, mixed, geographically limited, regional, part of a universal structure. But what *aims and activities* do these organizations support?

One way of answering this question is to examine the founding treaties of the organizations, documents that state the public reasons for their existence. These can range from the general to the specific. Many of the existing European organizations can be classified as 'multi-purpose' insofar as their activities cover a wide range of subjects – economic, social, cultural, political.

Charles Pentland has made the distinction between 'high political organizations ... most directly concerned with the sovereignty and security of their members' and 'low political' organizations which deal with 'the great volume of daily business conducted between states within that political order [the fundamental order of the political system] – concerning economics, social, cultural and technical issues' (1976, 528–9). An examination of European IGOs shows that this difference is no longer so apparent: NATO, an organization dealing with 'high political' questions has a programme covering the challenges to modern society and is certainly concerned with technical issues, whilst the European Communities – primarily an economic organization – concerns itself with the sovereignty of its members and with issues – such as currencies or the continuance of a coal and steel industry – which relate directly to the security of the member states. It should be remembered that organizations that start out with certain aims and activities may accumulate others during their lifetime. This has been the case with the European Communities which has widened its range from its prime aim of forming a common market to include actions in the political and social spheres.

Another method of judging the aims and activities of international organizations is to consider their purpose. Are they aimed at settling disputes among members by decreasing the level of conflict between them; are they intended to encourage cooperation between members that are not in a state of conflict; or are they supposed to produce or reflect confrontation between members and specific non-members?

Most organizations in Western Europe contain elements of conflict resolution and of cooperation as can be seen from their founding documents. A blend of these two elements can be seen in the preamble to the treaty constituting the European Coal and Steel Community (Treaty of Paris, 18 April 1951) in which the six founding governments

> Resolved to substitute for historic rivalries a fusion of their essential interests; to establish, by creating an economic community, the foundation of a broad and independent community among peoples long divided by bloody conflicts; and to lay the basis of institutions capable of giving direction to their future common destiny.

A more confrontational aim for a European international organization can be found in the preamble of the Treaty of Economic, Social and Cultural Collaboration and Collective Self-Defence (the Brussels Treaty of 17 March 1948) which showed the five member governments – those of Belgium, France, Luxembourg, the Netherlands and the United Kingdom – ready 'to take such steps as may be held to be necessary in the event of a renewal by Germany of a policy of aggression' (Peaslee, Part I, 1974, 129).

In any event such an attitude was already outdated by the time the treaty was signed as the main threat to the signatories was by then perceived to be the Soviet Union and not Germany. It just suited the member states to uphold the fiction that they were uniting to confront any revival of German militarism. Even in international treaties words do not always mean what they say.

It should be remembered that the aims and activities of international organizations change over time. For example, the Brussels Pact, mentioned above, was amended in 1954 to include Italy and the Federal Republic of Germany as members and the section of the Preamble cited was altered to read that the members were prepared 'to promote the unity and to encourage the progressive integration of Europe'.

However it is not always possible to ascertain a shift in aims and activities by studying treaty amendation. A study of the changing preoccupations of an organization and of its annual reports, resolutions, declarations and communiques will provide a far better appreciation of the dynamics of the organization in question.

A third method of identifying different types of European international organizations is by examining their *structure*. It is noticeable that over the years the institutional framework of international organizations has become more complex. The Central Commission for the Navigation of the Rhine, established in 1868, has a Central Commission composed of one representative from each member state. The general pattern of post-Second World War organizations was that they should have a Council of Ministers or states' representatives and a secretariat. This was the case for the Organization for European Economic Cooperation which also had an executive committee elected by the Council and which carried on work between Council meetings in accordance with Council instructions. There was also a host of technical committees. The Council of Europe set up in 1948, introduced a novel institution – a gathering of parliamentarians appointed by national parliaments and which formed a Consultative Assembly to complement its Council of Ministers. A similar institution was established by the creation of the Nordic Council in 1953. In this case the council of parliamentarians existed some 18 years before a Council of Ministers was established in 1971. The European Coal and Steel Community (ECSC) also had an Assembly of parliamentarians and made provision for it to be elected by direct universal suffrage by Community citizens. The ECSC produced three other institutional innovations on the European scene. The first was the High Authority the members of which, though appointed by the six ECSC governments, were supposed to 'exercise their functions in complete independence, in the general interest of the Community' (Article 9, Treaty of Paris). All member governments agreed 'to respect this supranational character and to make no effort to influence the members of the High Authority in the execution of their duties' (ibid). Secondly, the Treaty of Paris established a Court with jurisdiction over matters covered by the Treaty. Finally, the High Authority was assisted by a Consultative Committee which was representative, not of governments or parliaments, but of 'producers, workers and consumers and dealers in equal number' (Article 18).

Institutional development in European IGOs has produced a wide range of sophisticated structures. A number of these organizations now have parliamentary assemblies – the Council of Europe, the Nordic Council, the Western European Union, the European Free Trade Association and the European Communities. The last-named is the only organization to have a parliament elected directly by the citizens of the member states. Two organizations have separate judicial bodies – the Council of Europe and the European Communities. Two have advisory bodies consisting of functional representatives – the European Communities and EFTA. Secretariats range from the diffuse double secretariats of the Nordic Council to the more powerful and innovative successor of the ECSC's High Authority in the European Communities – the Commission.

In examining these institutions it is useful to ask the three questions laid down by Paul Reuter (1958, 248):

1 How do the organs balance the interests of one member or group against those of another member or group?
2 How do the institutions reflect the balance of power and influence between the members and the organization itself?
3 How is governmental and non-governmental representation balanced?

Dealing with each of these questions in turn, it can be seen that European organizations again offer a wide range of examples. In answering the first question, it must be admitted that institutions do not always reflect the realities of power and influence. Larger

and more powerful states *may* have greater institutional representation: until 1993 the Federal Republic of Germany, France and
the United Kingdom had 81 members each in the Parliament of the
European Communities whilst little Luxembourg only had six.
Sometimes such arrangements do not work – the elaborate system
of majority voting in the EC's Council of Ministers sometimes has
been placed aside because the national interests of members
demanded that decisions be arrived at unanimously. On other
occasions no effort is made to reflect power and influence in
organizational arrangements. The dominant position of the USA in
NATO does not leap out from the North Atlantic Treaty.

So one important aspect of the institutions of an international
organization is whether they treat all members equally – that is,
whether they are egalitarian – or whether they favour one or
more members by limited membership organs, by weighted voting
or by granting veto rights.

In examining the balance between the power and influence of
an organization's institutions and that of the members, it should
be remembered that the early public international unions such as
the Universal Postal Union (UPU) and the then International
Telegraph Union (ITU) allowed their secretariats (or bureaux) a
good deal of freedom. There was little tension between the permanent organ and the wishes of the member states as the day-to-day
activities were either routine or technical and policy decisions
would be made at the occasional meetings of member states'
representatives. Secretariats were quite often staffed by the civil
servants of one country – Switzerland in the cases of the UPU and
ITU. The League of Nations and International Labour Organization (ILO) created independent secretariats with civil servants
supposedly owing allegiance to the organization rather than to
their home governments. The United Nations Organization took
this independence one step further in Article 99 of the Charter by
adding a political role to its Secretary-General's administrative
and executive duties.

The European Communities has in the Commission an international body with wide responsibilities for initiating and implementing policy. The Commission of the merged Communities (European
Economic Community – EEC – Euratom and European Coal and
Steel Community) has thus had a more difficult task than did the
Commission of the EEC, and neither has had such powers as those
set down in the Treaty of Paris for the High Authority of the European Coal and Steel Community. Since the establishment of the

ECSC in 1951 and the EEC and Euratom in 1957, there has been a constant battle between the Community institutions – the High Authority, the Commission, the Court and the Parliament – and the governments of the member states as to which should be in the driving seat. As Chapter 6 will show, the match has so far been undecided.

Reuter's third question about the institutions of international organizations concerns the balance between governmental and non-governmental representatives. As has been seen, the latter have been prominent in a number of post-war West European organizations, especially in the form of parliamentary assemblies and consultative councils of functional representatives – people from unions, business, banking, agriculture, etc. Of course the purely international non-governmental organizations do not have any governmental representation in their organs and there have been a number of IGOs without a non-governmental presence – for example the Warsaw Treaty Organization. In the European Communities, a whole network of non-governmental organizations flourishes as the emphasis is on interest-group politics. This perhaps should be seen as less in contention with the governmental element (the Council of Ministers and the Committee of Permanent Representatives) but more as a potential ally and adversary for each governmental representative on each discrete issue.

To sum up, the international organizations in Europe are notable for their quantity and variety. Looking at their *type of membership* they embrace both international non-governmental organizations and intergovernmental organizations with a number of hybrids in between. The *extent of membership* ranges from those which cover the other continents as well as Europe, organizations which have a pan-European membership (and include one or two outsiders) through those spanning a half or a third of the continent down to the two- or three-member organizations. *Aims and activities* can be classified as ranging from the general to the specific and can be divided into those seeking to encourage cooperation between members, those lowering the level of conflict and those which may bring confrontation between members and sometimes with certain non-members. However it should be noted that most organizations contain a mix of the first two elements – cooperation and conflict resolution – in their aims and activities.

A study of the *structure* of international organizations may demonstrate whether they are egalitarian in the treatment of the membership, can show a degree of independence from that membership of the institutions of the organization and will also reveal the importance of non-governmental as opposed to governmental representation.

The various elements can be cross-checked against each other: Benelux has only three members and a narrow range of activities while the Council of Europe has extensive aims and membership.

Having established the wide range of international organization in Europe, it is now possible to examine the role and function of these organizations in the European system of international relations. Three major *roles* can be identified: those of instruments, arena and actor.

The most common role attributed to international organizations is that of an *instrument* wielded by its members. IGOs in particular are susceptible to pressure from sovereign state members that may wish to curtail any signs of institutional independence.

This limited view of international organizations has been expressed by Gunnar Myrdal, the former Executive Secretary of the UN's Economic Commission for Europe (ECE):

> [I]n the typical case international organizations are nothing else than instruments for the policies of individual governments, means for the diplomacy of a number of disparate and sovereign national states. When an intergovernmental organization is set up, this implies nothing more than that between states a limited agreement has been reached upon an institutional form for multilateral conduct of state activity in a certain field (1955, 4–5).

The equivalent can be said for most international nongovernmental organizations as they tend to reflect the wishes of the various churches, business groups, political parties or peace associations that form their membership. As a result of being instruments of their members' wishes, international organizations can become the battleground for individual members or groups vying for influence over and control of the organization. In such cases, the secretariat of the organization has to represent what Myrdal called 'the collective aspirations of the member governments'. In a number of organizations – ECE was one – this gives little room for manoeuvre though secretariats may find technical matters delegated to them (as did the secretariat of the ECE's Coal Committee in Myrdal's time) and they may earn respect as go-betweens and diplomats, as was the case with the EFTA secretariat during the years of British membership from 1960 to 1973 (Archer, 1976, 15–16). There is always a danger that an officer of an international organization might find that he or she no longer has the confidence of one or more member states, which may lead to early retirement from office similar to that of Etienne Hirsch who was not reappointed as a Euratom Commissioner in 1962 after a disagreement with President de Gaulle of France.

The decision-making machinery of organizations often demonstrates the requirement that they serve the interests of the membership. In particular the unanimity principle helps to protect those members finding themselves in a minority on any issue: a decision cannot be forced through against their wishes. It has been used in the Nordic Council of Ministers, and in the Council of EFTA on all issues except when there might be a complaint about the breaking of the EFTA treaty rules, in which case the 'accused' country cannot veto proceedings. Other variations are sometimes used. Myrdal claims that in the ECE's technical agencies, non-substantive issues were cleared with the members in advance by the secretariat whilst on substantive motions efforts were 'directed towards reaching a maximum agreement between a maximum number of governments' (1955, 19). Also 'one or several governments should not hinder two or more other governments from using the organization to reach a settlement among themselves'. This has often been the case in the Nordic Council of Ministers and in the Organization for Economic Cooperation and Development (OECD) where limited agreements bind those states voting for them but not members which abstain. While an international organization may act as an instrument for the policy of its membership, this does not mean that each and every decision has to serve the interests of all its members. Some members may allow action not in their favour to be taken as long as they consider the activities of the organization will benefit them in the long run.

A second role that European organizations have often fulfilled is that of providing an *arena* for the membership. In this case the organization acts as a platform from which members can espouse views and a forum in which they can confront each other. The most noticeable use of an IGO as an arena is that of the UNO where blocs clash, statesmen parade, diplomats display and countries are condemned. The European organizations – both governmental and non-governmental – also have such features. President de Gaulle showed a willingness to allow his ministers to use Council meetings of the European Economic Community to indicate French displeasure with the way the Community was progressing in the mid-1960s. Later on, the former Greek socialist government of Mr Papandreou was prepared to use both the European Communities and NATO Council meetings to signal its differences with other West European states on a number of issues including the siting of US nuclear missiles in Europe, the creation of nuclear-weapon free zones, sanctions against the Soviet Union over the issue of martial law in Poland and the condemnation of the shooting down in August 1983 of a Korean civil airliner by the Soviet airforce.

Apart from these more dramatic examples, the international organizations of Europe provide a meeting-place where members can discuss matters of common interest. Instead of irregular meetings between governments or interest groups from different countries called on an *ad hoc* basis, international organizations offer a regular basis for consultations with predetermined rules for the conduct of discussions. These European organizations have given a certain continuity and reliability to the conduct of social, economic and political life in the western part of the continent.

The third role played by some European organizations is that of independent *actor*. In such cases the organization, rather than being the tool of its membership or just a forum for discussion, participates in events as a separate actor. In Inis Claude's words: '[a]n international organization is most clearly an actor when it is most distinctly an "it", an entity distinguishable from its member states' (1971, 13).

The most striking case in Western Europe of an international organization acting as an 'it' in international affairs is that of the European Communities (EC). The EC's institutions make decisions separate from the collective decisions of the representatives of the member states, they can act contrary to the wishes of member states and can affect the actions of these states. Indeed the Commission of the EC is bound by Article 157 of the Treaty of Rome to act 'in the general interest of the Community', its members 'shall neither seek nor take instructions from any Government or from any other body', are appointed on the grounds of 'their general competence' and are people 'whose independence can be fully relied upon'. The task and powers of the Commission led some to visualize this body as the dynamic 'motor' of integration, whilst the wary considered it to be, in de Gaulle's words, 'an aeropagus of technocrats without a country and responsible to no-one' (Pentland, 1973).

The Court of Justice of the EC is another one of its institutions which acts separately from individual member-state interests. Any natural or legal person – not just the member governments – can have recourse in this Court against a decision of direct or individual concern to that person or body. Furthermore the Court can supervise the legality of measures taken by the Council and Commission (Article 173 EEC) and the member states are bound to take the measures required for the enforcement of Court judgements (Article 171 EEC).

Since it was directly elected in 1979, the European Parliament has shown a strong tendency to act as a separate political body divorced from national interests as expressed by the member governments. Parliamentarians sit in Community-wide political parties rather than in national delegations and, particularly over budgetary issues, the Parliament has shown its willingness to contradict the wishes of the member governments of the EC.

These institutions give substance to the claim that the European Communities act as an independent international actor, though the crucial role of the member governments should not be underestimated: it is still the key to the successful functioning of the EC.

Neither should the role of other international organizations as independent actors be forgotten. The wide range of economic interest-groups, INGOs, especially those that work within the framework of the EC, demonstrates how national functional groups can gain a new strength by uniting on a European or EC-wide basis. IGOs such as the Nordic Council, EFTA or Western European Union also make a contribution as organizations separate from the wills of their membership though – in the last two – this tends to be moderated by the absence of powerful non-governmental elements in their structures.

The three roles that can be adopted by European organizations – those of instrument, arena and actor – are not mutually exclusive and many international organizations take on two, or even all three. The European Communities have been used by member governments as instruments for the achievement of policy ends – for example, the support of French farmers has been championed by successive French governments. EC meetings have also been utilized as forums for member states as mentioned on p. 11, and the separate identity of the EC institutions as independent actors has been outlined above.

The extent to which each role can be adopted may depend on the constitution of the organization (whether institutions are allowed the possibility of independent action) and the balance of membership. An IGO such as EFTA after 1973 is more likely to be used as a genuine forum because the members are of about the same weight, whereas the North Atlantic Treaty Organization is dominated by the USA.

The *functions* undertaken by international organizations are manifold. The existence of both IGOs and INGOs in Europe clearly affects the functioning of international relations throughout the continent, and between parts of Europe and the rest of the world.

International organizations perform the function of *articulating and aggregating* their members' interests. The representatives of the various farming interests in the European Communities could no doubt make their own needs known to the Commission of the EC when it is considering agricultural policy, but the cacophony of different demands might lead to confusion in the Commission and possibly to individual points not being responded to satisfactorily. The existence of the EC farming organization, COPA, allows them to express their views in a comprehensible and comprehensive fashion. Some farmers may have to hold back on certain demands to allow more important issues to be given priority but in representing a number of disparate entities, COPA has to aggregate requirements, a process that may mean advancing certain requests to the detriment of others. The task of articulating and aggregating interests is one of the most widespread functions of international organizations in Europe. It should be noted that whilst articulation of needs through an organization may be more effective than individual effort, the process of aggregation by that organization could lead to the individual member sacrificing some of its interests.

Three associated areas where international organizations have contributed considerably to the working of international relations in Europe are those of normative activities, socialization and recruitment to the system.

Both IGOs and INGOs are involved in the establishment of *norms* – of values – in the politics of Europe. Some do this by setting standards for the behaviour of governments in relation to their citizens whilst other institutions also deal with the establishment of norms of behaviour between governments. Both activities were undertaken by the Conference on Security and Cooperation in Europe which has sought to institutionalize these norms of behaviour in a series of documents and in an increasingly complex organizational structure.

Agreement on rules of behaviour for international intercourse is not always easy and the means of enforcement are often lacking. Given that consent is better than subjection, one way of achieving acceptance for certain values and modes of behaviour is by *socialization*. By exerting group pressure and by teaching that certain creeds or activities are more desirable than others, organizations can influence the beliefs and behaviour of members.

That IGOs can only be established between sovereign states has provided encouragement to non-self-governing territories to obtain such a status. In a European context this function of IGOs helping *recruitment* into the international political system may not seem so relevant. The cases of Cyprus and Malta – which became independent in 1960 and 1964 respectively – can perhaps be cited as exceptions. It should also be noted that the process of bringing the Federal Republic of Germany to statehood was helped by the presence of international organizations such as the Council of Europe, the ECSC and the Western European Union. With the break-up of states in Central and East Europe after 1989, this recruitment function received a new impetus.

European INGOs have played their full part in the recruitment of new participants to the international systems. They have gathered together groups across frontiers and have created a web of contacts which has underpinned social, economic and political activity in Europe. Perhaps the strongest network is among the Nordic countries where the common culture and life-style provided fertile ground for INGOs.

Since the Second World War an increasing number of European organizations have taken on the functions of rule-making, rule-application and rule-adjudication. These are normally performed by state governments with their legislature, executive and judiciary undertaking the tasks.

At a national level, *rule-making* bodies subsidiary to the central government, such as local or regional bodies, the civil service and certain private associations, play an important role. In the absence of a world government at an international level, the source of rules for inter-European activities is more diverse. However, the European Communities provides a sophisticated system of rule-making with Community laws being created which member states and their citizens alike are obliged to observe.

The European Communities is also active in *rule-application*. Normally this is carried out at the international level by sovereign states – a country's coastguard or navy may enforce international anti-pollution regulations off its coasts, for example. However it is part of the task of the Commission of the European Communities to ensure that EC measures are carried out in member countries and, as mentioned, law-breakers could, ultimately, be taken to the EC's Court. It must be recognized that much Community law is still applied by national agencies and governments and it is only when these are at cross-purposes with the EC that the Commission has to enter the fray.

At national level the judiciary – courts, tribunals, panels, etc. – normally carries out the process of *rule-adjudication*. Europe lacks such a structure for all the continent but it does have a number of judicial and semi-judicial institutions such as the Court of the European Communities and the Court of the European Convention on Human Rights (the Council of Europe's Court).

European organizations carry out some other practical functions such as providing *information* and undertaking certain *operations*. Both the IGOs and INGOs provide a wealth of information whether it is the statistics of the ECE, the economic studies of the OECD, or the promotional material of the European Movement. Examples of operational activities are the peace-monitoring provided by the EC in former-Yugoslavia and the economic assistance provided to the Baltic states through the Nordic Investment Bank.

The roles and functions of international organizations in Europe are many and varied. They may not be active all the time across the whole continent. But throughout Europe there is evidence of their activities. Air transport will be dependent on International Civil Aviation Organization (ICAO) agreements. Farmers may be receiving money from the EC's Common Agricultural Policy for their vineyards. Factories may be having their smoke emissions studied in a Council of Europe survey. Citizens may be annoyed by the sight and sound of a NATO military exercise. Amnesty International may be investigating the ill-treatment of prisoners. A mayor may be hosting a delegation from the International Union of Local Authorities and so on. Europe without its international organizations would be a lot less complicated – but only in the sense that barren land is less complicated than a cultivated field.

This book is primarily about intergovernmental organizations in Europe, the rise of which will be covered in the next chapter. As has been remarked, not all the institutionalization of international relations has been in the form of international organizations. Other books deal with diplomatic relations in Europe (Taylor, 1963; Joll, 1976; Watson, 1982) and with economic and trade relations (Cipolla, 1976, a, b, c and d Lieberman, 1977; Milward, 1984 and 1992; El Agraa, 1982; Williams, 1987; McDonald and Dearden, 1992), all of which are important international institutions. Some of the institutions that will be covered in this book – for example, European Political Cooperation – are less formalized than international organizations, though an advance on bilateral diplomacy. It is of crucial importance to cover these developments especially as a series of conferences can easily be transformed into a formal IGO. One transnational – that is, across frontiers – set of actors that will not be covered is that of the multinational corporations. They are important in Europe and some are more powerful in their own areas than IGOs or even certain sovereign states. Again their influence is dealt with elsewhere (Tugendhat, 1973; Barnet and Muller, 1975; Vernon, 1977; Taylor and Thrift, 1986) and their profit-making nature distinguishes them from international non-governmental organizations.

Much of this book, from Chapter 2 to Chapter 12 inclusive, deals with the major European intergovernmental organizations. Each of the chapters dealing with particular IGOs will answer four questions about them:

1 By which governments were they established and for what reason?
2 What are the important institutional aspects and how do these reflect the nature of the organization?
3 What have been the major achievements of the organization since its establishment and to what extent has it lived up to expectations?
4 In what manner has the organization contributed to the functioning of the European political system?

By providing answers to these questions it is hoped that *Organizing Europe* will inform the student not only about European organizations but also about the institutionalization of international relations in Europe.

References

Archer, C. 1976: Britain and Scandinavia: their relations within EFTA, 1960–1968. *Cooperation and Conflict*, XI, 1–23.
—— 1992: *International Organizations*. London: Routledge.
Barnet, R.J. and Muller, R.E. 1975: *Global Reach: the Power of the Multilateral Corporations*. London: Cape.
Cipolla, C.M. (ed.) 1976a: *The Fontana Economic History of Europe. The Twentieth Century: Part One*. Glasgow: Collins.
—— 1976b: *The Fontana Economic History of Europe. The Twentieth Century: Part Two*. Glasgow: Collins.
—— 1976c: *The Fontana Economic History of Europe. Contemporary Economics: Part One*. Glasgow: Collins.
—— 1976d: *The Fontana Economic History of Europe. Contemporary Economics: Part Two*. Glasgow: Collins.

Claude, I.L. 1964: *Swords into Plowshares*, 3rd edn. London: University of London Press.

—— 1971: *Swords into Plowshares*, 4th edn. New York: Random House.

Duverger, M. 1972: *The Study of Politics*. London: Nelson.

El Agraa, A. (ed.) 1982: *International Economic Integration*. London: Macmillan.

Joll, J. 1976: *Europe since 1870. An International History*. Harmondsworth: Penguin.

Judge, A.J.N. 1978: International institutions: diversity, borderline cases, functional substitutes and possible alternatives. In Taylor, P. and Groom, A.J.R. (eds), *International Organization: A Conceptual Approach* (London: Frances Pinter), 28–83.

Lieberman, S. 1977: *The Growth of European Mixed Economies 1945–1970*. New York: John Wiley & Sons.

McDonald, F. and Dearden, S. 1992: *European Economic Integration*. London and New York: Longman.

Milward, A.S. 1984: *The Reconstruction of Western Europe 1945–51*. London: Methuen.

—— 1992: *European Rescue of the Nation State*. London: Routledge.

Myrdal, G. 1955: Realities and illusions in regard to intergovernmental organizations. In *Hobhouse Memorial Lecture 1955* (London: OUP), 3–28.

Peaslee, A.J. 1974: *International Governmental Organizations – Constitutional Documents Part I*, 3rd edn. The Hague: Martinus Nijhoff.

Pentland, C. 1973: *International Theory and European Integration*. London: Faber.

—— 1976: International organizations. In Rosenau, J.N., Thompson, K.W. and Boyd, G. (eds), *World Politics – An Introduction*. New York: The Free Press, 624–59.

Reuter, P. 1958: *International Institutions*. London: George Allen & Unwin.

Taylor, A.J.P. 1963: *The Origins of the Second World War*. Harmondsworth: Penguin.

Taylor, M. and Thrift, N. 1986: *Multinationals and the Restructuring of the World Economy*. London: Croom Helm.

Tugendhat, C. 1973: *The Multinationals*. Hardmondsworth: Penguin.

Vernon, R. 1977: *Storm over the Multinationals: The Real Issues*. London: Macmillan.

Watson, A. 1982: *Diplomacy – the Dialogue between States*. London: Eyre Methuen.

Williams, A. 1987: *The Western European Economy. A Geography of Post War Development*. London: Hutchinson.

2

A Brief History

Since 1945 a degree of political and economic order has been created out of the unpromising chaos left by the ravages of the Second World War. The rapid re-establishment of exiled governments and outside assistance – especially from the United States – were important factors in preventing the total collapse of the western part of Europe after 1945, and it is perhaps surprising how quickly the economies of the region returned to their former strength (Milward, 1984, Chapter 1). All this laid the ground for a longer-term process: the organization of that half of Europe into a prosperous, relatively peaceful, politico-economic entity covering some 20 sovereign states. Since 1989 efforts have been made to spread the web of these organizations across East and Central Europe and to institute more regional gatherings of states. The international organizations described in this book have formed the main institutional framework for Europe since 1945 and have underpinned the economic, political and military security of many of its countries. Each organization was created for specific reasons and was given the institutions seen appropriate for its tasks. The achievements of each have been varied, and have to be seen against their original aims and expectations; but the overall effect – especially in Western Europe – of the existence of such a wide range of institutions as the OECD, the European Communities, NATO, the Nordic Council, EFTA, the Western European Union and the Council of Europe was the creation of 'Western Europe', which was an adversary of – but also a magnet for – Eastern Europe. It was the existence of the two halves of Europe that typified the politics and economics of the continent for some 40 years. After 1989, the hope was that Europe would be 'whole and free'.

Pre-1945, Western Europe was a geographical expression covering France, the Low Countries (Belgium, Netherlands and

Luxembourg) and the western part of Germany. The United Kingdom was content to stand aloof from 'the Continent'; Iberia, Italy and Greece were regarded as Southern Europe; the Balkans formed another geographical grouping, as did Central Europe and Northern Europe. Eastern Europe covered the European part of the Soviet Union, the Baltic states, Poland, Romania and Bulgaria. Some of these geographical areas overlapped. Denmark could be seen as part of Western Europe and of the Northern region; Romania and Bulgaria had Balkan faces as well as East European aspects.

From 1945 to 1989 Europe was divided politically and economically into Western Europe and East Europe, with only a few states straddling the line in between. States with parliamentary democracies and a mixed economy have faced those with Communist-dominated, state-run economies across what became known as the Iron Curtain. The international organizations of Europe have contributed to and reflected this reality which was crystalized in the 1945 and 1949 period.

Since 1989 the barriers between East and West Europe, created by the Cold War, have fallen. Attempts have been made to cover the fault-line created by some 40 years of history – and, indeed, by deeper social, economic and religious divisions. It cannot be said that Europe is whole: there is still a tension between the factors of integration – including the organizations described in this book – and the forces of division ranging from regional particularism to ethnic differences, racism and intolerance. There is another tension between integration that offers the chance of the growth of democracy, a lessening of economic inequality, and the rights for minorities, and that which accentuates the social and economic divides in Europe and offers little effective freedom and democracy. The outcome of these battles is yet to be decided.

From Victory to Division

The meeting of the leaders of the victorious powers at the end of the war at Yalta and Potsdam sealed the fate of Europe. A devastated continent found itself occupied by liberating armies – mainly those of Britain and the United States in the West and Soviet Union in the East – and it was agreed that, with a few adjustments, these powers (plus France) would control defeated Germany and Austria and would maintain troops in the zones they had liberated, thereby giving them *droit de regard* over the governments of those areas.

The general pattern of the reconstructed administrations across Europe in 1945 was one of coalition governments that included most of the non-collaborationist parties, from the Communists and Socialists on the left to the Christian Democrats and Conservatives on the right of the political spectrum. Germany and Austria remained occupied and without their own national governments. Cooperation across frontiers was channelled in the first instance through the occupying armies or through the United Nations Relief and Rehabilitation Agency (UNRRA) which had spread its influence across Europe in the wake of these forces.

The origins of the Cold War have been traced back to nineteenth-century rivalry between America and Russia, to the Russian Revolution of 1917 and the subsequent intervention by Western troops, to wartime divisions between the Allies and to the antipathy of Communism and Capitalism. Manifestations of mistrust between the Soviet Union and the Western Powers began to show themselves fairly early in the post-war period and often involved Western concern about Soviet treatment of the East European peoples and their non-Communist representatives. As the United States and British armies demobilized, fear was expressed about the supposed continuation of the Red Army's presence – in strength – in Eastern Europe and the social unrest in Western Europe which, it was felt, was partly fomented by Soviet or Communist agents.

By 1947 it was clear to Britain, France and the United States that the Soviet Union was imposing its one-party Communist system on Eastern Europe and that cooperation over the running of Germany was breaking down. Britain and France had signed the Treaty of Dunkirk which, while overtly directed towards revived German aggression, could equally well be seen as the first stirrings of common action against a more immediate perceived threat – that of the Soviet Union.

A crucial turning point in the division of Europe into two blocs came in early 1948. Events moved quickly in February and March. Britain and France were joined by the three Benelux states (Belgium, Netherlands, Luxembourg) in the Brussels Treaty which bound the five countries together in common protection against an aggressor. That the feared power was the Soviet Union was in little doubt after a Soviet-inspired Communist coup ended democratic government in Czechoslovakia. The Soviet Union approached Finland to sign a treaty similar to the ones imposed on the East European satellite countries of Poland, Hungary, Bulgaria and Romania – although the Finns resisted such a one-sided agreement and also put down a Communist Party effort to take over power. The Norwegian and Danish governments feared they were on Stalin's list and mobilized their reserves at Easter 1948. Fear stalked Western Europe – fear of an end to democratic government and fear of war.

With the Communist takeover of Czechoslovakia, the emergence of a divided Europe was almost complete. After the three Western occupying powers of Germany – the United States, the United Kingdom and France – had introduced a common currency in their zones and the Soviet Union had imposed a Communist leadership on East Germany, the division was near complete. In an effort to isolate the Western-run island of West Berlin in the Soviet-dominated zone, Stalin imposed a blockade of Western land links to the city in June 1948. This helped to unite the Western powers in their resolve to resist Soviet action in Europe: they organized an airlift to West Berlin and speeded up negotiations for a wider collective defence organization that would include the United States and Canada.

The United States had indicated its willingness to become involved in the future of Europe. Despite massive demobilization after the end of the war, the US had troops occupying Germany and Austria and was heavily involved in the humanitarian and rehabilitation effort in Western Europe. In March 1947 President Truman enunciated his doctrine promising assistance to free people wishing to preserve themselves against tyranny. This had been mainly a response to the situation in Greece where the pro-Western government was fighting a fierce civil war against Communist-supported guerillas. The United Kingdom, which had been giving support to the Greek government, announced that, for economic reasons, it could no longer continue its assistance. The United States seemed willing to fill the void left by Britain (Dilks, 1985, 44; Gaddis, 1985, 68). Furthermore, Secretary of State George Marshall announced a massive aid programme in June 1947 to help rebuild Europe. Although the Marshall Plan was ostensibly aimed at all of Europe, the Soviet Union, fearing a spread of US influence to Eastern Europe, soon withdrew from discussions and ordered the Communist governments of Eastern Europe to do the same.

As a result of the Truman Doctrine and the Marshall Plan – and

of the responsiveness of West European governments – two important institutions were established in Western Europe.

The events of Easter 1948 and the Berlin Blockade had demonstrated to its governments the vulnerability of Western Europe.
They considered it essential to tie the United States to the defence
of Europe and the Truman Administration was willing to give suc-
cour to the democracies of Western Europe. Throughout 1948 and
early 1949, the USA, Canada and key West European governments
negotiated the form of this assistance in the Washington
Exploratory Talks. These led to the signing of the North Atlantic
Treaty which not only gave a guarantee of unspecified action
should a Treaty member be attacked in the North Atlantic area,
but was also associated with an American armament and materiel
programme for the West European signatories. At that stage, the
organizational manifestation of the Treaty was modest; there was
neither a great deal of common defence planning nor any promise
of US troops in Europe on a permanent basis.

It was the hope of the US Administration that the West Europeans would be able to manage their own defence after a few
years and that, meanwhile, arms and the American guarantee
would suffice (Wells, 1985, 181–2). In order to prevent the internal collapse of the West European governments, Marshall Aid
was provided. To encourage collaboration between governments
of Western Europe and to prevent the impression that the US was
imposing its will on the Europeans, a Committee of European
Economic Cooperation was established to plan the implementation
of Marshall Aid. This soon became a permanent organization –
the Organization for European Economic Cooperation (OEEC) –
with West European states as members and with the United States
and Canada as associates.

A political aspect was added to the military and economic
institutionalization of the division of Europe in 1948. Those countries that espoused democratic parliamentary ideals established
the Council of Europe, thereby providing a touchstone by which
European governments could be measured. As well as its intergovernmental aspect, the Council brought together parliamentarians, an innovation that helped provide a positive aspect to
Western Europe's identity.

By 1950 the political and economic division of Europe was complete and was institutionalized. No peace treaty was signed with
Germany which, divided, lay at the centre of the new East–West
schism. The Economic Commission for Europe, a United Nations

body established in the wake of the end of the war, lay moribund. Eastern Europe had little choice but to place its future in the hands of Moscow. Western Europe sought the road to peace and prosperity through cooperation with North America and with the North Atlantic Treaty and the OEEC as the vehicles. Its commitment to democracy was demonstrated by the establishment of the Council of Europe.

The Birth of the Community

The establishment of the OEEC and the Council of Europe and the signing of the North Atlantic Treaty may have given many of the states of Western Europe greater confidence in their future but major problems awaited resolution. Two unresolved questions were those of Franco-German relations and of Western Europe's contribution to its own defence.

In the years following the end of the war, French governments had resisted British and American efforts to rehabilitate Germany. France was afraid that the resources of a revived Germany could again – as in 1870, 1914 and 1939 – be turned against France. France had taken control of the Saarland and wanted to prevent Germany from recovering the Ruhr, thereby depriving any new German state of its industrial heartland and thus its ability to produce a war capacity (Frémaux and Martel, 1985, 92). The United Kingdom and the United States wished to return Germany to the comity of nations. They saw this as being the best guarantee of good behaviour and, furthermore, did not want an economic deadweight on their hands. They led the way in creating a single currency for West Germany and in providing it with a democratic government. Together with France they established the International Ruhr Authority to manage the resources of that area. However, unlike France, the United Kingdom and the United States were unable to resist the logic of the newly founded West German government that it was unfair to treat part of their industry – that in the Ruhr – as common property but not that in France or Belgium or Luxembourg. After all, the new West German government could not be held responsible for Hitler's war.

In early 1950, in response to ideas coming from American and German circles, the French government started to rethink its hard line on Germany. In this, it was helped by the work of Jean Monnet who had been the dominant figure in the post-war French economic planning process. He had seen that French economic revival could only take place in the context of a wider West European recovery and that this needed full-hearted West German participation. To make sure that this would not present the Germans with the opportunity to revive their military potential, he proposed the integration of the German industries then crucial to military strength – coal and steel – with those of France, Italy and the three Benelux countries. This functional approach to the problem of Franco-German relations offered the administrative ties between key industries as a means not only to create prosperity but also to build peace. In the eyes of the supporters of a federal Europe the plan for a Coal and Steel Community – adopted as the Schuman Plan by the French government in May 1950 – was also seen as a first step toward uniting Western Europe politically (Haas, 1968, 19–29).

However, while the Coal and Steel Community was soon put into place, the application of the Community method to political and defence questions was less successful in the early 1950s. Attempts to create a European Political Community and a European Defence Community proved to be too ambitious as they reached into the heart of the nation-state: political control and the defence of the realm. Furthermore, there was an important absentee from these schemes – the United Kingdom. British governments had accepted the intergovernmental nature of the OEEC, NATO and the Council of Europe and had even seen the utility of having meetings of parliamentarians in the Council of Europe, but neither Conservative nor Labour ministers were attracted by the potentially supranational nature of the Coal and Steel Community. If by 'supranational' it was meant that the Community would establish its authority above that of the nation-state members, then this was anathema to British governments that had struggled against the imposition of foreign rule (albeit by more warlike means) over the centuries. The Coal and Steel Community was anyhow seen as a means of solving the Franco-German problem (which, to an extent, it was) and therefore not something that needed direct British participation. When the chance arose, in 1954, the Conservative government obtained associate membership of the ECSC but showed reluctance to commit resources to a European Defence Community or to join negotiations for a wider Economic Community on the basis of control by a supranational authority. The notion of a Common Market, included in the plans for an Economic Community, also offended against Britain's trade preference which, because of its connections with the Commonwealth and North America, was in favour of a free trade area. By the time the treaty establishing the European Economic Community was signed in 1957 and the first steps towards a Common Market were taken by the end of the 1950s, Western Europe was divided into two trade groupings, one based on the Community method and aiming at a customs union, the other, led by the United Kingdom, looking to more modest intergovernmental institutions and aiming at a free trade area.

The second unresolved question at the start of the 1950s was that of Western Europe's contribution to its own defence. This issue became more sensitive after the invasion of South Korea by Communist North Korea in June 1950. It was feared in American and West European circles that this action, which was seen as being Soviet-inspired, was a feint meant to attract Western attention away from the expected main Soviet thrust – against West Europe itself. From the summer of 1950 United States, concern turned to the question of a suitable response. As well as improving NATO's organization, it seemed clear that Western Europe would need help in the form of US troops and aircraft if they were to resist successfully any attack by the supposed (and overestimated) might of the Red Army. For political as well as military reasons, it was felt necessary to match any US build-up in Europe with additional West European forces and, given the overstretched position of Britain and France in their colonial commitments, this was seen to necessitate German troops, and thus German rearmament (Wells, 1985, 185–7; Wiggershaus, 1985, 201–3).

French politicians were not ready for such a revival of German fortunes so soon after the Second World War. Instead, through the Pleven Plan of October 1950, they proposed that German rearmament be subsumed under a European Defence Community (EDC) – comprising France, West Germany, Italy and the three Benelux states as members – which would lead to a West European military force under a European defence minister, answerable to a West European parliament. The following four years saw a battle between those who wanted West Germany to be rearmed in a NATO context and those who preferred the EDC option. When the French National Assembly failed to ratify the EDC Treaty in 1954, a compromise was reached whereby a newly sovereign Federal Republic of Germany (and Italy) would subscribe to a revised Brussels Treaty, thereby forming the Western European

Union (WEU). It was within the constraints of the WEU that West Germany was to be rearmed and, as a result, the country joined NATO (Fursdon, 1980).

The prospect of West German troops, however, did not solve the problem of a West European contribution to its own defence. In the end, despite affirmations of increased conventional forces by the West Europeans at the Lisbon NATO Council meeting of February 1952, the most immediate and, it was felt by a number of European leaders, the most satisfactory answer to Western Europe's defence problems came from the Americans. It was not only in the shape of more troops and fighter aircraft: it was also a nuclear solution. From 1953, the US started to deploy dual-capability artillery – that could use either conventional or nuclear weapons – in Western Europe and in October 1953 the US National Security Council adopted NSC 162/2 which committed the country to the use of nuclear weapons in a wide range of possible conflicts. As a result '. . . questions of the role and uses of nuclear weapons in NATO, and therefore their design and deployment, continue to be among the most significant and divisive issues within the alliance' (Etzold, 1985, 285).

At the same time as this development, an effort was made after the death of Stalin to come to a better understanding between the West and the Soviet Union. In July 1953 an armistice was signed in the Korean War and in July 1954 the Geneva Protocols were agreed by the Great Powers, which allowed France to extricate itself from Indo-China. In May 1955, the Soviet Union, the United States, the United Kingdom and France ended their occupation of Austria, which was then established as a neutral, democratic state. Representatives of the four Great Powers met in Geneva later in 1955 but little came of their discussions. In the early part of 1956 the Soviet Union seemed to be conducting a political thaw internally with the new Secretary-General of the Communist Party of the Soviet Union, Mr Khruschev, repudiating Stalin and his work. However, this had little effect internationally as the Soviets denounced the Franco-British intervention in Egypt in October–November 1956 and were subsequently involved in the suppression of a 'revisionist' government in Hungary in November 1956. All the time, the Soviet Union had kept a wary eye on developments in Germany, opposing West German membership of NATO, establishing the Warsaw Treaty Organization as a riposte, recognizing as a state Soviet-occupied East Germany (all in 1956), and, in 1958, threatening to terminate the Four-Power Agreement on the status of Berlin.

These latter events tended to confirm to the member governments of NATO the necessity for an Atlantic Alliance. However, the late 1950s gave no relief in the debate within NATO about the West European defence effort, as measured against that of the United States. The dominance of the US and the United Kingdom as the two nuclear members of NATO began to be felt, particularly by the French, and efforts further to 'nuclearize' the defence of Western Europe were resisted in 1957 by smaller members such as Norway and Denmark by refusing to deploy Intermediate-Range Ballistic Missiles (Brundtland, 1985, 196). After the death of Stalin, the West had to think seriously about how to deal with the new leaders of the Soviet Union and their sometimes conciliatory offers. A response was normally decided by the Big Three – the US, the United Kingdom and France – but other members of NATO were consulted through the Alliance machinery. NATO as an institution had to start thinking about cooperation with the Soviet bloc as well as about conflict.

Divisions in the West

The structures established in Western Europe in the post-war years came under stress in the 1960s and had to face the results of the conflicts of interests of member states.

The division of Western Europe into two trading groups at the end of the 1950s was continued into the following decade. The United Kingdom, after deciding that it could not join the Economic Community, drew together some of the other West European countries also left outside and formed the European Free Trade Association in 1960. It was hoped that the transformation of the OEEC into the Organization for European Cooperation and Development (OECD) in 1960 – which demonstrated the decline of American economic domination of Europe – would allow the two groups to negotiate a wider settlement. That this did not happen was partly a result of political change in France that had brought President de Gaulle to power. Unlike many of the French politicians of the 1940s and 50s, de Gaulle did not believe that the ultimate aim of the European Economic Community (EEC) was a federal Europe. He accepted the workings of the EEC as benefiting France, especially French farmers, but considered that cooperation should be in the form of a Europe of nation-states ('Europe des patries'). Furthermore, he did not consider the United Kingdom to be ready for membership of the EEC and vetoed British entry in January 1963 and again in 1967. At the same time, de Gaulle was careful to nurture his country's relationship with the Federal Republic of Germany, signing a treaty of friendship and cooperation with West Germany the week after ending British hopes of EEC membership in 1963. This Franco-German relationship was the key to the working of the Communities during the 1960s and proved that the ECSC and the EEC had become useful tools in solving the problem of West Germany's relations with its Western neighbours. De Gaulle's attempt to downgrade the Communities to merely intergovernmental organizations was, however, resisted by the other members, including the Federal Republic, and the result was an agreement to differ about the powers of EEC institutions, the so-called Luxembourg compromise of January 1966.

The effect of the exclusion of the United Kingdom, together with Denmark, Eire and Norway, from membership of the EEC was felt by other organizations. After de Gaulle's veto of January 1963, the European Free Trade Association became more active as it seemed that its members would be in each other's company for longer than expected. The Nordic Council, formed in 1952 by common resolution of four of the Nordic parliaments, had already documented its cooperative efforts in the Helsinki Treaty of 1962 in order to safeguard the position of Nordic cooperation in any negotiations between Denmark and Norway on the one hand and the EEC on the other. By the end of the 1960s, with some of their number locked out of the Communities, the Nordic states considered closer economic coordination in a Nordic Economic Union, plans that came to nothing once the EEC option opened up again.

Despite any internal crises, it was clear that during the 1960s the EEC was a success. The creation of a customs union coincided with the rapid economic development of the six member states. Other West European institutions, such as the Council of Europe, the Western European Union, EFTA and the Nordic Council, were placed in a shadow by the EEC. The real accolade was the application for membership by the United Kingdom. Not only had the views about Community institutions been adjusted within the British government, but those institutions had also changed to become more acceptable to the United Kingdom. It was clear that the supranationalism of the Schuman Plan had been somewhat compromised by the time the Coal and Steel Community was established under the Treaty of Paris. The Treaty of Rome creating the Economic Community had not mentioned supranationalism and a balance had been struck between Community-based institutions and those in which the member states were dominant. France under de Gaulle had demonstrated that Community interest would not be placed above the important national interests of member states, a position that found favour with British ministers. Even when the three Communities – Coal and Steel, Economic and Atomic Energy – were merged in 1965 to 1967, the outcome did not strengthen the supranational element in the institutions.

By the end of the 1960s the newly merged European Communities (EC) – despite their success – failed to maintain unity in the face of the rising storms in the world currency markets. In 1968 France found its currency supported by the British and Americans rather than the Germans. The completion of the customs union in that year, 18 months ahead of time, brought the Communities of 'the Six' to a turning point. Political change in the following year in both France and West Germany allowed a fresh approach to the problem – the period of a divided Western Europe had to come to an end.

Division was also the catchword for NATO during the 1960s. By the end of the 1950s, France had increasingly felt the dominance of NATO institutions by the two Anglo-Saxon nuclear powers, the US and and United Kingdom. After failing to persuade these countries to establish a tripartite management of NATO, the French decided on their own nuclear weapons programme. Lack of allied support for France's war against insurgents in Algeria also rankled and the advent of President de Gaulle brought to the scene an element of French nationalism and distaste for the Anglo-Saxons, learnt during the Second World War (Horne, 1989, 179–90). The 'Special Relationship' of the United States under President Kennedy and the United Kingdom under Prime Minister Macmillan was seen as Anglo-Saxon hegemony. De Gaulle considered NATO to be a necessary alliance with a limited lifespan, not the forerunner of an Atlantic Community. He made sure that France stood by its NATO allies when a common enemy threatened them all – for example, during the Cuban Missile Crisis of November 1962 and the various Berlin crises in the early 1960s. When, at Nassau in December 1962, US President Kennedy offered British Prime Minister Macmillan assistance to continue the British nuclear deterrent, de Gaulle considered this proof of

Anglo-Saxon domination of NATO and of Britain's preference for America over Europe. Within a month he had stopped Britain's EEC membership negotiations. He followed up this action by decisions to withdraw France from NATO's integrated military structure in 1966 and to transfer Allied facilities, including NATO headquarters, out of France by April 1967.

In spite of this major division, NATO made progress during the decade. As mentioned, it kept a united front in the face of threats from the Soviet Union and uncertainty in East Europe. The institutions of the organization managed the successful transfer out of France. Most important was a series of decisions over relations with the Soviet Union and over strategy. By the end of 1967 NATO had adopted the concept of flexible response, by which members would respond to an attack at a more 'appropriate' level rather than with the threat of all-out nuclear war. This was a somewhat belated acceptance that the period of Western, mainly American, nuclear domination was over and that the Soviet Union could threaten a nuclear riposte to a Western nuclear attack. Secondly, the adoption of the Harmel Report on the Future Tasks of the Alliance, also in December 1967, committed NATO to matching their stance of deterrence with an offer of detente to their adversary, the Soviet Union. The idea was that as long as NATO countries stood guard against any Soviet attack, they could also afford to reduce tension and to deal with the Soviet Union over common problems.

The Soviet-led invasion of Czechoslovakia in August 1968 by Warsaw Treaty Organization troops was aimed at replacing a reformist Communist government by one supine to Moscow, but only served to unite NATO at a time when a post-war generation was questioning its necessity. It also postponed the process of detente with the Soviet bloc for a crucial year.

The Reaction to Change

The meeting of the Heads of State or Government in The Hague in December 1969 heralded a vital change for the European Communities. As well as deciding to journey further along the path of integration by deepening cooperation and coordination within the EC, especially by creating an economic and monetary union, the Six also agreed to widen their membership. By January 1973, the United Kingdom, Denmark and Eire had become full members of the EC and, by later that year, the other members of EFTA had signed free-trade agreements with the expanded Communities, thereby creating the potential for one West European market. The divide between the United Kingdom and continental Western Europe, opened up by the British government's negative response to the Schuman Plan in 1950 and subsequent British disinterest in, and sometimes downright opposition to, the Community idea, had closed. The process during the 1960s whereby British governments had become more accepting of the EC and the EC had become less based on supranationalism led to the synthesis of 1973. The journey was by no means complete: within two years a new British government, under a Labour prime minister, renegotiated some of the terms of entry to the Communities and placed the results before the British people in a referendum. The positive response did not prevent the Labour government – or its Conservative successor – from treating the Communities' institutions with scepticism and often interpreting British interests as being in direct opposition to what others saw as the Communities' welfare.

The extension of the Communities had an effect on other European institutions. The Western European Union, used briefly at the end of the 1960s as a contact point between the United Kingdom and the Six, became moribund. The Council of Europe was overshadowed by the enlarged parliament of the Communities. EFTA, without the United Kingdom, became an organization of equals and settled down to a more unexciting life. The Nordic Council revised its institutions to prevent Nordic cooperation from being undermined by Danish membership of the EC.

None of these institutions, the EC included, responded well to the major economic upheaval brought to the Western world by the steep rise in oil prices decided on by the OPEC members in early 1974. The subsequent recession, inflation and unemployment tested the political systems of West European states sorely and this was reflected in the international organizations. The EC failed to produce a common political response to pressure on one of its members – the Netherlands – which had supported Israel after the 1973 Yom Kippur War. The Communities also did not respond effectively to the economic and social malaise of the 1970s. This was not because the Communities' institutions – the Commission and the Parliament – lacked ideas or commitment but because disagreements between the member states – as demonstrated in the Council of Ministers – reached 'beggar thy neighbour' proportions.

The most noticeable institutional response to the Oil Crisis was the creation, within the ambit of the OECD, of the International Energy Agency (IEA). In the immediate aftermath of tough OPEC decisions, the IEA was given extraordinary powers to distribute oil and gas in times of shortage in the Western world, but it soon became clear that each member country would prefer to see to its own needs, even if others suffered, rather than trust to the vagaries of an international organization with real powers of distribution.

At the start of the 1970s, it had become apparent that the main driving factor of the post-war economy – the domination of the US dollar – could no longer be taken for granted. A similar decline seemed to have happened in US military strength. Withdrawal from a disastrous war in Vietnam had left the United States weakened and introspective and its allies concerned about its commitment to them. Economic pressures and the feeling that detente in Europe could lessen the need for a strong American presence there led first to calls for unilateral withdrawals of US troops from Europe and then to multilateral consideration of troops levels, East and West, at the Mutual and Balanced Force Reduction talks in Vienna. These negotiations were one of a number begun in the early 1970s. A Strategic Arms Limitation Treaty was signed in 1972 between the United States and the Soviet Union and talks on the subject continued. After West Germany had normalized its relations with Poland, Czechoslovakia and the Soviet Union in a series of treaties, a Basic Treaty between the two German states was signed in December 1972. This followed on a Quadripartite Agreement on Berlin between the US, the United Kingdom, France and the Soviet Union. In 1973, the Conference on Security and Cooperation in Europe (CSCE) opened in Helsinki with 33 European states (including the Soviet Union), Canada and the United States in attendance. This process led to the signing by these 35 states in July 1975 of the Helsinki Final Act which covered human rights questions as well as those of economic relations and European security. The Final Act was an end and a beginning. It represented a sort of peace treaty by which European countries recognized the status quo in their continent that had resulted from the Second World War. It also provided the instruments for pan-European relations, a broad set of principles for the behaviour of European governments towards their peoples, and a forum for future East–West contact.

The changes in Europe throughout the 1970s placed a strain on

NATO as an institution. The consequences of the adoption of the concept of flexible response in 1967 were being felt. This notion implied a commitment to produce the capabilities to respond in a flexible manner to a wide range of military threats but NATO members, faced with economic crisis, were unwilling to devote new resources to defence. Meetings of the political leaders confirmed the dual approach of the Harmel Report and supported aspects of detente with the Soviet Union and its allies. Throughout the 1970s concern grew among the Western military about the growth of Warsaw Treaty Organization military strength at a time when NATO members were struggling to maintain their existing force levels. There was also increasing concern about Soviet involvement in regional disputes throughout the world. The 1970s ended with the seizure by Islamic revolutionaries of the US Embassy in Tehran, a NATO decision in December 1979 to modernize theatre nuclear weapons in Europe at the same time as offering arms control negotiations with the Soviets, and the Soviet invasion of Afghanistan.

The Tehran action in November 1979 seemed to point to the limitations of the United States' 'global reach'. NATO's December 1979 'Dual Track' decision was a response to both Western fears about the growth of Soviet military power and European concern that the United States might be 'decoupling' itself from Western Europe. The Soviet intervention in Afghanistan seemed, at first sight, to confirm hawkish notions that the Soviet Union would use military power to achieve its ends. It led to an end to arms control negotiations between the Superpowers and opened a period of strong distrust between East and West.

An Emerging Europe

The early years of the 1980s were not auspicious for the European Communities. Oil price increases had aggravated the economic situation in 1979 and by 1983 unemployment in the EC was almost 10 per cent of the labour force. Member states continued to concentrate on solving their problems by national means. The United Kingdom considered its budgetary contribution to the EC to be too heavy for a country in its parlous economic state and this question, tied to that of farm prices, almost led to a breakdown of the Communities after the failure of the April 1980 Luxembourg Summit. Although a compromise was eventually reached, the issue of Britain's EC contribution seemed to dominate EC Council meetings for the following five years. Likewise it was clear that the expenditure on the Common Agricultural Policy had to be brought under control, a process started in March 1984 by a reform package.

The problems that the EC had to face should not mask an underlying trend that became more obvious in the 1980s. Throughout the 1970s hopes of a move towards a more integrated European Communities were kept alive in the Commission and by politicians such as Mr Tindemans of Belgium and Mr Spinelli of Italy. The direct elections to the EC's Parliament in 1979 represented an advance for those who sought Europe integration and those who wanted more democratic control of the Communities. The following decade saw progress – in the eyes of the integrationists – in a number of areas. Membership was expanded to include Greece, Portugal and Spain. The institutions of the EC were strengthened by the Single European Act allowing greater use of the weighted majority vote in the Council and more involvement in the Communities' decision-making by the Parliament. Progress was made towards a European Monetary Union. European Political Cooperation between the EC states became an accepted feature, especially in their foreign policies. The EC financed itself by its own resources and the British contribution question was settled. Agreement was reached on the completion of the internal market by the end of 1992. The aim was a much freer flow of goods, services, capital and people between member states than hitherto. The EC has emerged as one of the leading economic powers in the world and is attracting the attention of the United States, Japan, the Soviet Union and the Third World because of its economic potential.

The resurgence of Cold War feeling at the start of the 1980s bolstered NATO's activities, though at some cost. The implementation of the Dual Track decision was resisted at two levels. First, there was a vocal opposition within the countries chosen for the deployment of the Cruise and Pershing II missiles – Britain, West Germany, Italy, Belgium and the Netherlands – as well as in other NATO countries such as Norway and Denmark. This reflected a concern by some of the public in these countries about the increased nuclearization of Europe and a fear that the United States under President Reagan might be moving towards an acceptance of the possibility of fighting a nuclear war in Europe. Secondly, there was little positive response from the Soviet Union to the call to enter into negotiations about the control of all intermediate-range nuclear forces (INF) in Europe. The ageing

Soviet leadership, having made its dispositions in Eastern Europe, demanded an abstention from deployment by the West. However, it was faced by Conservative governments in the United States, Britain and West Germany that were quite prepared to rearm in response to what was seen as a threatening Soviet posture in Europe.

The advent of Mikhail Gorbachev as Secretary-General of the Communist Party of the Soviet Union (and later as President of that country) offered new opportunities for NATO. Gorbachev changed the diplomacy of his predecessors and started to accept many of the bargaining positions of his Western adversaries. Arms control negotiations, especially on strategic arms and on INF, were started in earnest. After 1986 the West was ready to respond positively. The political climate had changed once more. After some six years of increased expenditure on defence in many NATO states, their governments and people felt the time had come to talk about the limitation of any further need to arm up. In the October 1986 Reykjavik Summit between Gorbachev and Reagan, the way was cleared, despite disagreement about President Reagan's Strategic Defense Initiative, for negotiations on reductions in strategic weapons and in INF. The signing of the INF Treaty in December 1987 led to the abandonment of all the INF by the US and the Soviet Union and to a new round of discussions, starting in March 1989, concerning Conventional Forces in Europe. The NATO countries found themselves responding to a succession of arms control and disarmament proposals coming from Moscow, yet at the same time they were still faced by demands from their military to match the military build-up by the Soviet Union made in the late 1970s and early 1980s. NATO governments did not find this an easy circle to square.

Throughout the bleak days of the late 1970s and early 1980s, one institution allowed East and West to talk to each other on a wide range of subjects, apart from by the means of bilateral diplomacy. This was the CSCE, meeting first in Belgrade in October 1977, in Madrid in November 1980, and then in Stockholm in January 1984. This process, hardly formalized into an international organization, nevertheless presented a forum for detailed discussions about the nature of relationships between European states. The Stockholm meeting finally produced a document in 1986 that represented a significant advance in confidence and security building by the participating states insofar as it allowed intrusive inspection by members of each other's major military exercises. As the 'Helsinki Process' of the CSCE meetings has also dealt with human rights and economic relations, it has provided both a set of standards, however minimal, for European social and economic life, and the crude means by which progress might be monitored. It has also provided a significant roadblock to any use of force between European states and perhaps has contributed to limiting the conflict in former Yugoslavia to the republics of that country.

Certain European organizations saw a renewal in the latter half of the 1980s. The Western European Union found itself in favour again, this time as a platform for discussions about West European security both as a demonstration of European activity and as a backstop against the drawing down of US forces in Europe. The Council of Europe's court was active in protecting the rights of the citizens of Western Europe, particularly when they were infringed by their own governments, and the Council acted as a host to leaders and parliamentarians from some East European countries. The OECD continued its expert work on the Western economy and EFTA sought to confirm that the creation of a single European market within the EC will not be to the detriment of its own members. The Nordic Council concerned itself in particular with cultural and environmental factors and with safeguarding some of the more cherished elements of the 'Nordic Model' of social welfare and small-scale development.

Revolution and Evolution

The harmonious development of relations between the blocs of Europe that had been experienced from mid-1985 belied a deeper process at work in Eastern Europe. President Gorbachev of the Soviet Union had let the reformist genie out of the bottle in his own country and in the Communist-run states of Eastern Europe, but the inefficient and morally bankrupt regimes of those countries were unable to manage the subsequent economic and political change. During the summer of 1989 the pent-up demands of the populations of Eastern Europe came to the boil once it was realized that the Soviet Union would no longer back up the governments there with armed force. A successful change of government in Poland led the way to demands for greater responsiveness in other East European governments, a call met by vacillation or attempted oppression. In the end, popular movements swept away not only the old Communist governments but also that monument to East–West division, the Berlin Wall (Simpson, 1990, Parts 3, 4 and 5). By the end of 1989, non-Communist governments were installed in almost all the members of the Warsaw Treaty Organization, and the unification of Germany was on the political agenda of Europe. The 40-year-old political and security division between Western Europe and East Europe was over and international organizations – the EC, NATO, the Council of Europe, the Nordic Council, EFTA, OECD, the CSCE – were all apparently ready to help heal the scars left by this schism.

The process of uniting East and West Europe proved as difficult as the unification of Germany. While the task of bringing the former German Democratic Republic into the Federal Republic of Germany reached a climax with unification on 3 October 1990, the cost of such a move – and of the liberation of East Europe from Communist control – soon became apparent. The Federal German government found soon that – in order to pay the economic cost of unification – interest rates had to be kept high, thereby dampening wider European hopes of a quick recovery from the recession that was already emerging in 1991. The West European countries, increasingly hit by unemployment and budget deficits, felt unable – or politically unwilling – to provide the sort of capital assistance needed by the run-down economies of the former Communist-run states of East and Central Europe.

A series of efforts were made to bring the East and Central European states closer to the structures created by Western Europe since 1948. The NATO Heads of State and Government, meeting for the North Atlantic Council in London in July 1990, declared that 'Europe had entered a new, promising era. Central and Eastern Europe has liberated itself. The Soviet Union has embarked on the long journey toward a free society' (*Survival*, September/October 1990, 469). They went on to propose to the members of the Warsaw Treaty Organization a joint declaration in which they would state that they were no longer adversaries and would reaffirm their promise to 'refrain from the threat or use of force against the territorial integrity or political independence of any state . . .' (op. cit., 470). Emphasis was placed on a new, cooperative relationship with the East and Central European states and the Soviet Union; arms control and disarmament negotiations; the need for a new NATO force structure with less emphasis on nuclear weapons; and on a greater prominence for the CSCE in Europe's future (op. cit., 470–2).

This increased role for the CSCE (see Chapter 12) seemed to be a result of the Paris summit of that organization, in November 1990, when the hostility of the Cold War was declared to be at an end and new processes for dealing with conflict in Europe planned. Futhermore, the NATO and WTO states' representatives, meeting at the same time, undertook 'to maintain only such military capabilities as are necessary to prevent war and provide for effective defense' (Survival, January/February 1991, 79) and signed a Treaty on Conventional Armed Forces in Europe which not only limited the armed forces of both alliances in Europe but also instituted a strict verification regime.

In another development in the security field, the NATO members decided at their Rome summit in December 1991 to set up the North Atlantic Cooperation Council (NACC) consisting of the NATO countries, the former members of the WTO (which organization had been dissolved in 1991) and the successor states of the Soviet Union, which fell apart on the same day that NACC had its first meeting in December 1991. NACC was aimed at dealing with issues of common interest such as the implementation of NATO–WTO arms control agreements, and also at providing a forum within which some of the ex-Soviet states (such as Armenia and Azerbaijan) might sort out their differences.

The Council of Europe welcomed those states such as Bulgaria, Hungary, the CSFR and Poland, that had adopted democratic institutions and were seen to be upholding fundamental freedoms. Others, such as the Soviet Union and the Baltic Republics, that had not made such progress, were given special guest status and the Council offered the emerging democracies assistance on the road to freedom. The CSCE's interest in human rights was demonstrated in its attempts to safeguard minority groups in East and Central Europe and to monitor elections.

A major force in post-Cold War Europe has been the European Communities. It has established a series of programmes to assist the ex-Communist states of East and Central Europe and also signed 'Europe Agreements' with the CSFR, Hungary and Poland that gave those states some access – albeit limited – to the EC's market and the long-term hope of eventual EC membership. The Nordic Council and EFTA also undertook to help the East and Central European states both with economic aid and technical and other assistance.

The leaders of the EC countries were also instrumental in establishing the European Bank for Reconstruction and Development, which had its genesis in the meetings of the OECD and of the directorate of the most important Western states known as the Group of Seven ('G7'). This Bank has attempted to channel resources to East and Central Euorpe and to the states of the former Soviet Union, but has been unable to repeat the massive transfer of capital seen in the Marshall Aid to Western Europe after the Second World War.

The previous members of the WTO and Comecon found themselves without binding ties among themselves once these organizations were dissolved in the summer of 1991. They did not find it necessary to replace these organizations, but there was a poliferation of other more regionally-based institutions that emerged. The six-nation Hexagonale Group, consisting of Austria, the CSFR, Hungary, Italy, Poland and Yugoslavia was affected by the civil war and destruction of that last state. From Novemember 1991 Yugoslavia was excluded from the grouping which changed its name to the Central European Initiative and welcomed Croatia and Slovenia as observers. Another Central European initiative was that of the CSFR, Hungary and Poland at Visegrad in February 1991. The countries endorsed the notion of their 'total integration into the European political, economic, security and legislative order' and agreed to cooperate with each other to that end (Sherwen, 1991, 153). They have advanced plans for a free trade area among themselves, though this was more in response to EC prompting than because of any home-grown enthusiasm (Okolicsanyi, 1993, 19–22). Whether the agreement will make a positive contribution to the security of the member states remains to be seen (Spero, 1992, 58–83). With the break-up of the Czech Slovak Federal Republic on 1 January 1993, the 'Visegrad Three' extended its membership. Attempts have also been made at Balkan and Black Sea regional cooperation (Roucek, 1992, 26–7).

The three Baltic states (Estonia, Latvia and Lithuania) copied their Nordic neighbours by setting up a Baltic Council and Assembly, bringing together, respectively their prime ministers and parliamentarians. These three countries joined together with the Nordic states (except Iceland), Russia, Poland and Germany in the Council of the Baltic Sea states, with its first ministerial meeting in Copenhagen in March 1992. In January 1993, Russia joined with the Nordic countries to establish a Barents Euro-Arctic Council to cooperate on trade and environmental matters in the Barents Sea region.

Whilst all these regional efforts have their uses, in the end they have little to offer the states of East and Central Europe. For this area 'which is ethnically fragmented, politically unbalanced and economically weak, it is highly questionable whether regional cooperation alone, even if successful, can guarantee long-term security, stability and prosperity' (Roucek, 1992, 28).

With only a foothold in Europe is the Economic Cooperation Organization wherein the Islamic states of the former Soviet Union (Kyrgystan, Tajikistan, Uzbekistan, Turkmenistan, Azerbaijan and with Kazakhstan as an observer) have joined the previously moribund organization established by Pakistan, Iran and Turkey in 1963 (Clarke, 1992, 22).

One institution that can probably be categorized as an international organization using the definition on p. 18, is that of the Commonwealth of Independent States (CIS) established at the end of 1991 with the demise of the old Soviet Union. The original membership consisted of all the former republics of the USSR, except Georgia – which later joined – and the three Baltic republics. So far the CIS seems to have few permanent institutions apart from meetings of the heads of state or their representatives, which are not always attended by all 12 members.

If East and Central Europe has seemed to be fragmented since 1989, integration was the watchword in Western Europe. With the prospect of a Single European Market being created within the EC by the end of 1992, the 12 EC governments decided to convene two intergovernmental conferences (IGCs) to discuss the progress towards economic and monetary union – which, it was felt, should follow on the creation of the single market – and the prospect of political reforms that might take the EC members further down the road of European unity. By the time these two IGCs had merged with a final negotiating session in Maastricht in December 1991, hopes that the Maastricht Treaty on European Union might be a step towards a federal Europe were dashed mainly by the opposition of the United Kingdom government. However, the Treaty consolidated many of the changes brought about in the Single European Act, developed further the powers of the European Parliament and laid down a detailed route to economic and monetary union. The creation of a European Union rested not just on the evolution of the European Communities but also on cooperation between the 12 member states in the area of justice and home affairs, and in the implementation of a common foreign and security policy, including the prospect of a common defence policy.

With the signature of the Maastricht Treaty on European Union in February 1992, it seemed that the process of European integration which started with the Schuman Plan in 1950 had taken a decisive step forward. There was some discussion as to whether this 'deepening' of the Communities might mean that futher extension of EC membership – 'widening' – would be postponed. Austria and Sweden had already applied for membership and there was the prospect of other European states following this lead. However, the EC–EFTA Agreement – known as the European Economic Area – which was signed in Oporto in May 1992 seemed to offer a bridge for the EFTA members that might allow them to take up full membership by the mid to late 1990s.

The 'Europe Agreements', negotiated with the CSFR, Hungary and Poland in 1991, also provided the prospect of EC membership – maybe by the turn of the century – for those states. It did seem that, by early 1992, the EC – and the prospective European Union – was going to become the most magnetic of the European institutions, offering a model for political progress and economic development for both rich EFTA states and poorer East and Central Europeans alike. The European Union could form an enlarged security community within which the threat of the use of force between member states was not even contemplated and which would deal with a wide range of subjects from judicial affairs, through a common money and a Single European Market, to defence matters. Many of the other European organizations such as the WEU, EFTA and the Council of Europe, would either melt away beneath the rising sun of the European Union or would become mere satellites in its system.

This 'grand settlement' was not to be – at least, not by 1993. The economic recession that had already shown itself by 1991 was not improving by 1992. This led to disputes between EC members as it became clear that the cost of German unification had been passed on to citizens in the rest of the EC by high German interest rates, thereby slowing down recovery. It also increased the opportunity for conflict with the United States over trade matters and led to the inability of the two sides to conclude the 'Uruguay Round' of GATT – the world trade negotiations – well into 1993.

If the world economic downturn gradually eroded the fertile ground needed for the 'grand settlement', events both outside and within the EC combined to make it difficult for the European Union to take root.

The Gulf War of 1990 to 1991 when a coalition of Western and

Arab forces combined to roll back the Iraqi occupation of Kuwait in 'Operation Desert Storm', could be seen as a forerunner of a New World Order whereby threats to international peace and security would be met by determined action. However, the EC members were initially divided in their response to Saddam Hussein's occupation of Kuwait and only united (and then not completely) in 'Operation Desert Storm' under American leadership. Furthermore, what unity that existed in the response of European Political Cooperation (EPC) – the EC states' foreign and security mechanism – to Saddam Hussein did not seem to carry over into their response to a crisis much closer to home, that in Yugoslavia. The inability of EPC to prevent war and then to bring peace to the area of former Yugoslavia demonstrated the tentative nature of the New World Order and the limitations of the EC as an actor in international affairs.

Further evidence came in the unwillingness of the EC governments to adopt any imaginative scheme to assist the new and emerging democracies of East and Central Europe and of the former Soviet Union. Western response generally was hobbled by the economic recession and also by the unwillingness of major EC governments to act decisively through EC institutions. As a result the EC has seen the 'Iron Curtain' between East and West fall, only to be replaced by new barriers of trade and migration restrictions between the relatively rich EC and the economically struggling East and Central European states. The cost of this failure to offer decisive aid to the ex-Communist countries could be their sinking back into a mixture of nationalism and authoritarianism.

Within the EC a political crisis arose not long after the signing of the Maastricht Treaty. The Danish electorate refused to ratify the Treaty in June 1992 and had to be asked again in May 1993. Meanwhile the French electorate gave only a weak 'yes' in their referendum and the British government found the parliamentary road to ratification a long and arduous process. In Germany the Treaty was challenged in the Constitutional Court. The politicians who had agreed the Treaty seemed to be out of synchronization with their electorates which were more concerned about more basic questions of jobs, pay and crime. Even the EEA agreement between the EC and EFTA came unravelled after the Swiss electorate had rejected it in December 1992.

Thus it seemed that by early 1993 the European political system, far from benefiting from the aftermath of the end of the Cold War, was suffering from a sort of systems breakdown. States in East and Central Europe were fragmenting and the pursuit of the European Union had been severely curtailed. Nevertheless, the politicians attempted to climb back on to the road to European unity. The array of international organizations at their disposal may have confused the effectiveness of the choices available, but the countries and peoples of Europe do not yet seem ready to work within the framework of only one or two institutions – such as the European Union and NATO – to the exclusion of all other international organizations. The following chapters will outline why different structures have been used – and continue to be used – by European states wishing to work more closely together.

This brief history has been dominated, of necessity, by a few European organizations. This is a matter of judgement and does not detract from the activities of a range of other intergovernmental organizations in Europe. The *European Yearbook*, published each year under the auspices of the Council of Europe, will attest to the work of the Benelux Economic Union, the European Space Agency, the Central Commission for the Navigation of the Rhine, the European Civil Aviation Conference and of other European functional organizations. Even the Economic Commission for Europe, a regional body of the United Nations, has been revived from dereliction to play an important part in fighting transboundary pollution in Europe.

Neither should the impression be left that organizing Europe is only about intergovernmental organization. Far from it. The last three decades have seen an increase in non-governmental activity across frontiers whether it be tourism and travel or the work of organized non-governmental groups. These have sometimes attached themselves to the IGOs, such as the political parties participating in the parliaments of the Council of Europe and the EC or the pressure groups working within the EC. On other occasions they have tried to work in less institutional forms, as has been the case with the European Nuclear Disarmament (END) movement. Churches and professional organizations have also spread their influence across the frontiers of Europe, bringing assistance to the peoples of East and Central Europe.

This chapter has shown that the main international organizations of Europe have not been able to proceed unhindered towards whatever goals may be laid down in their founding charters. They have, to a great extent, been creatures of the governments of the member states. Even within the European Communities, where the institutions have some autonomy, it is not possible to disregard the opinions of the member states' governments. Neither have these governments, and therefore the organizations, been able to act independently of the wider strategic, political and economic situation in the world. Since the Second World War, Europe has no longer been the motor of world politics or the world economy. Whether a more organized Europe, free from many of the constraints of the immediate post-war period, can make a more positive contribution, remains to be seen.

References

Brundtland, A.O., 1985: Norwegian security policy: defense and non-provocation in a changing context. In Flynn, G. (ed.), *NATO's Northern Allies* (London: Croom Helm), 171–223.

Clarke, D.L. 1992: European multilateral organizations: an update. *RFE/RL Research Report* 1:12, 21–2.

Dilks, D., 1985: The British view of security: Europe and a wider world, 1945–1948. In Riste, 25–59.

Etzold, T.H., 1985: The end of the beginning: NATO's adoption of nuclear strategy. In Riste, 285–314.

Frémaux, J. and Martel, A., 1985: French defence policy 1947–1949. In Riste, 92–103.

Fursdon, E., 1980: *The European Defence Community: A History*. London: St Martin.

Gaddis, J.L., 1985: The United States and the question of influence in Europe, 1945–1949. In Riste, 60–91.

Haas, E.B., 1968: *The Uniting of Europe*. Stanford: Stanford University Press.

Horne, A., 1988: *Macmillan 1894–1956*. London: Macmillan.

Milward, A.S. 1984: *The Reconstruction of Western Europe 1945–51*. London: Methuen & Co. Ltd.

Okolicsanyi, K. 1993: The Visegrad Triangle's free trade zone *RFE/RL. Research Report* 2:3, 19–22.

Riste, O. (ed.) 1985: *Western Security: The Formative Years. European and Atlantic Defence 1947–1953*. Oslo: Norwegian University Press.

Roucek, L. 1992: *After the Bloc: the New International Relations in Eastern Europe*. London: Royal Institute of International Affairs, RIIA Discussion Papers 40.

Sherwen, N. (ed) 1991: *The Prague Conference on the Future of European Security*. Brussels: NATO.

Simpson, J. 1990: *Despatches from the Barricades*. London: Hutchinson.

Spero, J. 1992: The Budapest–Prague–Warsaw triangle: Central European security after the Visegrad summit. *European Security* 1:1, 58–83.

Survival 1990: September/October, 469–72.

——— 1991: January/February, 79.

Wells, S.F., Jr., 1985: The first Cold War buildup: Europe in United States strategy and policy, 1950–1953. In Riste, 181–97.

Wiggershaus, N., 1985: The decision for a West German defence contribution. In Riste, 198–214.

3

OEEC, OECD and EBRD

Establishment

The Organization for European Economic Cooperation was created as a result of the US government's wish both to help the West European countries and to encourage them to help themselves. It was motivated by the need to rebuild the European economies and to provide the economic backbone to prevent the internal collapse and possible outside takeover of Western democracies.

By early 1947 the attempt to rebuild Europe on a continental basis had slowed down and a repeat of the inter-war chaos was feared. The division between the Soviet bloc and Western countries had become apparent in Europe though the offer by US Secretary of State George Marshall of substantial American aid to Europe was made open to all the states on the Continent. Marshall did not want the US government to be responsible for drawing up the plans for European economic revival and considered that this was a task for the Europeans. After the failure of the June 1947 Paris summit meeting, the British and French foreign ministers, Bevin and Bidault, convened a conference to discuss Marshall's offer and invited all European governments, except those of occupied Germany and fascist Spain, but the governments of Eastern Europe refused to attend. The 16 states that did send representatives – Austria, Belgium, Denmark, France, Greece, Iceland, Ireland, Italy, Luxembourg, the Netherlands, Norway, Portugal, Sweden, Switzerland, Turkey and the United Kingdom – established the Committee of European Economic Cooperation (CEEC) to work on a four-year recovery plan.

After the war the West European economies were, in effect, bankrupt. They had either been stripped of their assets by occupying forces or, as in the case of Britain, had used them to finance their war effort. By 1947 there was a strong possibility that many European states would stop importing through lack of hard currency, thereby threatening US exports and the post-war American economic boom. The CEEC had the task of estimating how many dollars the West European countries – individually and collectively – would need from the US government, in what became known as Marshall Aid, in order to prevent this crisis of the Western economies. Technical committees were established for the detailed work but the political power-house was a five-country Executive Committee consisting of Britain, France, Italy, the Netherlands and Norway and dominated by the first two states.

The US Administration considered that if its aid to Europe was to be placed to best use, some form of customs union would have to be agreed by the West Europeans. As the countries were still settling their mutual trade accounts by annual, bilateral agreements, even a multilateral payments arrangement was some way off (Tew, 1977, 19). Together with British and Scandinavian opposition to such ideas, this meant the final CEEC report did not include a blueprint for a customs union but only mentioned that the question had been raised and needed further study. No European organization to administer Marshall Aid was recommended because the Scandinavians wanted cooperation with the ECE and the French had doubts about the role of Germany. US Under-Secretary of State Lovett characterized the CEEC report as '16 shopping lists'. The Europeans tried to mollify US government officials, even floating the idea of a European Customs Union Study Group (Milward, 1982, 543–69). Another compromise was the eventual agreement by the Europeans to establish an organization to continue the economic planning and cooperation started in CEEC. In April 1948 the 16 CEEC states established the Organization for European Economic Cooperation (OEEC). The original membership was joined by the Federal Republic of Germany in 1949, the USA and Canada became associates in 1950 and Spain in 1958.

The OEEC was established to help members promote production and trade, establish a multilateral payments system among the members as soon as possible, study the possibility of customs unions or free trade areas, reduce barriers to trade, maintain stable currencies, and make full and effective use of manpower (OEEC Convention, Articles 2–8). The OEEC had three functions: to encourage economic cooperation between West European states; to help member states fulfil their international obligations and national plans; to assist the US in implementing Marshall Aid.

By 1960 the conditions which had necessitated the OEEC had changed. Not only had Marshall Aid ended but the US had a trade deficit whereas the commerce of West European states had successfully recovered. There was still call for cooperation between the OEEC states but there were doubts whether OEEC was the appropriate institution for such activity. It had been established for aid-receiving countries: by 1960 the West Europeans were important aid donors to a growing list of newly independent states. It had not included the USA for fear of being seen as an instrument of the Americans: by 1960 the West Europeans could face the US on a more equal basis. Also the OEEC seemed to have achieved all it could hope to: most of its members had agreed to the convertibility of their currencies but the collapse of the Maudling Committee negotiations (see Chapter 6, pp. 91–2) signalled failure in the creation of a customs union or free trade area for all the OEEC states. The OEEC had also become affected by the Franco-British dispute in these talks. The French regarded the OEEC as British dominated and it was hoped that a new organization might be able to end the developing split between the EEC and the British-led supporters of a free trade area.

Late in 1959, the US, British, French and West German leaders agreed to appoint 'Four Wise Men' to suggest how OEEC might be improved. Any new organization would not have to trespass on the work done by the General Agreement on Tariffs and Trade (GATT) or upset the feelings of the US Congress if, as expected, the US was to be a member. The major emphasis of the new organization was not to be trade, but more economic cooperation (Aubrey, 1967, 26–7). A conference to discuss the reform of the OEEC met in May 1960 with representatives of the 17 OEEC states, the US, Canada and Spain. A Preparatory Commission under OEEC Secretary-General Kristensen drafted the detailed convention of the new organization. On 14 December 1960 the 20 countries signed the convention establishing the Organization for Economic Cooperation and Development and in December 1961 the Ministerial Council of OECD met for the first time. The organization's three main tasks were coordination of economic policy; the promotion of agriculture, science, technology, productivity and trade and currency liberalization; and the economic development of member and non-member states.

In 1964 Japan became a full OECD member, as did Finland in 1969, Australia in 1971 and New Zealand in 1973. Yugoslavia was an associate member until its fragmentation.

Institutions

The institutional structure of the OECD was based on that of the OEEC.

The wide membership of the OEEC meant that its institutions were intergovernmental with no hint of supranationalism: the role of the governments in the OEEC was very strong with large delegations. According to Article 15 of its Convention the ruling body of the OEEC was the Council 'from which all decisions derive', and which consisted of one representative from each member state. The Council normally met at official level (about once a week) with ministerial gatherings three or four times annually. The Council established a number of specialist committees from which it received proposals or reports.

The Council could adopt resolutions, agreements, recommendations and decisions, the last being obligatory. All such decisions are taken unanimously and are implemented by the members (Article 13).

The most important committee was the Executive Committee which prepared work for the Council and had delegated powers to take decisions. The technical committees included ones on Food and Agriculture, Coal, Iron and Steel, Raw Materials, Chemical Products and Maritime Transport, some of which had been CEEC study groups. There were also a number of boards for managing particular aspects of the members' economies. The most important of these was the European Payments Union Managing Board which consisted of seven experts and which ran the European Payments Union established in 1950. It is noticeable that the actual payments of the Union were made through the already existing Bank for International Settlement. The Council also established the European Productivity Agency (1953) and the European Nuclear Energy Agency in 1957 'within the framework of the Organization' and operated under Council authority.

OEEC's Secretariat played a servicing and coordinating role. The Secretary-General had influence rather than power and all three holders of the office were respected figures – Robert Marjolin (appointed 1948), René Sergent (1955) and Thorkil Kristensen (1958). The office was given added status from its inception when in 1948 the first Secretary-General and the Chairman of the OEEC Council were delegated the task of arbitrating the allocation of Marshall Aid to OEEC member states. The Secretariat performed the useful task of preparing studies on the West European economy and that of the individual states.

OECD's institutions demonstrate the continuity from the OEEC. The Council has on it the representatives of the member states, each with one vote, and may meet at ministerial or official level. Decisions and recommendations are to be unanimous, or, if a country's representative abstains, this shall not invalidate the decision which is then applicable to the other members. The Council can take decisions which are binding on members and must be implemented by them; it can enter into agreements with members, non-member states or international organizations; it can make recommendations for consideration by members or by other states or organizations; and it can pass resolutions concerning OECD's work. It has an Executive Committee similar to that of OEEC and a number of committees: Economic Policy, Economics and Development Review, Environment, Development Assistance, Technical Cooperation, Trade, Science Policy, Education, Manpower and Social Affairs, Industry, Energy, Oil, Agriculture, and Fisheries. There are also a number of committees covering financial affairs.

As with the OEEC, the Council appoints the Secretary-General who has a similar role to his OEEC predecessors. As well as heading the secretarial services for the Organization he also chairs the Council meetings held at permanent representative level. The Secretariat is divided into Directorates covering the issues dealt with by Council committees and also provides secretarial help for the OECD's Development Centre, the European Nuclear Energy Agency, the Centre for Educational Research and Innovation, and the Steering Committee for Road Research.

Achievements

It is easier to access the achievements of the OEEC than those of the OECD, not merely in view of the fact the latter is still working whereas the former ceased to exist over thirty years ago, but also because the OEEC's aims were more limited.

The most immediate achievement of the OEEC was to agree on the division of the pump-priming Marshall Aid to the West European economies. It has already been mentioned that the final division of these spoils had to be undertaken by arbitration – there was too much at stake for governments politely to give way on 'essential' requests. One positive result from this *impasse* was the development, after the end of Marshall Aid in 1952, of annual OEEC reviews of economic activity. Member states submitted memoranda on the economic situation in their country; the Secretariat prepared analyses of the outlook in each member state and in West Europe generally; the individual reports were commented on by all the other member states and the Secretariat's report was given detailed examination by the Economic Committee before being unanimously agreed. This work method – taken over by the OECD – produced informed economic commentary that had the ear of the member governments.

Another important aim of the OEEC was the encouragement of economic cooperation, in particular the promotion of trade, a freer system of payments, the reduction of trade barriers and the consideration of customs unions or free trade areas. Achievements here were mixed.

The early attempt to bring about the convertibility of sterling in July 1947 had failed because of large-scale transfers into dollars. Later in 1947 limited intra-European payments were allowed to states offsetting their various debts and credits and a part of Marshall Aid was used to help the West European countries allow drawing rights to their debtors. The establishment by the OEEC of the European Payments Union in 1950 permitted the member states, through the good offices of the Bank for International Settlement (BIS), to settle their accounts with each other on a multilateral basis. The capital fund that made the EPU 'giro' system possible was supplied by the USA (9th Report of the OEEC, 1958, 80). This system encouraged the liberalization of trade and helped states such as West Germany which in the early 1950s had a structural foreign debt problem. In 1955 the OEEC states signed the European Monetary Agreement and after a period of trading surpluses with the USA, the EPU was ended in December 1958 with most OEEC states deciding that their currencies could become externally convertible (Coffey and Presley, 1971, 22–3).

Associated with the liberalization of payments between members were the OEEC's attempts to free trade. The greatest success here was with the ending of quantitative restrictions (QRs) on trade through the Organization's Code of Liberalization which was inspired by the introduction of the EPU and the easing of payments between members. By the end of 1957, 82 per cent of OEEC trade had been freed from QRs. With QR liberalization, tariffs became more important as impediments to trade. Yet it was with this task that the OEEC had the most difficulty. By January 1948 the Benelux Customs Union agreed between Belgium, Netherlands and Luxembourg in 1944 had come into being. Attempts to extend the idea of limited customs unions to the Nordic Region and to Italy and France failed. After the Messina meeting of the 'Six' in June 1955, the differences of approach towards trade liberalization surfaced in the OEEC's Maudling Committee from 1957 to 1959. This attempt to obtain an agreed arrangement that would free trade in all the OEEC states only emphasized the divergence between those states that wanted the countries to present a common tariff to the rest of the world – the supporters of a customs union – and those that considered that member governments should be able to choose the rate of tariff on non-OEEC imports – the free trade area enthusiasts. It was distrust between the leaders of the two groups – respectively the French and the British – that contributed to the demise of the OEEC.

'The objectives of the OECD are broader than those of the OEEC. But the obligations are fewer and considerably less demanding' (Report of the Committee on Foreign Relations, 1961, 2). Because of this difference the OECD might be considered the less effective of the two organizations. It had difficulty in establishing a niche for itself: its birth coincided with the economic division of Western Europe between the EEC and EFTA and one of its stated tasks, that of encouraging the expansion of world trade on a non-discriminatory basis, was something the USA preferred to pursue through GATT in the 1960s. However, the OECD established itself in the 1970s as a useful consultative agency for the industrial states and it has spawned a family of related institutions, including the International Energy Agency (IEA) and the Group of Seven (G7) Summits, which have widened the network of cooperation among OECD states (Putnam and Bayne, 1987).

The OECD has developed a 'code of conduct' for trade and finance among the industrial states: non-tariff barriers to trade are considered by its Trade Committee and working party; the 1964 enlarged Code of Liberalization of Capital Movements covers that important area; the Committee of Experts on Restrictive Business Practices acts as a conciliation forum; the 1976 (revised in 1979) code on international investment and multinational enterprises is a guideline for firms (MacBean and Snowden, 1981, 136–8).

The OECD has established service agencies for particular policy areas. The Development Assistance Committee (DAC – formerly the Development Assistance Group) includes all OECD members – except Greece, Iceland, Luxembourg, Spain and Turkey – and the Commission of the European Communities. The organization has been active in three ways: it has set standards, it has harmonized action and it has undertaken its own aid activities. The most important standards have been those of the percentage of DAC states' GNP devoted to Official Development Assistance (ODA) and the proportion of grant element in these funds. The figures here have been respectively 0.7 and 86 per cent but the achievement has fallen short of this aim: the DAC states only give an average of 0.3 per cent of their GNPs for ODA, though only two have fallen short of the 86 per cent grant element. The DAC has harmonized aid policy by use of the confrontation technique pioneered by the OEEC and by the Annual Aid Review of members' performances and policies. The Development Centre gives actual help to aid-receiving states by its research programme, its transfer of specialized knowledge and by its statistical information.

The International Energy Agency was created as an autonomous body within the OECD in 1974 as an oil consumers' answer to OPEC's oil price increases and restrictions. Its aims were to reduce members' dependence on oil imports by energy conservation, by the encouragement of alternative energy sources and by research and development; to establish a system of oil allocation between members in an emergency; and to establish concerted relationships with oil producing and developing states. Its membership overlapped with that of the OECD except that Finland, France and Iceland did not join and Norway originally only became an associate. In November 1974 an International Energy Programme (IEP) was drawn up with the aim of cooperating in the use of emergency reserves, the equitable sharing of available oil and 'demand restraint during supply emergencies' (International Energy Agency, 1990, 51). The IEA states have managed to lower their dependence on oil imports, partly through a general decline in energy needs because of economic recession in the late 1970s and early 80s and partly because of the opening up of new oil and gas fields in the North Sea and North America. For similar reasons, IEA states have been able to increase their emergency oil reserves. The IEA also has a system of collective action to overcome any supply loss of oil. As well as using up emergency reserves members could cut their demand for oil. A decision to go over to this crisis-response would affect all IEA states but can be taken by a weighted majority, a factor that prevented sovereignty-conscious France from becoming a member. In 1984 the IEA Governing Body created the Co-ordinated Energy Response Measures (CERM) which could be implemented in times of disruption, short of a full crisis, triggering the energy-sharing system. This latter system has been tested seven times up to 1993 and CERM was tested in 1990 (International Energy Agency, 1990, 51).

The most important work of the OECD still remains 'the central problems of economic policy' (Aubrey, 1967, 150) and it is here that the Economic Policy Committee (EPC) is situated with its working parties and its sister Economic and Development Review Committee. It is from here that the much-quoted OECD Reports which receive both government and media attention often emanate. The EPC's Working Party No. 3 on international payments imbalances also doubles as 'The Group of Ten', a meeting of the 10 most powerful Western industrial states serviced by the OECD and working within the BIS and the IMF as a powerful pressure group. On many world economic questions it has proved to be an effective body for aggregating and articulating the interests of the Western industrialized states.

Since 1989 the OECD has attempted to encourage the countries of East and Central Europe to accept the rigours of the market economy. The Organization established the Partners in Transition Programme with the CSFR, Hungary and Poland, that allowed these states to participate in a number of the OECD's subsidiary bodies such as the Group of the Council on Rural Development and the Education Committee (OECD, 1992, 187). OECD members have seen the importance of fostering 'market disciplines' in East and Central Europe within a range of institutions such as the OECD itself, the EBRD, IMF, IBRD, the G24 process chaired by the EC Commission, CSCE, ECE, and ILO. Furthermore the OECD, together with the IBRD, IMF and EBRD, prepared a report on the economy of the USSR for the G7 Houston Summit, in which fundamental reform was seen as the only answer to the Soviet Union's underlying structural problems (op. cit., 155–6).

Another institution devised to help the emerging economies of East and Central Europe and the former Soviet Union has been the European Bank for Reconstruction and Development. This bank was established in May 1990 by the OECD countries meeting as the Group of 24 (G24) and chaired by the Commission of the European Communities, and was intended to foster 'the transition towards open market-oriented economics and to promote private and entrepreneurial initiative in the Central and Eastern European countries committed to . . . multi-party democracy, pluralism and market economies' (*Official Journal of the European Communities*, 1990, 33, C241, 1). The EBRD has attempted to harness private investment capital as well as government money for the ex-Communist countries, but has failed to inject the sort of sums that could make an impact on those states' economies. During 1992 the EBRD invested only ECU200 million in the target area. However agreement was reached in 1992 to invest ECU1.2 billion in projects, with a further ECU2.6 billion expected for 1993. Poland and Hungary accounted for 44 of the 71 projects approved by the start of 1993, with the Russian Federation taking only eight (*Financial Times*, 2 March 1993, 2). The EBRD is also the be involved in an ambitious ECU2 million programme to help privatization in the Ukraine by appointing a team of Western consultants (*Financial Times*, 25 September 1992, 2).

The EBRD has worked closely with other institutions. As well as helping the OECD, the World Bank and the IMF produce a report on economic reform in the Soviet Union (see above, pp. 38–9), it took on, in 1993, the administration of a fund of some ECU550 million to improve nuclear safety in the former Soviet Union. This idea came out to the Group of Seven (G7) meeting in Munich in 1992, when the leaders of the seven leading industrial powers – Canada, France, Germany, Italy, Japan, the United Kingdom and the United States – had their annual discussion of economic and other world affairs. The European Communities decided to contribute some 60 per cent of the fund.

While the EBRD has made a useful contribution to the move by the East and Central European states towards a market economy, especially in the cases of Hungary and Poland, it has essentially had an impossible task. In the case of the former Soviet Union, the adoption of capitalism has not only had to struggle against over 70 years of Communist bureaucracy and dogma, but against more deep-seated beliefs. If market conditions are absent from the CIS states, there are few incentives – apart from political ones – for Western countries to invest in these countries, especially in times of recession. Yet without substantial investment, there is little hope that markets will emerge there. This adverse circle has been reflected in the very modest activities of the EBRD up to 1993.

Contribution

Of the three major western international organizations created in 1948/9, the Council of Europe provided the political-legal force, NATO organized the military-security sinews and the OEEC helped channel economic and financial strength into the body of Western Europe. Unlike NATO, OEEC membership did not formally straddle the Atlantic though the induction of Canada and the US as associates in 1950 emphasized the close ties with North America which were formalized in the creation of the OECD. A critic of the OEEC has described it as 'being forced into being by America as a bold attempt to overcome the limitations of the European system of nation states, [but] within . . . three years it had become so depoliticized that it served only as a forum for registering international agreements made elsewhere, increasingly of a minor kind' (Milward, 1984, 207).

Despite the differences between the extensive membership – which includes rich, industrial, strong-currency states and relatively poorer, more agricultural, weak-currency countries – the OECD's institutions are effective in offering something to all its members. Comparing the ILO, Council of Europe and OECD, Harrison and Mungall thought that 'the OECD stands out as the most successful of the harmonizing organizations . . .' (1978, 190). However, it should not be thought that the other members are harmonizing to the US tune: the British, West German and Japanese delegations, let alone those from France, Sweden or Greece, would not stand for such gross domination.

Although the OECD has not created powerful institutions similar to the EC's Commission or Court, it has taken on the influential working techniques of the OEEC – especially that of confrontation of policy – and has added a family of committees and agencies that has built up the status of the OECD in the eyes of member states.

The OECD has no parliament or assembly and the influence of NGOs on its work is meagre compared to the cases of the Council of Europe or the EC, though it does listen to the views of labour and industry in its Trade Union Advisory Committee and Business and Industry Advisory Committee. It is primarily an organization of civil servants and experts – a strength in a policy area noted for its complexities and esoteric nature.

Given its restraints, it is understandable that the contribution of the OECD, and its predecessor the OEEC, to the functioning of the European political system has been cumulative and unspectacular. Both organizations have offered frameworks for cooperation that would anyhow have taken place: Marshall Aid would have gone ahead without the OEEC; market conditions rather than the IEA have provided the main counterweight to OPEC bargaining power. As well as running certain modest operations and providing a good deal of economic information, the OECD has helped to establish a code of economic norms for those European states belonging to the Western, market-oriented industrialized world, thereby linking them to its power-house, the United States. The EBRD has tried to spread these norms to East and Central Europe and the former Soviet Union, though its efforts have been consistenly less than that of a 'New Marshall Plan'.

References

Aubrey, H. 1967: *Atlantic Economic Cooperation*. New York: Praeger for the Council on Foreign Relations.

Coffey, P. and Presley, J. 1971: *European Monetary Integration*. London: Macmillan.

Harrison, R.J. and Mungall, S. 1978: Harmonisation. In Taylor, P. and Groom, A.J.R. (eds), *International Organisation* (London: Frances Pinter), 169–94.

International Energy Agency 1990: *Energy Policies and Programmes of IEA Countries. 1989 Review*. Paris: OECD.

Macbean, A.I. and Snowden, P.N. 1981: *International Institutions in Trade and Finance*. London: George Allen & Unwin.

Milward, A.S. 1982: The Committee of European Economic Cooperation (CEEC) and the advent of the Customs Union. In Lipgens, W. (ed.), *A History of European Integration, Volume 1 1945–1947* (Oxford: OUP), 543–68.

—— 1984: *The Reconstruction of Western Europe 1945–51*. London: Methuen & Co Ltd.

OECD 1992: *The Annual Report of the OECD. Report by the Secretary-General*. Paris: OECD.

The Organization for European Cooperation 1958: *9th Report of the OEEC. A Decade of Cooperation. Achievements and Perspectives*. Paris: OEEC.

Putnam, R. and Bayne, N. 1987: *Hanging Together. Cooperation and Conflict in the Seven-Power Summits*. London: Sage for Royal Institute of International Affairs.

Report of the Committee on Foreign Relations 1961: *Organization for Economic Cooperation and Development*. Washington, DC: Government Publications Office.

Tew, B. 1977: *The Evolution of the International Monetary System 1945–77*. London: Hutchinson.

4

Council of Europe

Establishment

Two major political forces were behind the creation of the Council of Europe in May 1949. One was the continental federalist movement that hoped the Council would become a parliament for a federation of democratic European states. This strand can be traced back to the writings of the seventeenth century onwards, advocating a united Europe (Hinsley, 1967, Part 1). During the twentieth century these viewpoints found voice with Briand's motion for a federal bond between European states, advanced at the League of Nations in September 1929, and in the Pan-European Union of Count Coudenhove-Kalergi which stressed the role of parliamentarians in uniting Europe. After the dark days of the 1930s and the Second World War, the Continental federalists felt that their time had come. From 1944 to 1946 the meetings of resistance leaders, the Economic League for European Cooperation, the European Union of Federalists (UEF), the European Parliamentary Union and the Christian Democrat Nouvelles Equipes Internationals, espoused various versions of a federal Europe and pressed for the early creation of federal European institutions (Lipgens, 1982).

The second strand rested in the hands of Winston Churchill. Spurred on by Briand's resolution and by the example of the United States of America, Churchill in 1930 commended the concept of the creation of 'the United States of Europe' in an article in *The Saturday Evening Post* of 15 February. He returned to this theme in 1938 in an article in the *News of the World* (29 May). During his wartime premiership Churchill appealed for the post-war establishment of a Council of Europe to promote European cooperation (broadcast, 22 March 1943) and he voiced ideas about this Council having judicial and economic powers and even a common airforce cohort under it (Colville, 1973, 126-7). In his speech at Zurich on 19 September 1946 Churchill relaunched his proposal for 'a kind of United States of Europe' with, as a first step, 'a Council of Europe'. By January 1947 he had become Chairman of the British United Europe Committee, later called the United Europe Movement. Churchill did not have a constitutional formula for building Europe, unlike many of the Continental federalists. He considered that a Council of Europe should first work towards a customs union, then move 'toward some common form of defence' and a uniform currency, but all this was to be achieved by stages (*Collier's*, 4 January 1947). Also Churchill was ambiguous about Britain's role in this process. He considered that 'France and Germany must take the lead together' whilst Britain was listed as one of 'the friends and sponsors of the New Europe' together with the Commonwealth, the USA and the Soviet Union (Zurich speech, 19 September 1946). Earlier that year he had written that Britain 'is also a part of Europe and intimately and inseparably mingled with its fortunes'.

Despite their differences, representatives of the predominantly Continental European federalists and the mostly British European 'Unionists' formed an international Committee of the Movements for European Unity which organized the Congress of Europe held in the Hague in May 1948.

This gathering of almost a thousand people from all over Europe, representing many aspects of life – workers, intellectuals, politicians, churchmen – was probably predominantly federalist but was dominated by the presence of Churchill. In its final session it adopted a 'Message to Europeans' calling for a Charter of Human Rights in Europe with a Court of Justice to implement it and 'a European Assembly where the live forces of all our nations shall be represented'. Furthermore a European Movement was created as a non-governmental body to promote 'the creation of a United Europe'.

Meanwhile the British, French and Benelux governments had signed the Brussels Treaty on 17 March 1948 establishing machinery for coordinating the 'economic, social and cultural collaboration' of the five states as well as their 'collective self-defence'. Moreover 16 West European countries had on 16 April 1948 signed the Convention for European Economic Cooperation to create the OEEC.

The French and Belgian governments took up the cause of the European Movement at the Brussels Treaty's Consultative Council later in 1948. They proposed a European parliamentary assembly but were faced with a counter-proposition from the British Labour Government for a European Council of Ministers dealing with questions of common concern except defence (to be dealt with by the proposed North Atlantic Treaty Organization) and economics (dealt with by the OEEC). In January 1949 the five foreign ministers reached a compromise: there would be a ministerial committee and a consultative parliamentary body for the proposed Council of Europe. Denmark, Ireland, Italy, Norway and Sweden were invited to join negotiations and on 5 May 1949 10 countries signed the Statute of the Council of Europe. The Statute entered into force on 3 August 1949.

The aims of the governments in establishing the Council are set out in its preamble. They reaffirmed their 'devotion to the spiritual and moral values which are the common heritage of their peoples and the true source of individual freedom, political liberty and the rule of law, principles which form the basis of all genuine democracy'. To achieve this, and in the interests of economic and social progress, they saw a need for closer unity of like-minded countries in Europe. Article 1(b) stated that the aims would be pursued by 'discussion of questions of common concern', 'agreements and common action in economics, social, cultural, scientific, legal and administrative matters'.

These aims reflected the will of the founder members to safeguard the democratic life that had been threatened or extinguished during the Second World War and, by 1949, was thought to be endangered by the Soviet presence in Europe. The aims were also those common to Western Europe and North America and had been set out in the North Atlantic Treaty. At a time when the world was becoming increasingly divided between 'East' and 'West', the Statute provided an ideological orientation for even the West European states that were unable to join NATO.

Since 1949 the Preamble and the aims of the statute have been the test for prospective new members. Democratic West European states have been allowed to join: Greece and Turkey (1949), Iceland (1950), the Federal Republic of Germany (1951), Austria (1956), Cyprus (1961), Switzerland (1963), Malta (1965), Liechtenstein (1978), San Marino (1988), Finland (1988). Spain and Portugal had to wait until after the end of fascist rule before becoming members in 1977 and 1976 respectively. Greece was suspended from membership of the Assembly from 1967 to 1970, left the Council from 1970 to 1974 and Turkish delegates were suspended

from the Assembly from 1981 to 1984, all because of military rule
in these two countries. The Saar was an associate member from
1950 to 1957 when it was amalgamated into the Federal Republic
of Germany. Finland had observer status up until 1988 when it
became a full member. Since the freeing of Eastern Europe in 1989
a number of states, formerly part of the old Soviet bloc, have
expressed their wish to join the Council of Europe. Hungary joined
in 1990, the CSFR and Poland in 1991, and Bulgaria in May 1992.
After the CSFR broke up and became the Czech Republic and
the Slovak Republic in January 1993, they were both obliged to
reapply for membership and go through the Council's vetting process. Special guest status in the Assembly was granted to Poland
and Hungary (which later became full members) and the Soviet
Union and Yugoslavia in 1989, and this was later extended to
Bulgaria (later a member) and Rumania. In September 1991 the
three Baltic states – Estonia, Latvia and Lithuania (later to be
members) – were given special guest status, as was Albania in
November 1991 and Slovenia in February 1992. Yugoslavia's
status was suspended in November 1991.

Institutions

The Council of Europe has two major institutions – the Committee
of Ministers and the Parliamentary Assembly – aided by a secretariat. Over the years it has also developed an important juridicial
instrument.

The executive organ of the Council is the Committee of Ministers. Each member state has one representative with one vote on
the Committee and Article 14 suggests that this should normally
be the Minister for Foreign Affairs. Alternates can take his or her
place and states have appointed civil servants as Permanent
Representatives to act in the minister's stead. Many of these
are resident in Strasbourg, the Council of Europe's usual
meeting-place.

The most important powers of the Committee of Ministers are
included in Articles 15 and 16 of the Statute. The Committee can
conclude conventions or agreements or encourage the adoption
by governments of common policy to further the aim of the Council
of Europe. The *conventions* – such as those on the Protection
of Animals for Slaughter of 1979 and on the Conservation of
Wildlife – are concluded within the framework of the Council and

are open for signature by Council members. By the end of 1992 there were some 140 such conventions. It may also make *recommendations* to all member governments asking them to report back on the action taken: such recommendations are made unanimously though this does not make them binding on governments. During the 1980s *declarations* have been issued to state publicly solemn principles which it is not possible or necessary to place in a treaty, examples being the Declaration of Freedom of Information adopted on 29 April 1982. Article 16 allows the Committee of Ministers to 'decide with binding effect all matters relating to the internal administration and arrangements of the Council of Europe' subject to certain Articles relating to the Assembly's powers. The Secretary-General is also responsible to the Committee for the Secretariat (Article 37). The Committee of Ministers can invite states to become full or associated members of the Council of Europe and can suspend states from membership (Article 8) though in both cases the Parliamentary Assembly should be consulted. The various conventions adopted by the Committee of Ministers – the European Convention for the Protection of Human Rights and Fundamental Freedoms being the best known – have added to the duties of the Committee of Ministers. The Council has also established a number of expert committees, now numbering over 50.

The Consultative Assembly (Parliamentary Assembly since 1974) consists of 177 representatives from 27 members in 1992: France, the Federal Republic of Germany, Italy and the United Kingdom each have 18 members; Spain 14; Poland and Turkey 10; the CSFR had eight (now divided); Belgium, Greece, Hungary, the Netherlands and Portugal seven; Austria, Bulgaria, Sweden and Switzerland six each; Denmark, Finland and Norway five; Eire four; Cyprus, Iceland, Luxembourg and Malta three; Liechtenstein and San Marino two. Since 1951 the representatives have been elected by the national parliaments 'or appointed in such manner as that Parliament shall decide'. They are to be nationals of the state they represent but not a member of the Committee of Ministers. In practice the parliaments elect the representatives in some states, in others the government draws up the list in consultation with the main political parties. The representatives are seated in alphabetical order and since the mid-1950s they have formed political groupings that cut across the national frontiers.

Under Article 22 of the Statute, the Parliamentary Assembly

is the deliberative organ of the Council of Europe which can debate matters within the competence of the Statute and can make recommendations to the Committee of Ministers. Assembly debates also have the aim of influencing political opinion by publicity and by educating the representatives from the national parliaments.

Article 23 allows the Parliamentary Assembly to recommend action upon matters referred to it by the Committee of Ministers. The Assembly, can also pass resolutions, some of which relate to the workings of the Assembly, others express Assembly opinions not requiring Ministerial action and a third type is addressed to a limited number of governments – such as those of the EC (Manual of the Council of Europe, 1970, 38). A recommendation needs a two-thirds majority to be adopted whilst a resolution only requires a simple majority.

The Assembly holds an annual session at Strasbourg, though this is now divided into three parts. Debates are held in public and the Assembly has established a number of committees.

The Secretariat of the Council of Europe plays an important role in coordinating activities and organizing meetings. The Secretary-General and Deputy Secretary-General are 'appointed by the Consultative Assembly on the recommendation of the Committee of Ministers' (Article 36b) and are served by an international staff drawn from the nations of the member states. The term of office of the Secretary-General is normally five years and past holders of this post have been: Jacques-Camille Paris (France, 1949–53), Leon Marchal (France, 1953–6), Lodovico Benvenuti (Italy, 1957–63), Peter Smithers (Britain, 1964–9), Dr Lujo Toncic-Sorinj (Austria, 1969–74), Georg Kahn-Ackerman (Germany, 1974–9), Franz Karasek (Austria, 1979–84), Marcelino Oreja (Spain, 1984–9) and Catherine Lalumière (France, from 1989). The Secretary-General can make oral or written contributions to Council discussions, and, since Benvenuti, has been able to take part in an advisory capacity in Committee of Minister's discussions and even place questions on their agenda. Smithers introduced the notion that the Secretary-General should also submit to the Ministers an Annual Programme of Work.

The Assembly appoints its own Clerk who has the status of a Deputy Secretary-General.

Certain non-governmental organizations (NGOs) have consultative status with the Assembly: those in 'category 1' may, after consulting the Secretary-General, suggest subjects for the Assembly's agenda. The help of NGOs such as Amnesty International has been particularly valuable for the work of the Council of Europe in human rights.

The work pattern of the Council of Europe is as follows: a Recommendation or Resolution, backed by a number of members, comes before the Assembly whose Bureau – made up of the President and Vice-Presidents – refers it to the relevant committee where most of the work is done. The committee's work in the form of a rapporteur's report is referred to the Assembly where, after a debate, it is voted on. A Resolution ends there but a Recommendation to the Committee of Ministers is taken up by the Committee or their Deputies and referred to one of the governmental committees. The Committee of Ministers and the Assembly hold Joint Committee meetings to examine common problems, to make proposals for their agendas and to decide how to give effect to Recommendations. Colloquies are also held between the Committee of Ministers and the Assembly on subjects such as 'the balanced development of Europe' (held in 1979). Since the 1960s the Secretariat has presented a Programme of Work which is agreed to by the Committee and the Assembly. This helps to concentrate the Council's work around a motif such as 'Man in a European Society' and sets down discrete targets for intergovernmental action.

An important institutional development has been added to the Council of Europe through its involvement in human rights. Given that the horrors of the Second World War – rehearsed in the Nuremberg Trials – were still fresh in people's minds in 1949 and that governments had a year earlier agreed on the Universal Declaration of Human Rights at the UN, it was not surprising that the first convention of the Council of Europe was the European Convention on Human Rights of 4 November 1950. This is now subscribed to by all Council members.

One of the most significant innovations established by this Convention is the creation 'of machinery and procedures which specially enable the individual victim to institute proceedings on his own behalf . . . [to obtain] redress in respect of the violation of one of the rights protected by the Convention' (Fletcher, 1980, 144). As well as inter-state proceedings, therefore, individuals can lodge their own complaints through the Council of Europe machinery (Article 25). Article 19 established the Commission of Human Rights (ECHR) with one member each drawn from the contracting parties to the Convention. The Commission's task is to winnow out all the complaints for admissibility, to attempt friendly settlements and to set out the merits of the case. At this stage, the case can either go to the Committee of Ministers who can judge whether a violation of the Convention has occurred and what measures should be taken or, alternatively, the Commission or state party can refer the issue to the Court of Human Rights. The Court consists of one judge from each member of the Council of Europe though it normally sits in chambers of seven judges. The Court gives a juridicial judgement with the supervision of execution of judgement being undertaken by the Committee of Ministers (see Fig. 4.1).

Achievements

The Convention on Human Rights was an early achievement of the Council and has proved to be the most public and perhaps the most important part of the organization's activities. In Articles 2 to 14 inclusive of the Convention and the subsequent First and Fourth Protocols, a number of rights and freedoms are laid down: for example, freedom to life protected by law; freedom from torture and slavery; the right to a fair trial; the right to private and family life; the freedom of thought, conscience, religion and expression; the freedom of peaceful assembly and association; the right to marry and found a family. Most of these articles are balanced with derogations or by matching responsibilities and Articles 15 to 17 inclusive add further exceptions.

From 1955 to June 1980, 9016 individual and 10 inter-state applications were made to the Commission of Human Rights. From when the Court was first constituted (January 1959) to the end of 1978 only 27 cases were referred to it, whereas 45 had gone to the Committee of Ministers (Fletcher, 1980, 150). In 1991 alone, 1658 decisions on individual applications were made, with only 217 being ruled admissable (Council of Europe, 1992, 6). By 1993 the Secretary-General of the Council of Europe was calling for a reform of the Commission and the Court to deal with a six-year delay in rulings and a backlog of 2500 cases (*The Guardian*, 12 March 1993, 9). All of the member states of the Council (except the new East and Central European members) have ratified the European Convention on Human Rights and accept the right of individual petition to the Commission and the compulsory jurisdiction of the Court. Some countries have incorporated the Convention into their constitution. This is the case with the

Schema of the implementation machinery of the Convention

First stage — Individual or state application

Examination of the admissibility

Admissible ← → Inadmissible ▶ End of the case

Second stage — Establishment of the facts

Attempt to reach a friendly settlement

No settlement ← → Friendly settlement (on the basis of respect for human rights) ▶ End of the case

Third stage — Report containing legal opinion on alleged breach

Report transmitted to Committee of Ministers of the Council of Europe: beginning of the three months

Final stage
Within the prescribed period of three months the Court may be seized of the case by: — The European Commission of Human Rights *or* The state or states concerned

Judgement of the Court

The judgement is transmitted to the Committee of Ministers which supervises its execution. End of the case

Final stage
If the court is not seized of the case within the period of three months: — The Committee of Ministers decides whether there has been a violation

Decision made public

If necessary, the Committee supervises the carrying out of measures required by its decision by the state concerned. End of the case

Note: The right of individual petition (Article 25 of the Convention) and the Court's compulsory jurisdiction (Article 46 of the convention) are optional.

Fig. 4.1 Short guide to the European Convention on Human Rights (Gomien, 1991, 152)

Netherlands where the new constitution of 17 February 1983 contained a provision thought to be contrary to the Convention – as a result of which the Commission has accepted a case which could possibly lead to a revision of the new Dutch constitution.

A number of cases have come before the Court which have affected the way governments treat their subjects. The Greek case of 1969 and that of Ireland v UK in 1978 distinguished degrees of conduct – torture, inhuman treatment or punishment, and degrading treatment or punishment – prohibited by Article 3 (Gomien, 1991, 19). In the case of the Dutchman, Winterwerp (1979), the Court decided that a person detained in a psychiatric hospital should have access to a court, so should a woman wishing to obtain a separation decree in Ireland (the Airey Case 1979); the Isle of Man's use of birching was found to be unsuitable (Tyrer v UK 1978); the laws concerning adult homosexuals in Northern Ireland were brought into line with those of the rest of the United Kingdom; the right of non-trade unionists to keep their job has been upheld; the rights of prisoners (Golder v UK 1975) have been upheld as have those of the press to publish articles considered to be in the public interest (*Sunday Times* v UK 1979, Lingens v Austria 1986, and Weber v Switzerland 1990). Extradition has been affected by the landmark Soering Case of 1989. During the period of martial law in Turkey from 1980 to 1984, the Council took a close interest in the denial of human rights in that country. In July 1982 France, the Netherlands, Denmark, Norway and Sweden filed complaints with the Commission about Turkey's breaches of the Convention and Turkey was saved from expulsion by a return to democracy, however limited. As a result of the Convention, people in Western Europe are slightly less the objects of state action. Certainly the Council of Europe's human rights system is the most effective international one and is a source of aspiration for less fortunate politicians and jurists in, for example, Latin America.

Another important aspect of the Council's work consists of the number of agreements between member states it has helped to foster: indeed it has been described as a 'treaty factory'. To the end of 1984 the Council had produced 115 treaties. The style of the Council has been to obtain general agreement among members before launching a treaty and, in drafting it, not to be too specific about enforcement. Often a committee of experts can be established to deal with specific workings of a convention – for example, the Frontier Formulation Committee has dealt with the problems of gypsies. In the case of the Convention on Information on Foreign Law, an NGO – the Institute of Comparative Law – collates this information. NGOs are important in initiating treaty activity – either directly or through parliamentarians.

The Council has interested itself in legal questions. More generally conventions on the Suppression of Terrorism (entry into force 1978), on the Legal Status of Children born out of Wedlock (1978) and the Data Protection Convention (1984) are examples of the wide range covered. The aim is not to create a unified code of European law, more to lessen the inconveniences of there being different national laws. To this end the Council hosts regular meetings of Ministers of Justice to discuss, for example, suppression of terrorism, drug trafficking ('the Pompidou Group') or the less publicized aspects of legal cooperation.

In the social and socio-economic field, one of the noticeable achievements has been the European Social Charter, drafted between 1955 and 1958, signed in 1961 and in force in 1965. The Charter itemizes economic and social rights, the core ones being the rights to work, to organize, to collective bargaining, to social security, to social and medical assistance, to protection of the family and to the protection of migrant workers. The supervisory procedure consists of certain aspects being examined in two-yearly cycles first by a Committee of Independent Experts and then by a Committee of Ministers' Deputies. At the end of this cycle their reports will go to the Assembly and to the Committee of Ministers which can make recommendations by a two-thirds majority. Whilst these may be directed at an individual state, often they are more general such as their recommendation in 1978 to amend the Charter to include rights of non-discrimination between men and women in job recruitment. The Council's main task in this area has thus been standard-setting though in such transnational questions as migration they have undertaken independent activity with the help of a Resettlement Fund.

The Council's role in education, culture and sport has been to act as a clearing station and point of contact. The European Cultural Convention of 1954 has few binding articles but was important in stressing both the unity and diversity in European culture and in establishing in 1962 the Council for Cultural Cooperation (CCC) which included representatives of the member states plus Finland (not then a member) and the Holy See. The CCC makes proposals to the Committee of Ministers and adopts and executes an annual programme which is financed by a Cultural

Fund. Since the signing of the convention there has been a greater official acceptance of a shift from just making traditional 'high culture' more accessible towards a broader definition of culture itself. There is also a move away from seeing culture as having 'the political purpose of promoting greater unity among the member states' (Haigh, 1974, 194). More emphasis has been placed on sport with the establishment of a Sports Fund in 1978, and on education, especially in the area of languages, adult education and greater mobility for students. In most of this area, as in European Heritage Year and European Music Year (1985), much of the work is national but the Council offers a framework for action.

In 1960 the Council inaugurated a youth programme which at first emphasized cooperation between youth NGOs in European Youth Centres the first of which was permanently established in 1972. The following year the European Youth Foundation was established 'to promote youth cooperation in Europe' through financing youth organizations.

The importance of local authorities in Europe was an early interest of the Assembly – Chaban-Delmas of Bordeaux tabled a motion in 1951. In 1957 the first European Conference of Local Authorities – now called the Conference of Local and Regional Authorities of Europe (CLRAE) – took place, bringing together representatives of these authorities in the Assembly building. More specialist conferences of historic towns, alpine regions, border areas and island regions, among others, have since been held and in 1992 CLRAE approved two new charters, one on youth participation in local life and the other being an urban charter (*Forum*, May 1992, 8). Intergovernmental cooperation has emphasized special studies of local problems, such as the flight from the land, and is supervised by senior officials in the Steering Committee for Regional and Municipal Matters.

A more recent interest of the Council has been that of conservation and environmental problems. The Assembly, in 1960, and Committee of Ministers in 1962 recommended joint action in this area. An expert Committee for the Conservation of Nature and Natural Resources was set up, the issue was included in the Council's Medium Term Plan and the European Information Centre for Nature Conservation established in 1967 to help coordinate national efforts. The main Council activity has been in facilitating symposia, studies and some common activities. In 1979 a Convention on the Conservation of European Wildlife and Natural

Habitats was signed by the Council members, Finland and the EC, providing an all-round approach to nature conservation, including lists of protected plants and animals. In 1968 the Committee of Ministers adopted the European Water Charter on all aspects of water management, and 25 years later in the spring of 1993 the Assembly set itself the task of producing specific proposals for a pan-European water policy.

The European Public Health Committee, formed in 1966, consists of the national heads of public health departments and experts from member states, the World Health Organization's European office and the League of Red Cross Societies. Exchange of medical students, agreements on medical subjects and coordinated research has been encouraged. A blood bank and a European Pharmacopoeia have been established.

The federalists at the 1948 Hague Congress hoped that the Council of Europe would lead the way on economic and political cooperation. In their first session the assembly recommended convertibility of European currencies, a move towards European economic union, control of international tariffs and a European Patents Office. It was hoped that the OEEC's work would be extended and specialized agencies with discrete powers in particular fields – such as those suggested for a coal and steel authority by Schuman in 1950 – would be established. The creation of the ECSC and the Franco-British disagreements about a customs union overshadowed the Council of Europe in this area from the 1950s onwards and since the formation of EFTA the Assembly has normally been content to hear reports from the EC, EFTA and OECD and discuss the progress of economic cooperation in general terms.

At the first Assembly meeting it was unaminously agreed that the goal of the Council of Europe was the 'creation of a European political authority with limited functions but real powers'. Attempts to bring this about and to interweave the institutions of the Council with those of the Brussels Pact and the OEEC – made most notably in the 'Mackay Protocol' and 'La Malfa Proposals' of 1950 – petered out after opposition from the British and Scandinavian governments. The Schuman Plan and the EDC caused a flurry of discussion in the Assembly. The 1952 plan of the British Foreign Secretary, Anthony Eden, to envelop the nascent Communities within the Council of Europe was opposed by the neutrals, and even attempts to create close consultation between the ECSC's Assembly and that of the Council of Europe came to little (Robertson, 1961, 81–99). In the end, all the discussion led to the Council taking on the social and cultural work of the WEU in 1959. Since then the Council has continued to discuss important political questions, including foreign and security matters (though 'matters relating to national defence do not fall within the scope of the Council of Europe', Article 1d).

In 1989 the Council granted observer status to Hungary, the Soviet Union, Poland and Yugoslavia in an effort to open a dialogue with Eastern Europe. Both the Committee of Ministers and the Assembly have passed resolutions and made recommendations about detente in Europe, the development of the European Communities, events in Eastern Europe, the Soviet invasion of Afghanistan, trouble in the Middle East and, in July 1989, the Assembly was addressed by Mr Gorbachev on his vision of a future Europe. Generally the Council has been most vocal where human rights have been undermined or peace threatened. It is therefore not surprising that the Committee of Ministers strongly supported the democratization process in East and Central Europe, establishing the Demosthenes programme to provide expert advice to the states of that part of Europe on 'every aspect of the organisation and functioning of a pluralist democracy' (Ouchterlony, 1991, 9). In 1990 a special commission for democracy through law was established, and ministers from East and Central European states have been invited to specialist meetings, whether their country is a Council member or not.

The Council has also considered its relations with other European organizations. On the occasion of the fortieth anniversary of the Council, the Committee of Ministers, in May 1989, adopted a solemn Political Declaration within which relations with the EC had pride of place. It was decided that relations between the two institutions should be intensified but that they should be complementary. Quadripartite meetings were to be arranged between the EC's Presidents of the Council and of the Commission and the Council of Europe's Chairman of the Committee of Ministers and Secretary-General. The EC has also become a party to a number of the Council's conventions and other instruments (Ouchterlony, 1991, 7). The Council has played an active part in CSCE meetings involving minority rights and the cultural heritage and the 1990 Paris Charter of the CSCE recognized the important role of the Council of Europe in promoting human rights, democracy and the rule of law (op. cit., 11).

Contribution

The Council of Europe has not lived up to the expectations of the federalists involved in its creation: it has not provided the legislative, executive and judicial institutions for a federal Western Europe. It has, however, fulfilled useful functions in the development of the West European political systems since 1949.

The democratic norms for West European countries were provided by the statute of the Council and the Convention of Human Rights. Within the Council, member governments have been socialized into a pattern of behaviour towards their citizens based on these values. Recruitment into the West European political subsystem was based on the acceptance into the Council of those states with parliamentary democratic institutions. This has set a standard for East and Central European states. The Council, lacking enforcing institutions itself, has depended on the member states to implement its decisions though the Commission and Court of Human Rights provide an extra layer of rule-adjudication above the national courts. The bulk of the Council's work has consisted in providing a network of information, cooperation and coordination on a wide variety of subjects.

The institutions of the Council of Europe work for extensive functions between 31 European states but have not had the power given to those of the European Communities. The Committee of Ministers has been able to make decisions but has had to be content with agreements that could attract unanimity. The Assembly has had the advantage of covering a spectrum of political views for all the democracies in Western Europe but has not attracted the attention, or influence, of the EC's directly-elected parliament. Neither has the Council had the driving force of the Community's Commission behind it though the Programme of Work system has given greater shape to Council activities. Its Assembly has provided a stage from which the officials of other international organizations lacking such an institution (for example, the Secretary-General of the OECD) may from time to time ventilate their views to a wider audience. The Council has also given non-governmental organization a focus for their activities on an all European-wide basis. It is perhaps the extent of its membership – and its commitment to democracy – which gives the Council to Europe a special position in the pantheon of European institutions.

References

Colville, J. 1973: Churchill as Prime Minister. In Stansky, P. *Churchill: A Profile*. New York: Hill & Wang.

Council of Europe, 1992: *European Commission of Human Rights, Survey of Activities and Statistics 1991*. Strasbourg: Council of Europe.

Fletcher, I. 1980: The Council of Europe and human rights. In Twitchett K.J. (ed.) *European Co-operation Today*. London: Europe.

Forum May 1992: Strasbourg: Council of Europe.

Gomien, D. 1991: *Short Guide to the European Convention on Human Rights*. Strasbourg: Council of Europe.

Haigh, A. 1974: *Cultural Diplomacy in Europe*. Strasbourg: Council of Europe.

Hinsley, F.H. 1967: *Power and the Pursuit of Peace*. Cambridge: Cambridge University Press.

Lipgens, W. 1982: *A History of European Integration. Vol. 1 1945–47*. Oxford: Oxford University Press.

Manual of the Council of Europe 1976. Strasbourg: Council of Europe.

Opsahl, T. 1978: The protection of human rights in the Council of Europe and in the United Nations, *European Yearbook*, XXXVI, 92–4.

Ouchterlony, T. 1991: *The Council of Europe in the New Europe*. Edinburgh: Europe Institute.

Robertson, A.H. 1961: *The Council of Europe: Its Structure, Functions and Achievements*, 2nd edn. London: Stevens.

5

The European Coal and Steel Community

Establishment

By the end of the 1940s, institutions had been established in Western Europe to tackle some of the economic and political problems: the Council of Europe helped strengthen the democratic sinews of societies threatened from outside and within, the Marshall Plan and the OEEC had pointed the way towards economic recovery and NATO had brought the promise of American assistance against the threat of Soviet attack. There remained, however, a series of interrelated problems that, by 1950, had not been satisfactorily covered by these organizations.

The basic problem was that of what to do with Germany. With the division between the Eastern Soviet zone and the three Western zones and the creation out of the latter of the Federal German Republic in 1949, it became clear that suppression was not an answer, at least for West Germany. However, the French in particular had doubts about West German economic revival: they feared that, unrestrained, the Germans might come to dominate, politically and militarily, the continent of Europe as they had done within two decades of the end of the First World War. De Gaulle expressed this concern: 'The current of German vitality is thus turned westwards. One day German aggressiveness might well face westwards too' (*The Times*, 10 September 1945). French governments had subsequently tried to sap Germany's strength by resisting German control of the Ruhr industries and concluding an economic union of the Saarland and France in 1948. After facing increasingly hostile British and American (and German) attitudes towards this restrictive approach to the industrial mainstay of the West German economy, the French government satisfied itself with the creation of the International Ruhr Authority (IRA) in April 1949. This was to make sure that 'the resources of the Ruhr shall not in the future be used for the purpose of aggression', in the words of the Draft Agreement of 9 January 1949 and which established an Authority of Britain, France, USA, Benelux and Germany, on which the Germans were in a minority and even had their votes cast by the three occupying powers until the establishment of the Federal Republic in December 1949. The task of the IRA was to control the distribution of the coal, coke and steel of the Ruhr 'taking into account the essential needs of Germany'. In reality the IRA fell between two stools. It upset the West Germans who, particularly after achieving statehood, considered it unfair that only their resources should be subject to international control: it seemed too much like punishing the new democratic government for the sins of its Nazi predecessor. Neither did the IRA satisfy French demands as they quickly found that the British and American representatives, conscious of German criticism, were unwilling to constrain coal and steel production in the Ruhr.

By 1950 the quest was for a better solution to the problem of how to allow German recovery without undermining France's sense of security. There was no lack of ideas. As seen in Chapter 4, the federalists had been active in promoting plans for a united Europe in the post-war period. A crucial figure among the federalists was Jean Monnet who had been French representative to the Inter-Allied Maritime Commission during the First World War, had been one of the authors of Churchill's proposal for a Franco-British Union in 1940 and in the immediate post-war years had headed the organization carrying out the French economic plan.

The US Administration, through the Marshall Aid administrator Paul Hoffman, called for 'an integration of the Western European economy' (31 October 1949). Karl Arnold, Minister-President of North Rhine–Westphalia which included the Ruhr, asked in 1949 whether the international arrangement for the Ruhr should not be extended to French Lorraine, the Saar, Belgium and Luxembourg, an idea taken up by John McCloy, the American Commissioner in Germany, and supported in variations by socialists and businessmen alike (Diebold, 1959, 35–46).

The coal and steel industries of Western Europe offered an attractive target for the integrationists. First, they represented the sort of heavy industry needed to fight a war and which could cause concern if built up in former Axis countries. Secondly, these industries in continental Western Europe had important linkages. The Saar steel industry was linked to France but the new Federal German government wanted the Saarland to be reintegrated into

Germany. The French steel mills of Lorraine depended on the Ruhr for their coking coal and coke. The French steel industry was larger than that of Germany but was concerned by the German potential, just as the French coal producers feared competition from German mines (Willis, 1968, 88–94). Finally, there was a more general threat – that a post-war depression, similar to that which had followed the First World War, would hit Europe's coal and steel industries and that its owners would be forced into larger cartels which national governments would find hard to control.

Coal and steel thus presented the ideal functional area for an experiment in European integration. In the words of Monnet's memorandum prepared for French Foreign Minister Robert Schuman on 4 May 1950, there was one way of escape from the problems: 'concrete, resolute action on a limited but decisive point' (Vaughan, 1976, 51). Schuman, on the basis of Monnet's work, proposed on 9 May 1950 'to place all Franco-German coal and steel production under a common High Authority, in an organization open to the other countries of Europe'. This would be 'the first step toward European Federation', 'a first decisive act in the construction of Europe' (Willis, 1968, 80). The West German government, followed shortly by those of the Benelux states and Italy, accepted the Schuman Plan. The United Kingdom's Labour Government found itself unable to join negotiations based on a Franco-German agreement where the participants were aiming 'at peace, European solidarity and economic and social progress by pooling their coal and steel production and by the institution of a new higher authority whose decisions will bind them' (Diebold, 1959, 49). Monnet took charge of the negotiations and aimed at 'upgrading the common interests' of the six states. He succeeded in persuading the member governments to accept a supranational authority to control the coal and steel industries in the European Coal and Steel Community (ECSC). The Treaty of Paris, establishing the ECSC, was signed in April 1951, ratified by the French, West German, Italian, Belgian, Dutch and Luxembourg parliaments by June 1952, allowing the Treaty to come into force on 25 July 1952. The Treaty, valid for 50 years, consisted of a hundred articles, six protocols, a convention on transitional provisions and an exchange of letters between France and West Germany about the Saar. The preamble stated that the parties were 'resolved to substitute for historic rivalries the merger of their essential interests; to lay, by establishing an economic community, the foundations of a broader and deeper community among peoples long divided by bloody conflicts'.

To this end the six states established the ECSC 'founded upon a common market, common objectives and common institutions' (Article 1). The common market in coal and steel meant that, within the Community, import and export duties and quantitative restrictions were to be abolished, as were discriminatory and restrictive practices affecting price or delivery terms, and state subsidies (Article 4). The objectives of the ECSC were to create an orderly supply to this common market taking into account third countries; to ensure that comparable consumers within the common market had equal access to production; to ensure the lowest possible reasonable price; to encourage expansion of production and rationalization of natural resource exploitation; to promote improved working conditions; to promote international trade and equitable limits in export pricing; and to promote orderly expansion and modernization of production. Such a list of aims often meant in reality a clash of policy choices, for example between lower prices and better work conditions in the coal and steel industries.

Institutions

In his proposal, Robert Schuman had suggested that Franco-German production of coal and steel should be placed 'under a joint High Authority, within an organization open to the participation of other European nations' (Documents on International Affairs, 1949–50, 316–17). The nature of this High Authority was fleshed out in the Treaty of Paris. It was to consist of nine members appointed for six years and chosen for their general competence. They would be nationals of the member states (though with not more than two coming from any one state), eight would be appointed by the member states and the ninth elected by these eight (Article 10). The members of the High Authority were to be 'completely independent in the performance of their functions, in the general interest of the Community' (Article 9). Furthermore this Article stated that they would neither seek nor take instructions from any government or other body nor would member states seek to influence them in the performance of their duties. This would preserve 'the supranational character of their functions'. In order to understand this supranational character it is necessary to examine the other institutions established by the Paris Treaty and the powers entrusted to them.

It was originally intended that the ECSC would be run by the High Authority which would abjure individual state interests and instead deal in terms of the Community's needs. During the negotiations for the Treaty this idea was adapted. Monnet suggested that there should be an Assembly of parliamentarians from the member states, which would have the power of voting the High Authority out of office and would generally exercise a supervisory role. Originally the Assembly had 78 members nominated from the members' parliaments, though the possibility of direct election was left open (Article 21). The Assembly could discuss the annual report of the High Authority and, by a two-thirds majority of votes cast (representing a majority of Assembly members), could dismiss all the members of the High Authority. The Assembly had no other power, no budgetary control, no legislative duties and its power of dismissal was less threatening than it seemed as, in theory, the member states could reappoint the censured High Authority.

Another institution added during the treaty negotiations was the special Council of Ministers suggested by the Dutch and Belgian representatives (Diebold, 1959, 63). Articles 26 to 30 of the Paris Treaty set out the powers and composition of the Council. It consisted of the representatives of the six member states, each with one vote. This body was established in order to mediate between the High Authority and national interests, harmonizing Community action with that of the individual governments. Furthermore, the Council had to concur in certain actions by the High Authority and be consulted on others. On some matters the Council had to be unanimous – for example the fixing of customs duties on coal and steel as against third countries (Article 72) – whilst others were decided by a two-thirds majority – as in Article 88 which dealt with non-fulfillment of obligations by states, and by a simple majority vote for decisions other than those by qualified majority or unanimity (Article 28). On certain matters the Council could itself take decisions: altering the number of High Authority members (Articles 9) or Court Judges (Article 32) fixing High Authority and Court members' salaries (Article 29), fixing customs duties (Article 72), appointing the Community's auditor (Article 78(6)), adding to the list of coal and steel products (Article 81) and making amendments to the powers of the High Authority (Article 95) and to the Treaty (Article 96).

The task of the Court of Justice was to 'ensure that the law is observed in the interpretation and implementation of the ECSC, Treaty and of regulations made thereunder' (Article 31). The Court consisted of seven judges assisted by two Advocates-General, all of whom were chosen by common accord between the six governments from persons whose 'independence can be fully relied upon' and who fulfilled the conditions for exercising the highest court functions or 'who are legal experts of universally recognized ability' (Article 32b). Security of tenure was insured for the judges' six years of office as their appointments could only be terminated by death, retirement or by the unanimous opinion of all the other judges that 'they no longer fulfil the required conditions' (Articles 6 and 7 of the Protocol of the Statute of the Court of Justice).

The remit of the Court was widely drawn. It had extensive compulsory powers in areas covered by the Paris Treaty. Its jurisdiction covered controversies concerning the application of the Treaty between member states and the ECSC institutions, and between the various organs of the Community. It also protected individuals and enterprises against wrongful action by the ECSC institutions, awarding damages to injured parties (Article 40). The Court could give preliminary ruling on the validity of High Authority and Council actions where these were in question before a municipal court or tribunal (Article 41). Finally the Court had two interventionist powers – it could review High Authority action if member states brought the matter before the Court, claiming that the action provoked 'fundamental and persistent disturbances in its economy' (Article 37); it could intervene if it considered a government had abused its right of veto over the appointment of members of the High Authority (Article 10).

A final institution of the ECSC was the Consultative Committee advisory to the High Authority. It consisted of between 30 and 51 members, comprising equal numbers of producers, workers, consumers and dealers, all appointed by the Council for a period of two years (Article 18).

The original idea of a supranational High Authority deciding coal and steel policy on a Community-wide basis was already watered down by the Treaty of Paris. The Council of Ministers represented an input by the member governments; the Assembly allowed for democratic advice and, in theory, ultimate accountability; the Court provided for judicial review; and the Consultative Committee presented the viewpoints of functional groups. The High Authority had considerable potential powers, though the exercise of these was to be by no means unchallenged.

Achievements

The newly formed Community had to face the question of its relationship with United Kingdom, a major coal and steel producer. The Labour Government had not felt able to join in negotiations for a Coal and Steel Community based on supranational institutions. After the Conservatives came to power in 1951, Sir Anthony Eden, the Foreign Secretary, tried to incorporate the ECSC into the work of the Council of Europe but withdrew his plan in the face of neutral nations' hostility. Churchill's Conservative Government wanted a closer relationship with the ECSC and on 21 December 1954 a Treaty of Association was signed between the Community and the United Kingdom, to come into force in September 1955. This brought about a practical working agreement between Britain and the ECSC (Haas, 1968, 101–2).

To promote the common market in coal and steel, the ECSC has taken measures to achieve a unified market among member states and to create competitive conditions, removing restrictive practices and state subsidies (Article 4).

In pursuit of the unified internal market, the ECSC took on the task of coordinating commercial policy for coal and steel, overseeing trade agreements with third countries. Trade restrictions on coal, iron ore and steel among member states were scrapped and common tariffs agreed for external trade. From the beginning, the High Authority implemented a fair pricing policy and prevented illegal rebates by governments, which would have interfered with the creation of a common market. The High Authority also tried to prevent hidden subsidies through the pricing mechanism for coal and steel loads on the various state railway systems. From the mid-1950s the High Authority tried to tackle the problem of free movement of miners, at that time complicated by a surplus of unskilled Italian workers. It had more success with conditions for mine and steel workers and created a house-building programme for them. Spurred on by the Common Assembly and its vocal socialist members, the High Authority in 1957 declared its aim was 'to bring about a levelling-up in working conditions'.

To increase competition, the High Authority first had to tackle the difficult topic of cartels. Such arrangements whereby large companies fixed market conditions rather than compete against each other were forbidden by Articles 65 and 66 of the Treaty of Paris but it was 1956 before the High Authority took action against the most entrenched cartels (Haas, 1968, 76–7). The High Authority aimed to eliminate state subsidies which would otherwise distort the creation of a common market.

Such measures were difficult even in the years of general economic expansion of the 1950s and 60s, partly because the coal industry in the Six was in decline, swamped by cheap oil imports. However, the massive rise in oil prices in 1973/4 and again in 1979/81 had a negative effect on coal and steel in the expanded Community because of its dampening of industrial demand.

The Community was also facing competition from other producers. From 1946 to 1974 world steel production grew from 112 to 709 million tonnes, providing enough demand for all producers. The highest growth was in Japan whose share of the market increased from 2.5 to 16 per cent. By 1981 this had stabilized at 15 per cent whereas the ECSC share had dropped to 18 per cent, compared with 23 per cent in 1970. Within the Community demand for steel fell by 15 per cent from 1964 to 1980, leaving the industry running at a 63 per cent capacity compared with the USA's 80 per cent and the 85 per cent needed to be profitable. From 1974 to 1981 almost a quarter of a million jobs were lost in the Community's steel industry, a decline of some 31 per cent. By the end of 1984 there were 446,000 employed in the industry.

By 1993 the Braun Report had found that the Communities' steel industry was in overcapacity by 30 million tonnes of crude steel and between 19 and 26 million tonnes of rolled products. Steel producers agreed to reduce crude capacity by 25.8 million tonnes and rolled products by 17.9 million tonnes. The Communities intended to ask the East and Central European states to agree to export restraint of cheap steel products, though this seemed contrary to the wish to open up EC markets to the Europe Agreement states.

In response to this downturn in the steel industry, the ECSC adopted a number of policies. From May 1977 to July 1980 compulsory minimum prices or guide prices were in force with the strict application of Article 60 concerning unfair and discriminatory pricing and marketing. This was to prevent one Community steel industry from insulating itself against the market to the disadvantage of others by undercutting their prices. In July 1981 these rules were extended. Despite its action the ECSC had to declare a 'manifest crisis' for certain steel products, under Article 58(1), and it brought in compulsory restrictions on production and deliveries.

Since 1978 the ECSC had negotiated agreements with its principal suppliers to maintain these supplies and to keep their prices close to those of the Community. The major problem internationally has been with the United States which has threatened to exclude Community steel exports to protect its own.

In 1993 the Clinton Administration imposed dumping duties on US imports of steel from 19 countries, including ECSC members. The highest tariff was on steel plate from British Steel – 109 per cent. This was particularly resented as the Communities had been acting under a voluntary restraint code agreed with the US.

There has also been a Community policy of restructuring the steel industry. Planned investment has to be notified to the Commission (the High Authority's successor) and public aid is only permitted if it is aimed at restructuring. The aim is to reduce the amount and intensity of aid, eventually phasing it out, to allow fewer distortions of competition and fewer grounds for complaint by the United States (*European Yearbook*, 1988, EC 23). The ECSC has continued its policy of giving loans to aid investment and the European Regional Development Fund has provided non-repayable aid for such activities as scientific research in the steel industry.

Social aid has aimed at the redeployment of steel workers by retraining (158,000 in the 1975–81 period), creating new jobs and supporting early retirement and part-time work schemes. In 1983 the Commission called for the closing down of a further 8.33 million tonnes of productive capacity and by 1985 such reductions were being achieved. The reduction of output in 1993 was also accompanied by an aid package of some ECU900 million to alleviate the worst effects.

The coal industry has also been affected by the world economic conditions since 1974. The Community's dependence on imported oil has lessened as total energy consumption decreased with industrial depression and with the more efficient use of fuels. The position of coal has declined only slightly.

Since 1969 the policy of concentration prohibition under Article 65 has given way to one of support allowing concentration. There are production subsidies for coking coal and subsidies for total or partial pit closure (Commission Decisions of 22 December 1970 and 10 December 1971). In 1975 the Council approved the ECSC's

Medium-Term Guidelines for Coal, 1978–1985, which were aimed at stabilizing coal production and increasing productivity. In 1983, the Commission proposed a restructuring of the industry over five years with investment being channelled into the most promising mines. By the 1990s the aim was to allow financial support only if it improved the competitiveness of the coal industry. At the same time there was a move to ease the resulting social problems and in July 1984 the Council voted money to the ECSC budget to help with the social consequences of restructuring the coal industry.

While major changes were taking place in the coal and steel industries, the ECSC itself was also undergoing reconstruction. The Economic Community and Atomic Energy Community, established by the Treaties of Rome in 1957, were based on the blueprint of the Coal and Steel Community but with modifications to make the balance of the institutions quite different from the achieved in the Treaty of Paris. From the beginning, all three Communities had the Court of Justice and the European Parliament as common institutions. The major institutional differences was that the Commission of the two new Communities did not have the same autonomous powers as the ECSC's High Authority.

By April 1965 the six member countries had decided to merge the Commission and the High Authority and that there should also be one Council of Ministers for the three Communities, an agreement that eventually entered into force in July 1967. Whilst the High Authority no longer has a separate existence, its powers live on. When acting as the Commission for the Coal and Steel Community, the merged Commission still has the benefit of those powers granted to the High Authority by the Treaty of Paris. Furthermore there is still an ECSC Consultative Committee, as established by Article 18 of that Treaty. These institutions were left untouched by the Maastricht Treaty of 1992, though the ECSC – with the EEC (renamed the European Community) and Euratom – would become part of the European Union.

The merger has meant the integration of Community coal and steel policies into the wider context of the Communities' actions in the realms of industry and energy.

Contribution

The importance of the ECSC was in being the first Community institution. It held all the hopes of creating a new Europe, starting only five years after the Second World War. The Preamble of the

Treaty of Paris and the statements of the founders of the Coal and Steel Community demonstrate high aspirations many of which have not been fully achieved.

More than any other European institution, the Coal and Steel Community reflected a vision which inspired its authors. As seen at the start of this chapter, the Schuman Plan was a response to European integrationist calls, the needs of Franco-German politics and the economic requirements of the day. The Community represents a keystone in the edifice of Franco-German reconciliation and in the construction of a West European economic entity.

At a crucial time in the post-war West European period, the ECSC attempted to establish new norms of behaviour between countries that had a long history of warfare by making the sinews of war unavailable for exclusively national use. It provided institutions for the articulation and aggregation of the interests of functional groups and political representatives in the member states and established a system of rule-making and adjudication for the coal and steel industries of those countries.

However, the ECSC has failed to fulfil the grander designs of some of its mentors. It has not led to the sort of political unity hoped for by the federalists – 'the European federation which is indispensable to the maintenance of peace', to quote the Schuman Plan. Neither did it lead to further victories for the functionalist approach to integration. Plans for an agricultural Green Pool, a health White Pool, a European Political Community and a European Defence Community did not materialize and when two new Communities were created in 1957 – the EEC and Euratom – their institutions were less supranational than those of the ECSC.

What the ECSC represented was an alternative approach towards tackling the broad problems of peace and prosperity in post-war Europe. Subjugation of former enemies no longer proved efficacious. The British approach of supporting broad-based institutions with modest powers won out in the creation of the OEEC and the Council of Europe. The Schuman Plan was much more an act of faith, one which the British felt unable to uphold.

So, despite the United Kingdom's Treaty of Association, the ECSC was the first step down the road of West European schism with the Continental Six going along the Community track and the United Kingdom, plus its Scandinavian allies, sticking to its familiar inter-governmentalist path. It would be 20 years before the two could be brought together.

References

Diebold, W., 1959: *The Schuman Plan*. New York: Praeger.

Documents on International Affairs 1949–50 1951, London: Royal Institute of International Affairs.

European Yearbook 1988: European Communities: *European Yearbook 1986*. Dordrecht: Martinus Nijhoff, EC 1–47.

Haas, E. 1968: *The Uniting of Europe*. Stanford: Stanford University Press.

Vaughan, R. 1976: *Post-War Integration in Europe*. London: Edward Arnold.

Willis, F.R. 1968: *France, Germany, and the New Europe, 1945–1967*. Stanford: Stanford University Press.

6

The European Communities

Establishment

The signing of the two Treaties of Rome in March 1957 created the European Economic Community (EEC) and the European Atomic Energy Community (Euratom) to add to the European Coal and Steel Community (ECSC). It was seen as a major step in the move towards West European integration, and the three organizations, now expanded with unified institutions and called the European Communities (EC) form the bedrock of much economic and political cooperation among the countries of Western Europe.

Chapter 5 showed how the European Coal and Steel Community was set up by France, West Germany, Italy and the three Benelux states to deal with some of the problems left unsolved by international organizations and their West European member governments in the period from 1945 and 1950. The main challenge was to allow West German economic and political recovery without creating French feelings of insecurity. The ECSC was the first move to lay 'the foundations of a broader and deeper community among peoples long divided by bloody conflicts' (ECSC, 1987, Preamble). It covered two industries – coal and steel – which, although important, represented only part of the economic activity of the ECSC's member states and the Community's membership excluded what was then Western Europe's largest economy – the United Kingdom – as well as a host of other smaller but nevertheless thriving countries such as Switzerland and Sweden.

From the start it was clear that the ECSC might spawn other Community organizations and that there might be 'supranational' institutions for other sectors of the economy. The idea of Jean Monnet and those around him was that 'the "spill-over" effect in sector integration was believed to lead inevitably to full economic unity' (Haas, 1968, 283). Their reasoning was that an integrated coal and steel industry in the Community states could not exist without bringing a common transport policy, the equalizing of conditions in other heavy industries and a unified approach to agricultural production. Thus progress in the integration of one area of economic life would 'spill-over' into others. By using the 'Community idea' – the notion that policies should be carried out for the benefit of the inhabitants of a group of states as if frontiers did not exist between them – it was hoped to bring economic and social benefit and to contribute to peace and security. This represented a use, on a regional basis, of the functionalist notions of David Mitrany, whereby the functions of everyday societal life – transport, health care, agriculture, industrial development, education and so on – are no longer carried out on a basis limited by the boundaries of each sovereign state but are undertaken across frontiers, thereby indirectly contributing to the prevention of warfare between states (Archer, 1992, 88–9).

The supporters of the Community idea saw it as something more than a way of knitting together previously hostile societies with Lilliputian economic threads. There were those, like Monnet and Schuman, who considered the ECSC as being 'the first step toward European Federation' (Schuman, 9 May 1950). The European Federalists had been working hard to attract support for their ideas but the immediate post-war period had found them weak and divided in a period when European national governments were struggling to establish their legitimacy (Lipgens, 1982, 685). The realists among them knew that if a united Europe was to be created it had to be with the consent of governments and peoples and not by edict (Hallstein, 1962, 11). It was hoped that by establishing the ECSC, the benefits of European unity could be positively demonstrated. But more was needed.

At almost the same time as a Coal and Steel Community was being mooted, other proposals were being advanced for an agricultural community (a 'Green Pool'), a transport authority, and a health community (a 'White Pool'). Most important were the inter-related plans for a European Defence Community (EDC) and a European Political Community (EPC) which both sought to advance European integration 'in a jealously guarded domain that was highly and patently political' (Hallstein, 1962, 14). The Pleven Plan, in which the French Prime Minister proposed the EDC, called for a West European army – including units from the Federal Republic of Germany which was not then remilitarized – controlled by a European Minister of Defence who would be responsible to an elected assembly. From 1952 to 1953 an 'Ad Hoc Assembly' – in fact a bolstered version of the ECSC's Assembly – considered a draft EPC treaty and produced a plan for a political framework to control the ECSC, EDC and any other community ventures. It proposed a bicameral parliament – one chamber being elected by universal suffrage, the other by the national parliaments – to which a European Executive would be responsible. There would also be a single European Court and Council of Ministers and, eventually, a common market in goods, capital and persons would be established between the member states. Discussions about the EDC continued throughout 1953 and early 1954 but finally, in August 1954, the French National Assembly decided not to ratify the EDC Treaty (Fursdon, 1980, 295–7). The 'Ad Hoc Assembly's' plan for an EPC had already been sidestepped by the ECSC's foreign ministers meeting at The Hague in November 1953, when it was decided that any further advance should be on the basis of a 'Community of sovereign states' and institutions with less specific powers than those foreseen in the Assembly's plan (Camps, 1964, 15).

The collapse of the EDC and its subsequent replacement by the British-inspired Western European Union marked a decline in the fortunes of the Community idea inspired by Monnet and espoused by Robert Schuman in his proposals for a Coal and Steel Community in May 1950 (see Chapter 5, p. 75). The rejection of both the EDC and EPC, the acceptance of the WEU and the signing, in December 1954, of a treaty of association between the ECSC and the United Kingdom seemed to suggest that the Community method was giving way to the more traditional forms of inter-state relationships commended by British governments. It even appeared that French–West German relations were taking on a distinctly bilateral aspect to the detriment of the Coal and Steel Community which, in 1954, was hit by recession (Haas, 1968, 265).

In November 1954 Jean Monnet announced his resignation from the presidency of the High Authority of the ECSC, not as an act of desperation but in order to help the 'relance' – the relaunching of Community Europe. In this process he was aided by the foreign ministers of the three Benelux countries who had become concerned by the way that closer Franco-German relations were undermining the original intention of the Schuman Plan that the ECSC should be 'the first step toward European Federation'. Early in 1955, the Dutch Foreign Minister, Beyen, produced a plan for further integration of transport, oil and atomic energy in the six

ECSC states. These ideas were expanded in the Benelux Memorandum drawn up in the spring and summer of 1955, which proposed not only the inclusion of the above three functional areas
into a plan for European integration, but also the creation by
states of a common market among the Community countries. New
supranational organs would be needed for both the Atomic Energy
Community and the Economic Community. These ideas were
strongly supported by Monnet who by October 1955 had created
the Action Committee for the United States of Europe which
included representatives of many of the major political parties
and trade unions in the six ECSC states, and which aimed at the
creation of a federal Western Europe by the Community method.
This meant that they supported the creation of new institutions
that would deal with particular policy areas – trade, energy,
transport – on a Community-wide basis rather than try to aggregate the different policies of six governments in those functional
areas. This approach would benefit the ordinary citizen who, the
Action Committee hoped, would become more amenable to fully-
fledged federal schemes.

The 'relance' was also helped by a pro-'European', Edgar
Faure, becoming Prime Minister of France in February 1955. His
government took a positive approach to the Benelux Memorandum
which formed the basis of discussion for the Messina Conference
of representatives of the six ECSC states held on 1 and 2 June
1955. The ground was prepared at Messina for the creation of two
new Community organizations – one for the common economic
market of the Six and the other for their fledgling atomic energy
industries. The most important decision at Messina was that a
committee of the representatives of the six governments should be
established with the aim of creating the two Communities, an
objective that was not disputed. The Europeanist Belgian Foreign
Minister, Paul-Henri Spaak, was chosen to head the group which
consequently became known as the Spaak Committee. The key
features of the common economic market emerged at Messina.
The six governments committed themselves to the creation by
stages of a 'European market' without customs duties or quantitative restrictions to trade between the member states. Consideration was also given to other elements of a common market,
apart from a customs union, such as harmonization of economic,
financial and social policies. The Italians advanced ideas about
investment in poorer areas as well as funds for readjusting to the
common market. Discussion about institutional arrangements

tended to accept that this wider arrangement would be controlled by a common authority endowed with the necessary powers but one that was less 'supranational' in nature than the High Authority of the ECSC. It was also agreed at Messina that the United Kingdom should be invited to participate in discussions from the beginning (Camps, 1964, 24–8).

The Spaak Committee met from July to December 1955 with delegates from the six ECSC states and a representative of the British government who had not, however, been delegated to negotiate on behalf of the United Kingdom. It seemed to be accepted that the British would be associated with a common market of the Six in the same way as they were with the ECSC and that their involvement with an Atomic Energy Community might be much closer as at that stage the British nuclear energy industry was one of the most advanced in the world (Camps, 1964, 28).

There were a number of major differences between the British and the Six during the Spaak Committee discussions. Most important was the British preference for a free trade agreement over a customs union. The former meant an end to trade restrictions between members of such an arrangement but with each member being allowed to have different trade barriers (tariffs, quantitative restrictions – QRs) with non-member countries. This was of particular importance for the United Kingdom which had a network of special trade arrangements with Commonwealth countries. It feared that these might be jeopardized by membership of a customs union which would create free trade between the members of that union and also a common external tariff and common set of QRs for trade with all other countries. The British also wanted the removal of trade restrictions to be undertaken more within the OEEC context whereas the Six were wary of the delay that the more permissive OEEC machinery might cause. This hinted at a third, more important difference, that of institutions. The supranationalist institutions of the ECSC had received something of a knock from the defeat of the plans for Defence and Political Communities and, by 1955, some of the ECSC governments were having second thoughts about allowing such an independent authority as the High Authority a prominent position in the institutions controlling the Economic Community. However, they still wanted new and strong institutions with some prospect of taking decisions by a majority vote. The British wanted to use the OEEC with its emphasis on unanimity.

The Spaak Committee negotiations were not typified by a

permanent majority of the ministers of the Six against the British representative. On a number of issues it was the French who were at odds with their colleagues. The French were reluctant to specify the length of the transitional period during which trade restrictions would be abolished and they wanted to keep open the possibility of reimposing tariffs and QRs even after such a transition. They also wanted harmonization of social policies almost as a precondition of the customs union and they pressed for a high common tariff around the common market, something opposed by the more low-tariff Benelux delegates and the free-trading Germans (Camps, 1964, 34–8).

However important these differences between France and the other members of the Six may have been, the French government remained committed to the creation of an Economic Community, and was especially unwilling to reject plans for such an organization so soon after the EDC debacle. The British government, on the other hand, was highly sceptical of Community schemes. They regarded the Messina talks as being about trade and thus sent a Board of Trade official while other governments sent ministers. Senior British ministers considered efforts to involve the United Kingdom in the Spaak Committee negotiations as 'a bore' (Charlton, 1983, 197). When, in November 1955, it became clear that the Committee was going to proceed on the basis of a customs union, the British representative withdrew. In the words of Lord Butler, then British Chancellor of the Exchequer, 'we just thought it was not going to work' (Charlton, 1983, 195). After leaving the Spaak Committee the British attitude towards the negotiations changed, for a while, from 'one of indifference to one of opposition' (Camps, 1964, 49).

Despite internal wranglings and British rejection, the Spaak Committee continued its work and, in April 1956, the Spaak Report was presented to the governments of the Six. It represented a blueprint for the Treaty of Rome which was to establish the European Economic Community. Central to the plan was the creation of a Common Market among the Six, within which goods, capital and labour would eventually be able to move with almost as much ease as between different regions of a country. Such a Common Market would be based on a customs union and on a common economic policy and would be supervised by common institutions implementing agreed rules for the whole Community area. The Report allowed for the possibility of close relations with other European states, with Britain obviously in mind (Camps, 1964, 59).

In May 1956, the Foreign Ministers of the Six met in Venice to receive the Spaak Report. They accepted it with one amendment: the French insisted on the addition of a section on Algeria, the French Overseas Territories and Colonies.

Europe was now at 'Sixes and Sevens': on the one side were the six Community countries with their plan to found a customs union and common market with strong central institutions; on the other side was an assortment of mainly Scandinavians and neutrals led by the United Kingdom, all of which preferred a free trade area within the OEEC context. In July 1956, the British government supported the idea of establishing a Working Party within the OEEC to examine how the customs union of the Six might be associated with other members of the OEEC. This represented a new British approach of 'if you cannot join them, smother them'. The intention was to create an OEEC-wide free trade area which would include the emerging European Economic Community as one entity. This notion had not been ruled out by the Spaak Report but the clear priority of the Six was the creation of their customs union rather than allowing across-the-board exceptions from the beginning. Furthermore, there were differences between the Six and the British on how the Community's customs union might coexist in an OEEC free trade area: Britain wanted only industrial free trade with agricultural products excluded and also wanted arrangements for their own Commonwealth preferential trade.

The OEEC Working Party reported in January 1957 that a free trade area of West European states including a customs union of the Six was possible but it would first be necessary to solve a number of problems. Further working parties were established but these could not disguise the very real difference of approach between the British and the French who were anxious to make the European Economic Community a *fait accompli* before reaching any compromise with other OEEC states. The French felt that any disadvantages from entering into an economic union with their five neighbours would be far outweighed by the advantages of EEC membership – cementing their new relationship with the Germans, benefits to French agriculture, the possibility of Community help to French overseas territories and the hope that their country's economic growth would be spurred on by creating a united market of the Six. The balance sheet of an OEEC-wide free trade area, as advocated by the British, was quite different in French eyes. French industry would have to compete in a larger market but without the assurances that the conditions of competition regarding social and industrial policy would be in any way standardized, as was planned for the EEC. The British insistence on keeping its 'cheap food' policy was seen by France as a way of subsidizing British industry's wage costs as well as excluding Continental farmers from the British market.

With the signing of the Treaty of Rome in March 1957 and its ratification during the summer by the parliaments of the six member states, drastic action was needed to avoid a trade division of Western Europe. In October 1957 the OEEC Council passed a resolution expressing the wish to establish a West European free trade area taking effect 'parallel with the Treaty of Rome' and comprising all their members, thereby associating the EEC with other OEEC states. As a result, an intergovernmental committee was set up with the relevant British minister, Reginald Maudling, as chairman and with the remit to put the October resolution into effect. Discussions in this committee once again demonstrated the fundamental – and growing – differences between the British and the French in particular. The French government was afraid that, by the creation of an OEEC-wide free trade area, the British and their supporters would obtain 'the advantages offered by the Rome Treaty, without imposing upon them its obligations' (*Financial Times*, 15 November 1957). The situation was further complicated by the fall of the French Fourth Republic in the summer of 1958 and the rise to power of General de Gaulle who, though he was sceptical about the supranational aspects of the Treaty of Rome, realized that the agreement hammered out by the Six was in the French interest and was not prepared to see it watered down to suit the British. In the words of de Gaulle's Foreign Minister: 'France has never been a free-trade country, and it believes more in organization' (Charlton, 1983, 226). Mr Maudling, at the October 1958 meeting of the OEEC, told the assembled representatives that the conditions agreed by the Six were 'quite unacceptable to us' (*The Times*, 25 October 1958). On 1 January 1959, the Six made their first tariff and quota reductions among themselves and any attempt to bring together the EEC and the other OEEC members in a West European free trade area was buried in February 1959.

The division that was to haunt Western Europe for the next 14 years was manifest. How had it happened? At the end, there is little doubt that a robust French attitude prevented any compromise between the free trade idea and the principles behind the European Economic Community. But the major share of the blame must rest with the British politicians who in the second half of the 1950s failed to realize that the Six were earnest in their endeavours and that there was a willingness to include Britain in any scheme. One of the leading British politicians at the time, R.A. Butler, later admitted that the British approach to the Messina talks showed 'a definite lack of foresight on the part of myself, and a much bigger lack of foresight on the part of the Treasury, and a very big lack of foresight on the part of the Foreign Office' (Charlton, 1983, 195). The issues mentioned as those which divided Britain from France – the question of the inclusion of agriculture, customs union versus free trade, Commonwealth preference, and the powers of the institutions – could have been adjusted to suit British tastes during the early negotiations had the British shown the willingness to be part of the Community enterprise. Lord Thorneycroft, then President of the Board of Trade in the British government, later considered that a deal could have been made on agriculture and the Commonwealth (Charlton, 1983, 192), and on the customs union issue Britain would have had strong support from the Benelux states and the West Germans for some form of compromise solution. The British instead had been concerned with Commonwealth affairs, the Middle East and relations with the United States and considered little economic advantage to be gained from a customs union with the Six. In Thorneycroft's words: 'The Cabinet had really decided against the European concept' (Charlton, 1983, 182).

Thus the European Economic Community and the European Atomic Energy Community were born. The ideas seen in the European Coal and Steel Community were to be tried in the wider economic field of the Six, but in creating the EEC its members had found themselves in an undignified tussle with other West European countries, in particular the United Kingdom.

What were the important elements of the Treaty of Rome, signed by the Six on 25 March 1957 and to which the British and the Scandinavians were so reluctant to append their signatures?

The Preamble of the Treaty was less histrionic than that of the European Coal and Steel Community (see above pp. 75-6) but nevertheless carried over the theme of European unity. The six governments were 'determined to lay the foundations of an ever closer union among the peoples of Europe' and were 'resolved to ensure the economic and social progress of their countries by common action to eliminate the barriers which divide Europe' (EEC, 1987, Preamble).

The improvement of living and working conditions was set as a goal and it was recognized that concerted action was needed to guarantee 'steady expansion, balanced trade and fair competition'. Other objectives were the reduction of differences between the various regions, the abolition of restrictions on international trade, and the confirmation of solidarity with overseas countries in order to ensure their development and prosperity. It was resolved to pool the resources of the Six 'to preserve and strengthen the cause of peace and liberty' and a call was made to the other peoples of Europe who shared these aims to join in.

The ideals of the Preamble were expanded upon in Part One of the Treaty of Rome (Principles), were fleshed out in Part Two (Foundations of the Community), and can be seen in a wider context in Part Three (Policy of the Community). Part Four of the Treaty dealt with the Association of Overseas Countries and territories and the Community's institutions were covered in Part Five. Part Six included the general and final provisions and was followed by a series of lists defining some of the headings referred to in the Treaty, protocols and conventions covering such matters as internal German trade, the statutes of the European Investment Bank and the Community's Court of Justice, and the tariff quota for bananas. The Final Act brought together all these documents establishing the European Economic Community, the separate treaty establishing the European Atomic Energy Community and a convention on institutions common to the European Communities and appended the signatures of the representatives of the six states. There then followed a number of declarations about matters of particular interest to individual members such as the Franc area (France), the status of Libya and Somalia (Italy), Surinam and the Netherlands Antilles (the Netherlands), and the definition of German nationals and the question of Berlin (West Germany).

Part One of the Treaty establishing the European Economic Community gave the broad outline of how the common market between the member states might be created. Eleven activities of the Community were listed which would achieve this common market. They were: an end to customs duties and quantitative restrictions on trade between the member states; the establishment of a common external tariff and common commercial policy towards third (that is, non-member) countries; the abolition of obstacles to freedom of movement of persons, services and capital between the Six; the establishment of a common agricultural policy; the adoption of a common transport policy; a system to ensure that competition in the common market was not distorted; coordination of members' economic policies; the approximation of laws to ensure the proper functioning of the common market; the creation of a European Social Fund to improve the employment opportunities and living standards of workers; the establishment of a European Investment Bank to help the expansion of the Community's economy; and the Association of Overseas Countries and Territories 'in order to increase trade and to promote jointly economic and social development' (Treaty of Rome, Article 3).

The first two activities were essential for the creation of a customs union. The next six activities would lead to a *common market* – to be established during a period of 12 years (Article 8) – wherein goods could be produced, bought and sold from one member state to the next more or less on the same basis as within one country. The last three activities would perhaps establish a *community* of concern among the Six that went beyond a common market. This element was bolstered by common institutions to help carry out Community tasks, and by Article 7 which banned any prejudice on the grounds of nationality in the field of application of the Treaty.

Part Two of the Treaty – Foundations of the Community – was divided into four sections. The first dealt with the free movement of goods, the significance of which was explained in Article 9: 'The Community shall be based upon a customs union which shall cover all trade in goods and which shall involve the prohibition between Member States of customs duties on imports and exports and of all charges having equivalent effect, and the adoption of a common customs tariff in their relations with third countries'. The details of the elimination of customs duties between the member states were covered in Articles 12 to 17 and those concerning the establishment of the common customs tariff in Articles 18 to 29. Articles 30 to 37 dealt with the elimination of quantitative restrictions (such as quotas) between the Six. Each of these sections set out a timetable of activity, which in many cases was to be completed by a decision of the Community institutions.

The second section of Part Two covered agriculture. Article 38 laid down that '[t]he common market shall extend to agriculture and trade in agricultural products' and that '[t]he operation and development of the common market for agricultural products must be accompanied by the establishment of a common agricultural policy among the Member States'. The objectives of a common agricultural policy were set out in Article 39 as being

- to increase agricultural productivity by technical progress and efficiency,
- thereby to ensure a fair standard of living for those in the agricultural community,
- to stabilize markets,
- to provide certainty of supplies
- and to ensure supplies to consumers at reasonable prices.

The need was expressed to consider agriculture's social structure and regional disparities in working out the details of the common agricultural policy, which was to be implemented by degrees during a transitional period. The forms of organization to achieve these objectives were listed in Article 40 as common rules for competition, compulsory coordination of the various national marketing organizations, or 'a European market organization', and the measures that could be adopted were price controls, production and distribution subsidies, stock-piling and carry-over systems (what later became known as Community 'mountains' or 'lakes' of farm products such as butter and wine) and common arrangements for the stabilization of imports or exports. An important sentence in Article 40 read: 'Any common price policy shall be based on common criteria and uniform methods of calculation'. It was clear that the Six wanted a Community-wide agricultural policy, not just one that was cobbled together from existing national policies.

The third section of Part Two covered the free movement of persons, services and capital. By the end of the transitional period (mentioned in Article 8), freedom of movement for workers was to be secured within the Community, according to Article 48. This would abolish any discrimination based on nationality between workers in the Six, as regards employment, pay and other work conditions. Workers in Community countries would be able to move freely throughout the Community to obtain employment. Exceptions were made for employment in the public service and restrictions justified on grounds of public policy, public safety or security and public health. Articles 52 to 54 gave the right to nationals of a Community state to establish firms, agencies, branches or subsidiaries and to engage in self-employed occupations in the territory of another Community country. However, this provision was limited in a similar fashion to the freedom of movement of workers, only the clause on public service was widely drawn to exclude any occupation connected 'even occasionally, with the exercise of official authority' (Article 55). Articles 59 to 66 made way for an end to restrictions on the freedom to provide services within the Community. These services included occupations of an industrial or commercial character, work in the small craft industries and professional occupations. Restrictions on the movement of capital belonging to persons resident in the Community and discrimination based on nationality or place of residence or on the place where the capital was invested were to be abolished according to Articles 67 to 73. Article 70 foresaw 'measures for the progressive coordination of the exchange policies of Member States in respect of the movement of capital between those States and third countries'.

The last section of Part Two dealt with a common transport policy. In Article 75 it obliged the Community institutions to lay down common rules for international transport affecting Community territory and the conditions under which non-resident carriers could operate transport within a member state.

Part Three of the Treaty of Rome covered the policy of the Community and gave some of the bare bones of what was needed to establish the more vital economic and social aspects of the Community. An important section was that on the rules of competition (Articles 85 to 94) which broadly banned practices that affected trade between the member states and which prevented, restricted or distorted competition within the common market (Article 85). It was left to the Community institutions to flesh out the details of the prohibition. Furthermore, state aid distorting competition between undertakings and affecting trade between member states was deemed to be incompatible with the common market (Article 92). Exceptions were made for aid having a social character, granted to individual consumers; disaster aid; and aid to certain areas of West Germany, required to compensate for the economic disadvantages caused by the inner-German border. Consideration would also be given to aid for regions with a low standard of living or serious under-employment; help to promote important projects of common European interest or to remedy serious disturbance in a member state's economy; and aid to develop certain economic activity or economic regions.

Articles 95 to 99 in Part Three dealt with tax provisions and forbade the imposition of internal taxes on products of other member states that were not placed on similar domestic products (Article 95). Under Article 99, further consideration was to be given to the harmonization of legislation on various indirect taxes and duties.

Other national laws affecting the operation of the common market were to be considered for approximation – that is, they would be brought closer together – under Article 100.

The section of Part Three under the heading of 'Economic Policy' provided for consultation over current trends in the economy (Article 103) and for coordination of economic policies in order to maintain an equilibrium in members' balance of payments and confidence in their currency (Articles 104–5). Specifically, cooperation between administrations and between central banks was mentioned, as was the liberalization of payments between members (Article 106). Each member's policy towards rates of exchange was declared to be a matter of common interest under Article 107 and the following two articles made provision for Community involvement should a member state have serious balance of payments difficulties.

The next section in Part Three was on commercial policy and committed members to 'the progressive abolition of restrictions on international trade and the lowering of customs barriers' (Article 110). Article 111 allowed for the coordination of commercial relations with third countries to bring about a common policy in the field of the external trade of the Six.

The section of Part Three dealing with social policy (Articles 117–28) established the need to 'promote improved working conditions and improved standard of living for workers' so as to obtain their progressive harmonization and improvement (Article 117). The signatories believed that this would result from the operation of the common market – which would favour the harmonization of social systems – and from the approximation of laws and regulations. Such close collaboration was to be promoted in the employment and social field (Article 118). Furthermore the principle of equal remuneration for the same work as between male and female workers was established in Article 119. Article 123 set up a European Social Fund with the task of increasing employment facilities and the geographical and occupational mobility of workers within the Community. The last section of Part Three established the European Investment Bank which, by recourse to the capital market and by use of its own resources, would contribute to 'the balanced and steady development of the common market' (Article 130) by helping projects for the less developed regions, those called for by the establishment of the common market and those of common interest to several member states but which could not be financed by the individual members.

Taken as a whole, Part Three set out the policies of the Community that would complement the common market, ensuring that it could not be circumvented by the use of other economic policies or by widely differing social policies. By doing this, it was to take the Six members beyond mere membership of a common market and closer to a Community with common institutions and policies.

Part Four of the Treaty of Rome concerned the Association of Overseas Countries and Territories with the Community. The non-European countries and territories were listed in Annex IV and consisted of the colonies, trusteeships and overseas territories of France, Belgium, the Netherlands and Italy. Article 131 stated that association would have the purpose of promoting the economic and social development of these countries and of establishing close economic relations between them and the Community as a whole. The objective of Association was that member states should 'apply to their trade with the countries and territories the same treatment as they accord each other pursuant to this Treaty' (Article 132.1).

Likewise each of the Associated countries would trade with the members of the Community and with the other Associates as if they were the European state with which they had a special relationship. However, for a period, the Associates could levy customs duties to meet their needs of development and industrialization or to contribute to their budgets (Article 133.3).

Member states were to contribute to the capital investment needed for the development of the overseas countries and territories. Indeed, in the Implementing Convention attached to the Annex of the Treaty, the members of the Community established a Development Fund to finance social and economic projects in the Associates. Both this Fund and the Association agreement were intended to work for an initial period of five years, before which it would be decided, in the light of experience, what provision would be made for a further period (Article 136).

The Association agreement gave the other Community members access to the primary products of the vast French colonial possessions, but it also provided a mechanism whereby the development of these territories could be underwritten by France's Community colleagues, not least the Federal Republic of Germany.

Part Five of the Treaty of Rome contained its institutional arrangements which will be discussed in the next section (pp. 101–7). The General and Final Provisions were in Part Six (Articles 210 to 248).

Article 210 gave the Community a legal personality and its legal position in the member countries was entrenched in Articles 211 and 218. Article 223 stated that the Treaty would not oblige a member state to disclose information it considered contrary to the interests of its security, and members could take measures to protect 'the essential interests of its security and which are connected with the production of or trade in arms, munitions and war material;' though such measures should not affect market competition for products not meant for specifically military purposes. Article 224 allowed for measures to be taken to prevent the common market being affected by any emergency measures a member state might take.

Article 228 provided for the conclusion of agreements between the Community and one or more states or an international organization and Articles 229 to 231 dealt with the Community's relations with the United Nations and its specialized agencies, the General Agreement on Tariffs and Trade, the Council of Europe and the Organization for European Economic Cooperation.

Article 225 afforded steps to be taken to achieve the objectives of the Community even when the Treaty had not provided the necessary powers to do so. This seemed to allow the Community's institutions to expand their operations beyond those mentioned in the Treaty.

Article 237 dealt with European states wishing to become members of the Community: the conditions of membership would have to be agreed between the applicant and the member states. Article 238 said that the Community could agree an association 'involving reciprocal rights and obligations, common action and special procedures' with a third country, a union of states or with an international organization.

Article 240 stated that the Treaty was concluded 'for an unlimited period'.

In the various attachments to the Treaty, the Protocol dealing with internal German trade defined trade between the Federal Republic of Germany and East Germany (then a separate state) as being 'internal', in effect giving East German trade with West Germany preferential Community treatment.

France, Italy and Luxembourg had protocols relating to particular aspects of their economic life – on export aids, import taxes and overtime payment in the French case; on the development of southern Italy; and on Luxembourg agriculture.

The Treaty of Rome was a mixture of high ideals and political necessity. The vision was that of a community of states within which people could work and live and businesses could flourish as if there were no frontiers. The plan was to establish a customs union, complement it with a common market and consummate it with a fully-fledged economic and social community. The immediate tasks of a customs union, the early stages of a common agricultural policy, and the Association with Overseas Countries and Territories were set out in some detail: these were essential parts of the Franco-German political deal that formed the basis of the Economic Community. For many of the other activities needed to achieve even a common market, the Treaty gave only some general guidance, leaving the detail to be filled in by the institutions established in Part Five of the Treaty.

Institutions

The institutions of the European Economic Community were set out in Part Five of the Treaty of Rome but there have been important changes since the establishment of the EEC. The nature of these institutions can be explained by reference to those of the European Coal and Steel Community and to the experience of the Six since the ECSC's establishment. As mentioned in Chapter 5, the High Authority of the ECSC was given real powers to create a framework for the functioning of the coal and steel industries in the Community member states, though extra institutions – a Council of Ministers and an Assembly – had been added during the negotiations for the Treaty of Paris. By the mid-1950s the work of the High Authority was coming under pressure from national governments and its success as an independent entity was by no means assured. However, in the Benelux Memorandum and the work of Jean Monnet's Action Committee which helped relaunch the idea of Community Europe in 1955, a place was found for supranational institutions for the suggested new European Economic Community (see p. 88). The six Community countries, when negotiating at Messina, agreed that the new organization would need strong institutions and that the ability of member states to sidestep their obligations in a common market should be curtailed, but they did not seem ready to place the management of such a wide range of economic and social policies as those covered in the Treaty of Rome in the hands of an institution unchecked by national considerations. Part Five, and the powers given to the various institutions throughout the Treaty of Rome, represented a compromise between this desire to have some national input into Community policy-making and the requirement for an effective body that would see through the creation of a common market.

Article 4 of the Treaty of Rome established that the European Economic Community would have four major institutions: an Assembly, a Council, a Commission and a Court of Justice. These reflected the institutions of the ECSC, with the Commission taking on the role, but not the equivalent powers, of the High Authority. The Council and Commission were to be assisted by an Economic and Social Committee in a consultative capacity. The institutions of the European Atomic Energy Community were to be the same as those of the European Coal and Steel Community and, by virtue of a Convention attached to the Treaty of Rome, the Assembly, Court of Justice and Economic and Social Committee were to be common to these two organizations and the European Coal and Steel Community. It was more in the balance of powers between the two remaining institutions – the Council of Ministers and the Commission – that the Economic Community and Euratom differed most from the ECSC, and thus, to start with, these were kept separate from the Council of Ministers and High Authority of the Coal and Steel Community.

The part of the Treaty of Rome covering the Community's institutions was divided into Title I, covering institutional provisions, and Title II on financial provisions.

In Title I, Chapter 1 dealt with the Economic Community's four main institutions: the Assembly, the Council, the Commission and the Court of Justice.

The Assembly, according to Article 137, was to consist of representatives of the peoples of the Community states, and was to have advisory and supervisory powers. To start with, the Assembly would have delegates nominated by the respective parliaments – 36 each from France, Germany and Italy, 14 each from Belgium and the Netherlands, and six from Luxembourg – but provision was made for it to draw up proposals for 'elections by direct universal suffrage in accordance with a uniform procedure in all Member States' (Article 138.3 EEC). Members of the Council and the Commission could be heard by the Assembly, and the Commission was obliged to answer questions posed by the Assembly or its members. Under Article 144, if the Assembly passed a censure motion on the Commission by a two-thirds majority of the votes cast, representing a majority of all the members, then the Commission would have collectively to resign office. It should be noted that the Assembly could not apply such a stricture to an individual member of the Commission, neither could it prevent the censured Commission from being reappointed – except by another vote of no confidence.

The Council (often called the Council of Ministers) was to ensure the attainment of the Treaty objectives by coordination of the general economic policies of the member states and by its power to take decisions (Article 145). It represented the governments of these states and consisted of one delegate from each. The Presidency of the Council was to rotate among the membership each six months, according to alphabetical order of the member states. Article 148 stated that, 'save as otherwise provided in this Treaty', the Council's decisions had to be taken by a majority of its members. Where a qualified vote was provided for, the members' votes were to be weighted according to Article 148.2 – four for France, Germany and Italy, two each for Belgium and the Netherlands and one for Luxembourg. Decisions then needed 12 out of the 17 votes in favour to carry a Commission proposal but 12 votes cast by at least four members in all other cases. This meant that the 'Big Three' countries could not push through proposals without the support of either the Commission or one of the smaller members. Under Article 149, when the Council agreed to a measure on a Commission proposal, it could only be amended by a unanimous vote of the Council, though the Commission could amend its proposal, especially after having consulted the Assembly.

According to Article 155, the Commission was to ensure the working and development of the common market by:

– seeing that Treaty provisions and pursuant measures were carried out;
– making recommendations or giving opinions on Treaty matters, where it was expressly provided or if the Commission considered it necessary;
– having its own powers of decision and participating with the Council and the Assembly in the shaping of measures;
– exercising powers given by the Council to ensure enforcement of rules laid down by the Council.

The Commission was to consist of nine members, chosen 'on the grounds of their general competence' and whose independence could be fully relied upon (Article 157). The Commission was not to have more than two members having the nationality of the same state. In the general interests of the Community, its members were to be completely independent in performing their duties, and they were neither to seek nor take instructions from any government or from any other body. The member states were to respect that principle and not seek to influence Commission members in their work. The Commission membership was to be decided 'by common accord of the Governments of Member States' every four years, with the possibility of appointment being renewable (Article 158). In effect this allowed each government to appoint one member of the Commission. A member could be compulsorily retired by the Court of Justice if he no longer fulfilled the conditions required for the performance of his duties or because of serious misconduct (Article 160). The President and two Vice-Presidents of the Commission were to be appointed for a two-year term by 'common accord', that is by agreement of all the governments concerned. Commission decisions were to be taken by a majority of its members (Article 163): it was to work as a collegiate system. Article 162 contained the requirement that the Council and Commission should consult each other and settle 'by common accord' their method of collaboration. This placed the emphasis on cooperation between the two institutions and demonstrated that, in the Treaty of Rome, the Council had advanced from the mainly harmonizing role it had in the Treaty of Paris.

The Court of Justice was one of the institutions already established by the Coal and Steel Community and – as in the case of the Assembly and Economic and Social Committee – it was also to be used by the EEC and Euratom. The section in the Treaty of Rome on the Court thus reflected the equivalent part of the Treaty of Paris which established the ECSC. The Court of Justice was to see that the law was observed 'in the interpretation and application of this Treaty' (Article 164) and consisted of seven judges chosen by common accord by the member states' governments for a term of six years and from persons whose independence could be relied upon and who were competent to the highest court level nationally or who were 'jurisconsults of recognized competence' (Article 167). The court was to be assisted by two Advocates-General whose duty it was to 'make, in open court, reasoned submissions', with complete impartiality and independence (Article 166).

The Commission could bring before the Court a member state for non-compliance with its obligations under the Treaty (Article 169); one member state could bring another before the Court for the same reason (Article 170); the Court was to supervise the legality of measures taken by the Council and the Commission (other than recommendations and opinions) and to rule in cases instituted by member states, the Council or the Commission on questions of jurisdiction, procedures, Treaty infringement and the use and misuse of powers; and any 'natural or legal person' could have recourse against a decision directed to them or of direct and individual concern to them (Article 173). The Court could also give preliminary rulings on the interpretation of the Treaty, the validity and interpretation of measures taken by Community institutions and the interpretation of the statue of bodies set up by the Council. A court or tribunal of a member state could request a Court ruling on such matters and, where all domestic appeals had been exhausted, they were obliged to bring such matters before the Court of Justice (Article 177).

Chapter 2 of Title I dealt with provisions common to several institutions. Under Article 189 the Council and Commission were empowered to make regulations, issue directives, take decisions, make recommendations or give opinions. A regulation applied generally, was binding in its entirety and took direct effect in each member state. A directive was binding as to the result to be achieved upon each member state to which it was directed, though the national authorities were left with the choice of method of implementation. A decision was binding in its entirety upon those to whom it was directed. Recommendations and opinions had no binding force. Directives and decisions were to be notified to those to whom they were directed. It should be noted that Article 187 tied the enforcement of Court of Justice judgements to Article 192 whereby enforcement was to be governed by the rules of civil procedure in force in the relevant state. A specified national authority was to attach an enforcement order to a decision. This meant that the Community institutions relied on national enforcement agencies rather than on establishing a parallel system of law implementation.

An Economic and Social Committee with a consultative status, similar to that in the Coal and Steel Community, was established under Article 193 and consisted of representatives of various categories of economic and social activity such as farmers, workers and the professions, with special mention being made of those from the agricultural and transport sector. According to Article 198 the Committee had to be consulted by the Council or Commission where the Treaty provided, otherwise the Community institutions were free to consult it as they deemed appropriate.

Title II of Part Five covered financial provisions. Article 200 set down that budget revenue – apart from any other income – would include financial contributions from the member states. The scale of each member's contribution was set for both the general budget and for the European Social Fund. It is noticeable that Italy, the country most likely to benefit from the Fund, was expected to contribute a much reduced share to the European Social Fund compared with the other large countries (20 per cent as against France and Germany's 32 per cent each).

The Commission was exhorted by Article 201 to examine how this system could be replaced by the Community's own resources, especially those accruing from the common customs tariff. Article 203 gave the Commission the task of consolidating estimates into a preliminary draft budget which they would then submit to the Council. The Council would consult the Commission and other Community institutions whenever it intended to depart from the preliminary draft and would forward a draft budget to the Assembly which had the right to propose amendments to the Council. If within a period of a month of receipt of the draft budget, the Assembly had given its assent or had not made its opinion known to the Council, the draft budget was to be considered as adopted. If the Assembly proposed amendments, then the Council had to discuss these with the Commission and other appropriate institutions, and had finally to adopt the budget by a qualified majority decision. Article 206 established a control commission of auditors to verify the Community's accounts. Article 209 was an enabling section whereby the Council, by unanimous decision on a Commission proposal, made specific regulations for the budgetary process, determined the methods and procedures of member state contributions and laid down the rules and supervisory measures of the authorizing and accounting officers.

The major changes in the institutions of the Economic Community from those of the Coal and Steel Community concerned the relative powers of the High Authority and the Commission. The High Authority had been the driving power of the Coal and Steel Community with the Council of Ministers acting as a liaison committee between the High Authority and national interests. It seemed that the six member states were not prepared to hand over such powers to a supranational body similar to the High Authority for the wide range of vital policy areas covered by the Treaty of Rome. Furthermore, experience with the High Authority had not been trouble-free (Haas, 1968, 251–72). Perhaps for this reason and for ease of coordination, the institutions of the functionally limited European Atomic Energy Community were identical to those of the Economic Community which was established in Rome at the same time, rather than mirroring those of the Coal and Steel Community. The relationship of the Commission and Council of the Economic and Atomic Energy Communities was one of two institutions in harness providing the motive power for the organizations. In most cases, the Council could not act without the Commission initiating a proposal, and most action had to be agreed by the Council.

The above description of the institutions of the Treaty of Rome has been given in the past tense partly because changes were made to the Treaty, mainly when the institutions of the three Communities were merged and when the Single European Act was agreed (see pp. 114–15), and partly because the expansion of the European Communities' membership necessitated changes in Treaty articles covering the institutions. Furthermore, the Treaty on European Union, 1992, has brought institutional development. There have been a number of adjustments in the relationship of the Communities' institutions since the signing of the Treaty of Rome in March 1957.

What Part Five of the Treaty laid down was an institutional framework: the reality of the power relationships between the major parts of the organization had to await the functioning of the Economic Community and is understandable only in the context of wider West European political events.

When the European Economic Community began work on 1 January 1958, the new Commission – headed by Walter Hallstein of West Germany – was faced with a busy programme of activities set out in the Treaty of Rome. The main work was in the areas of the creation of a customs union and of a Common Agricultural Policy. Stage One of the transitional period to a common market was to take four years and the move from the first to the second stage was 'conditional upon a finding that the objectives specifically laid down in this Treaty for the first stage have been in fact attained in substance' (Article 8.3 EEC). The Commission was thus working to a deadline of completing Stage One by January 1962. This was helped by the decision of the member states, taken in 1959, to accelerate progress to the customs union. Much of the time of the Commission was taken up in dealing with trade relations with other countries (not least because of the negotiations over the expansion of membership from June 1961) and with the introduction of the Common Agricultural Policy (CAP). The CAP was described by Hallstein as 'vital to the future Community' (1962, 54). Agreement had to be reached by the

Council of Ministers and Hallstein described this process vividly: '45 separate meetings, 7 of them at night; a total of 137 hours of discussion, with 214 hours in subcommittee; 582,000 pages of documents; 3 heart attacks – the record is staggering' (p. 55). Nevertheless, the first stages of the CAP were agreed on 14 January 1962, and the Economic Community was launched into the second stage of its transition.

Because of the success of the Commission in this initial period and because of the determined character of Dr Hallstein, the Commission had established a record of activity and initiative by 1962. It had been in the common interests of all six member states to see the foundations of their organization laid and solidified – not least because critics were waiting for the enterprise to falter – and the Commission seemed to undertake that task competently.

President de Gaulle of France, while supporting the implementation of the Community's essential policies, was not as enthusiastic about certain aspects of the Economic Community as his predecessors in the French Fourth Republic who had signed the Treaty of Rome. In particular, he was wary of any challenge to national sovereignty and considered some of the activities of the Commission to be high-handed and usurping the rightful powers of governments. Matters came to a head in 1965. According to the Treaty of Rome, certain questions associated with the creation of the common market could be decided by a majority vote in the Council from 21 January 1966. Dr Hallstein and his Commission pressed to associate advances in the creation of the CAP – which was in the interests of the French farmers – with a start to planning for the Community's own resources, and greater budgetary powers for the Assembly in order to oversee the money raised. The French government wanted these issues separated so that progress might be made with the CAP but a stop placed on further powers and resources for Community institutions. When the other five members opposed this separation, French representatives were withdrawn from the Council of Ministers and the main decision-making institutions of the Community. By this 'empty chair' policy, de Gaulle had effectively prevented the organization from moving to decision by majority vote (whereby France could be outvoted on crucial matters) and from becoming more supranational. In December 1965, a 'Europeanist' candidate in the French presidential elections showed up favourably against de Gaulle, who was re-elected on a smaller majority than foreseen; the French attitude to the Community seemed to soften; and in January

1966 all the ministers of the Six reached a compromise at a meeting in Luxembourg.

The Luxembourg Accords – or Compromise, or Agreement to Differ – was to affect the balance of power between the institutions of the Community for the next 20 years. The essential points of the Accords which affected the question of majority voting in the Council were as follows:

I Where, in the case of decisions which may be taken by majority vote on a proposal of the Commission, very important interests of one or more partners are at stake, the Members of the Council will endeavour, within a reasonable time, to reach solutions which can be adopted by all the Members of the Council while respecting their mutual interests and those of the Community, in accordance with Article 2 of the Treaty.

II With regard to the preceding paragraph, the French delegation considers that where very important interests are at stake the discussion must be continued until unanimous agreement is reached.

III The six delegations note that there is a divergence of views on what should be done in the event of a failure to reach complete agreement (Hartley, 1988, 18).

There was also agreement that decisions on certain agricultural matters should be taken by common consent. On the question of finance, a more restrictive arrangement was made – based on direct national contributions – compared with the Commission's proposals.

Important elements in this settlement affected the balance of power between the various institutions of the Community and between the member states and the Community itself. The financial arrangements did not, as the Commission had hoped, presage a shift towards the Community having its own resources, thereby depending less on the member states. It also meant that the appointed Assembly (which had changed its name to 'European Parliament' in 1962) had missed the opportunity to take on even rudimentary powers of the purse. The Commission had its wings clipped. As well as losing, at the insistence of President de Gaulle, some of its ceremonial trappings, the Commission had been seen to be forestalled not only by the Council but by one member of the Council: thenceforward this must have changed the calculus of what was acceptable when the Commission drafted its proposals and entered into a dialogue with the Council. The Accords – which, it can be seen, reflected a basic difference between the French and the other five members – indicated that, whatever the Treaty of Rome might say, sovereign governments were not going to allow themselves to be outvoted on matters which they felt affected their interests. (It should be noted that while it was the French government that made this point in January 1966, other governments subsequently took advantage of the formula.) Admittedly, majority voting in the Council was used from an early stage for the Community budget, but this was a case of the ends having been agreed, the means had to be found.

On joining the Community, the United Kingdom government seemed to think that the right of veto in the Council still existed and was somewhat surprised in 1982 when an agricultural price increase was agreed on a qualified majority vote against British insistence. Whether this broke the Luxembourg Accords is moot, but the trend in the 1980s has been away from a restrictive interpretation of this agreement (Nicoll, 1984, 40–1). Furthermore, the Single European Act (Article 16) extended the use of the qualified majority and, in certain cases, allowed states to safeguard their interests by opting out of harmonization rather than having to resort to the veto in Council meetings. As long as there were member states with governments which were not prepared to allow ministers of the other member states to decide their policy on certain matters covered by Community treaties, then the right of veto – however circumscribed – had to be respected in the Council. In this political truth lay the importance of the Luxembourg Accords.

One major institutional change that had come about in this period was the merging of the institutions of the three Communities. A Merger Treaty was signed in Brussels on 8 April 1965 and came into force on 1 July 1967. This left the three Communities – the Coal and Steel Community, the Economic Community and Euratom – intact but brought together their separate institutions. The ECSC's High Authority and the two Commissions of the Economic Community and Euratom became a single Commission of the European Communities and likewise the three Councils formed a single Council of the European Communities. The three Communities already shared the Court of Justice and the European Parliament (Assembly) and further rationalization seemed a logical step. As noted, the powers of the High Authority and the Commission and their relationships with their respective Councils differed somewhat (see p. 106), and these differences were maintained after the merger. So the single Commission uses the powers granted to the High Authority by the Treaty of Paris when dealing with Coal and Steel matters and those given by the two Treaties of Rome when covering EEC or Euratom business.

An institutional development that the Merger Treaty recognized was that of COREPER, the Committee of Permanent Representatives. This had not been specifically mentioned in the Treaty of Rome, but it had soon become apparent that the work of the Council could not all – or mostly – be done at a ministerial level and that the ambassadors of the member states and their deputies would have to undertake a lot of the preparatory activities. Meetings at this level became known as the Committee of Permanent Representatives – or; using the French acronym, COREPER – and the technical discussions at deputy level as COREPER I, with COREPER II being the ambassadorial meeting discussing more politically sensitive questions. Questions agreed at COREPER level are placed on Part A of the Council's agenda to be adopted without debate, while contentious matters form Part B. The Merger Treaty formalized the existence of COREPER in Article 4 and this institution has become an essential part of the day-to-day working of the Communities.

The next changes in the institutions of the European Communities – as they had become by then – were brought about by the expansion of membership on 1 January 1973, when Denmark, Eire and the United Kingdom joined. Since then, further amendments have been needed to accommodate Greek membership (from 1 January 1981) and that of Portugal and Spain (from 1 January 1986). This expansion in the number of member states in the Communities has necessitated an increase in the size of the Commission, the Council, the Court, the Economic and Social Committee and the European Parliament, as well as of a member of other related institutions (such as COREPER). Each extension of the Communities has also provided the potential for a shift in the relationship between the Communities' institutions (in particular the Commission and the Parliament) and the member states as represented in the Council. It might be thought that the new members would be more cautious in allowing the Communities' institutions to take on any supranational powers and would be more jealous of their rights than states that had been part of the Community method since 1951. This seemed to be the case for Britain, Denmark and, to a much lesser extent, Greece, but Eire, Portugal and Spain have been content to see Community power grow. This may be because these countries had hoped to gain more by a strengthening of common policies on, for example, regional aid or fisheries. It may also reflect an attitude in these traditionally Catholic countries about being part of a wider European polity that is not found in Protestant Britain and Denmark

(Kerr, 1986, ch. 2). It is also noticeable that both the United Kingdom and Denmark have close links with countries outside the Communities' framework: the United States and the Commonwealth in the former's case; the Nordic countries in the latter's. It should, however, be remembered that during the 1960s it was France under President de Gaulle that attempted to tip the balance between Community furtherance and state power in favour of the latter. Since 1973 it has been successive British governments that have – at least in public – espoused a Gaullist reserve towards having powerful Community institutions (Thatcher, 1989, 7–8).

One institutional innovation brought by the extension of 1973 was that of the European Council (not to be confused with the Council of Europe – see Chapter 4). Meetings of the Council of Ministers were held with the appropriate representation – agriculture ministers met to discuss agricultural policies, industry ministers to decide on industrial policy and so on. In 1974 it was agreed that the Heads of State or of Government of the members of the European Communities (such as the French President, the German Chancellor, the British Prime Minister) would hold regular summits. These became known as the European Council, though they were not formally part of the European Communities process. They tended to deal with subjects of high politics, such as the international situation (see, pp. 113–14), and with contentious matters unresolved at the Council of Ministers level. Once taken at this highest level, decisions could be translated into Community action through its normal decision-making channels. The position of the European Council as an institution auxiliary to the European Communities was established in February 1986 in the Single European Act, Title I, Article 2, whereby the Heads of State or of Government were to be assisted by their Foreign Ministers and by the President and one other member of the Commission of the European Communities and would meet at least twice yearly.

One of the main concerns of the European Council has been the development of European Political Cooperation. This is a process and a set of institutions that have run parallel with the development of the European Communities. The notion of the Communities going beyond functional and economic cooperation to include a wide range of political subjects could perhaps be read into the Preamble of the Treaty of Paris, establishing the Coal and Steel Community, which resolved 'to lay, by establishing an economic community, the foundations of a broader and deeper community among peoples long divided by bloody conflicts'.

Attempts to establish a European Political Community at the same time as the doomed European Defence Community failed, as did schemes for political union in 1961. At that time, proposals under the Fouchet plans to give the Economic Community greater direction of foreign affairs foundered on disagreement between the larger members, in particular France, and the smaller Benelux states over institutional arrangements. The idea surfaced again at the Hague Summit in December 1969, which also agreed to the extension of membership of the Communities. The Luxembourg Report of 1970 formed the basis of political cooperation, especially over foreign affairs, that was taken on by members of the expanded Communities of the Nine in 1973. European Political Cooperation was to be separate from the European Communities and their institutions, though the two enterprises were clearly interdependent. The Single European Act of 1986 dealt with the European Communities (Title II) and 'Provisions on European cooperation in the sphere of foreign policy' (Title III), and in Title I, on common provisions, it was stated that 'The European Communities and European Political Cooperation shall have as their objective to contribute *together* to make concrete progress towards European unity' (Article 1, emphasis added).

The structure of European Political Cooperation has been laid down in a number of reports (Luxembourg 1970, Copenhagen 1973, London 1981), by the Solemn Declaration on European Union of 1983, by established practice and by Title III of the Single European Act. The highest form of European Political Cooperation is the European Council (see above, p. 112) which may also discuss European Communities matters and meets biannually. Foreign Ministers also meet twice yearly as well as having an informal weekend put aside for more relaxed discussions. Ministers can also convene a meeting at 48 hours notice at the request of three members (Article 30, 10d SEA). The day-to-day continuity of European Political Cooperation is ensured by its Political Committee which consists of the 'Political Directors', or senior foreign ministry officials, who hold regular monthly meetings (as well as any emergency sessions) and smooth the way for the ministerial gatherings. The European Correspondents Group is also a grouping of foreign ministry officials who, under the direction of their superiors on the Political Committee, monitor the implementation of European Political Cooperation. The Political Committee also directs a number of Working Groups – 15 to 20 in all – that meet between four to six times a year. The task of initiation and coordination of European Political Cooperation is largely in the hands of its Presidency. This post is taken over every six months by the same country that holds the Presidency of the European Communities and, as well as convening and chairing meetings, it also represents the 12 European Political Cooperation states in certain international gatherings and in relations with the European Parliament.

Since the start of 1987, the Presidency has been assisted in administrative matters by a small Secretariat, based in Brussels. Previously all the administrative burden was taken on by the foreign ministry of the country holding the Presidency and was thus shifted from capital to capital every six months. The Secretariat, the Commission of the European Communities and all 12 foreign ministries are linked by a confidential telex system, 'Coreu', which allows for rapid exchange of information. It should be noted that, in accordance with the commonality of the two institutions expressed in Article 1 of the Single European Act, the Commission of the European Communities is 'fully associated with the proceedings of Political Cooperation' (Article 30b SEA) and is represented at all of its meetings.

The Maastricht Treaty on European Union (see p. viii) substantially retained the procedures for a Common Foreign and Security Policy (CFSP) laid down in the Single European Act, though under Article J.3.2, the Council can define those matters on which decisions may be taken by a qualified majority. Article J.7 requires the Presidency of the Council to consult the Parliament on 'the main aspects and the basic choices of the Common Foreign and Security Policy' and to ensure that these views are taken into consideration, and the Parliament may ask questions of the Council on such matters. Article J.9 associates the Commission with the work in the Common Foreign and Security Policy field. However, this policy is not open to judgement by the Court.

The Single European Act, which was agreed by all the 12 members of the European Communities in February 1986 and came into force on 1 July 1987, contained a number of changes to the institutions of the Communities.

First, the Single European Act introduced a Cooperation Procedure (Articles 6 and 7 SEA), by which the European Parliament was brought more into the decision-making process for some (but not all) of the Communities' legislative procedures (see below,

p. 120). This strengthened the element of democratic control and allowed the Parliament to become a more active, and constructive, partner in the formulation of the Communities' legislation.

Secondly, the Single European Act, under Article 10, amended Article 145 of the Treaty of Rome to allow the Council to confer powers on the Commission to implement Council rules. This had been done previously but the amendment provided more specific terms for this process.

Finally, the 1986 Act provided for the establishment of a court of first instance for the Court of Justice for certain cases. It would not deal with actions brought by member states or by Community institutions, neither would it settle questions referred for a preliminary ruling under Article 177, but could deal with a number of other complicated, time-consuming questions.

To summarize the major institutions of the European Communities, *before* the enactment of the Treaty on European Union, they consist of the Commission, the Council (assisted by COREPER), the European Parliament, the Economic and Social Committee and the Court of Justice. The European Council also deals with Communities' issues.

The Commission has 17 Commissioners appointed by the member states with two each coming from the five largest countries – Germany, France, Italy, Spain and the United Kingdom – and one each from the other seven states. The President of the Commission is appointed by common accord of the member states for a renewable term of two years. At the beginning of the four-year life of the Commission, portfolios are allocated among the Commissioners. There are 20 such portfolios, called Directorates General (DG). These range from External Affairs (DG I), through Agriculture (DG VI), Science, Research and Development (DG XII), Regional Policy (DG XVI), to Financial Control (DG XX), are headed by a Director-General – responsible to the relevant Commissioner – and are run by a civil service. Each Commissioner also appoints their own *Cabinet*, with a *Chef de Cabinet* in charge, which acts as their personal staff.

The Council of the European Communities consists of one voting representative of each member state. The ministers for a particular sector – say, agriculture or transport – meet together on a regular basis with the relevant Commissioner also present. The Presidency of the Council is responsible for its smooth running, for chairing the meetings (and for providing chairmen for other Council bodies) and for representing the Council to the outside world.

The Presidency rotates among the membership of the Communities every six months. The Council has a small General Secretariat. Preparatory work for the Council is undertaken by COREPER.

The European Council is a biannual meeting of the Heads of State and of Government of the members of the Communities, attended also by the President of the Commission and one other Commissioner. These meetings may discuss matters related both to the European Communities and to European Political Cooperation.

The European Parliament has been directly elected since 1979. Elections are held on fixed dates every five years with an allocated number of Members of the European Parliament (MEPs) being chosen by the electorate in each member country. The number of MEPs from each state were, by 1993, as follows:

Germany, France, Italy, United Kingdom	each 81
Spain	60
Netherlands	25
Belgium, Greece, Portugal	each 24
Denmark	16
Eire	15
Luxembourg	6
TOTAL	518

MEPs sit according to political party in the European Parliament, which meets in Strasbourg, holds a number of committees in Brussels and has its Secretariat in Luxembourg, all as a result of the inability of the member states to agree on its unified home. The main parties represented are the Socialists, the European People's Party (Christian Democrats and Conservatives), the European Democratic Alliance (Gaullists and Irish parties), European United Left (Communists and Allies), Liberal Democratic and Reformists, the Greens, the Rainbow Group (mainly regional parties) and the Group of the European Right (extreme right-wing parties). The Edinburgh European Council decided to increase the number of seats for Germany post-unification, and gave other countries extra seats, though fewer than those for Germany.

The Economic and Social Committee represents functional interests from within the Communities. It brings together spokesmen for employers, employees and other groups such as the self-employed, farmers, professions and consumers, who are chosen on a basis of national allocation by the Council in consultation with the Commission.

The Court of Justice consists of 13 judges, one from each member country and one extra, normally from one of the larger countries. The Court sits either in full plenary session or as a Chamber consisting of either three or five judges. The Court is assisted by six Advocates-General whose task it is to bring before it reasoned submissions on the cases. The Single European Act allows for the creation of a new court of first instance which is intended to deal with some of the more time-consuming and less important cases.

The Treaty on European Union signed at Maastricht in February 1992 (see p. viii) proposed a number of institutional changes that will affect the EC. The Treaty had certain innovations, but it also included many of the changes – mentioned above – that had affected the European Communities since their foundation. The Union is to be founded on these Communities (Article A, Treaty on European Union) and thus its institutions, as amended by the Treaty itself. As well as provisions covering the three Communities, there are titles on a Common Foreign and Security Policy – served by its own institutions (see above, pp. 112–4) – and on cooperation in the field of justice and home affairs, which is to be intergovernmental in nature.

The Treaty's tidying up of EC institutions made the Court of Auditors – the EC's financial watchdog, in being since 1977 – a full institution in its own right, on par with the Parliament, the Council, the Commission and the Court.

Perhaps the most important institutional change in the Maastricht Treaty is the increased powers for the European Parliament. The Co-decision Procedure of Article 189b is a development of existing practice and the Cooperation Procedure of Article 189c mirrors a change introduced by the Single European Act. The Assent Procedure entrenches powers that the Parliament had sought for some years (see p. 121). These changes have placed the Parliament more squarely as a partner with the Council and the Commission in the EC decision-making process. The Parliament also gained the rights, under Articles 138b and 138c respectively, to request the Commission to draft new legislation and to establish a Committee of Enquiry to investigate alleged breaches of EC law or maladministration by EC institutions. Under Article 138d the right was established of anyone residing in the EC to petition the European Parliament on EC matters that affect that person. The post of an Ombudsman to be appointed by the Parliment was set down in Article 138e. This person can receive complaints from citizens of the European Union concerning maladministration by the EC's institutions, excepting the Court, and can report on such matters to the Parliament.

The Commission remains largely unchanged by the treaty, except that its term of office had been extended to five years. Also the European Parliament is to have a greater say in the appointment of the Commission. The governments of the member states, in making the appointment of President of the Commission, are now to be obliged to consult the European Parliament. The whole Commission is then subject to a vote of approval by the Parliament.

In the section on the Court of Justice, the powers of the Court of First Instance – established by the Single European Act – is clarified.

An entirely new institution established by the Maastricht Treaty on European Union is the Committee of the Regions, consisting of representatives of regional and local bodies. Germany, France, Italy and the United Kingdom are to have 24 members of this Committee; Spain 21; Belgium, Greece, Netherlands, Portugal 12 each; Denmark and Ireland nine and Luxembourg six. The Committee is to be consultative, similar to the Economic and Social Committee.

The part of the Treaty dealing with Economic and Monetary Union (EMU) introduce a number of new institutions. (These are dealt with on pp. 144–7 in the section on EMU.)

How do these institutions work together to make decisions in the European Communities?

The process is a complex one which may differ from subject to subject. The Single European Act and the Maastricht Treaty (see p. viii) brought some changes in procedure but the basic pattern is still one of the Commission initiating legislation for the Council's decision, with the European Parliament providing democratic control and the Economic and Social Committee giving the input of the sectional interests.

In some cases the Commission alone can legislate: it is the main source of legislation for the Coal and Steel Community; it can legislate to effect tasks delegated to it by the Treaties of Rome and the Council; and it has some direct powers of decision under these treaties (for example, on turnover tax under Article 97 EEC).

Since the beginning of the European Economic Community the normal form of EC decision-making has evolved with the major Community institutions vying for power and influence. Despite the existence of 'Community' institutions such as the European Parliament and the Commission and of the interest-group-based Economic and Social Committee, there are a number of opportunities for the governments of the member states to influence the decision-making process and they can exercise their final say when the decision is taken in Council. As mentioned above, the use of majority votes has become more common in the Council, though by far the overwhelming number of decisions are still taken with the consent of all members and contentious issues are more often than not laid to one side. This is not just because of the Luxembourg Accords (see p. 109 above), but because in the founding treaties of the three European Communities, unanimity in the Council is required in 48 articles, while majority voting is the case in 25 articles (Nicoll, 1984, 42). The current system allows the following weighting when a qualified majority is needed:

Germany, France, Italy, United Kingdom	each 10 votes
Spain	8 votes
Belgium, Greece, Netherlands, Portugal	each 5 votes
Denmark, Ireland	each 3 votes
Luxembourg	2 votes

Fifty-four out of the 76 votes are needed to obtain the qualified majority, but when the proposal is not one deriving from the Commission the decision also needs the support of at least eight members. It should be noted that if Council members abstain, then their votes are effectively cast against a resolution needing a qualified majority, but this is not the case for decisions requiring unanimity.

The early usual pattern of EC decision-making, involving the Council acting on a proposal of the Commission, with the European Parliament and Economic and Social Committee being consulted developed into the Consultation Procedure (see Table 6.1) under which the Parliament gained greater prominence. In 1973, after the first extension of EC membership, both the Council of Ministers and the Commission agreed to extend their consultation process and in the 1980 Isoglucose case the EC's Court struck down legislation adopted by the Council but on which the Parliament had not given its opinion as required under the Treaty of Rome. This gave the Parliament greater leverage in, for example, having its amendments to proposed legislation considered by the Commission (Jacobs, Corbett and Shackleton, 1992, 178–82).

In March 1975, the Commission, the Council and the Parliament agreed a convention between the Parliament and the Council known as the Conciliation Procedure. This was an attempt to deal with the possiblity that the Parliament might exercise its then newly-found budgetary powers by delaying legislation with

Table 6.1	Consultation Procedure
Commission Initiates	Commission working group reports after discussion with governments and interested groups Commission drafts its proposals for the Council
The Council Consults	Proposal is sent by the Council to European Parliament (EP) and its relevant committee(s) for its opinion (obligatory in some cases) It may also go to the Economic Social Committee (ECOSOC) Commission may amend proposal in light of advice from EP and ECOSOC
COREPER sifts	Proposal goes to the Committee of Permanent Representatives (COREPER) which, with a group of national representatives, prepares a report for the Council If agreement is reached by COREPER, the matter is placed on Part A of the Council agenda; if not, it goes on Part B
The Council decides	Part A of agenda – barring any change of mind – adopted without debate Part B contains the contentious issues which are debated in the hope of reaching agreement
If no agreement	The proposal may be amended by the Commission to obtain a compromise The issue may be sent to the Council of Foreign Ministers or to the European Council for a political deal, perhaps involving other policies A vote may be taken and the proposal – in some cases – can be adopted by a weighted majority of the Council.

revenue and spending consequences. The intention was that 'acts of general application which have appreciable financial implications' should be submitted to a Conciliation Committee of representatives of the Parliament and the Council, with the Commission participating. The aim was to 'seek an agreement between the European Parliament and the Council' (OJ 1975, No. C89/1, cited in Foster, 1992, 74–5). The evidence seems to suggest that this conciliation, together with the Consultation Procedure, has led to a greater respect of Parliament's views by the Council (Jacobs, Corbett and Shackleton, 1992, 183–4). Furthermore, the Conciliation Committee has been included in the Co-decision Procedure of Article 189b of the Treaty on European Union.

The Cooperation Procedure (Table 6.2) was introduced by Article 6 and 7 of the Single European Act for some of the cases in the EEC's Treaty where there was a requirement to consult the European Parliament. These 10 articles cover much of the single market legislation, regional fund and social policy questions.

Table 6.2	The Cooperation Procedure (Articles 687 SEA, 189c Maastricht)
	As Table 6.1 for the first three stages, that is **Commision initiates** **The Council consults** **COREPER sifts** Then
The Council decides with Parliament's consent	Council adopts a 'common position', if necessary by a qualified majority The common position, with Council's supporting statement and the reasons for the Commission's position, is sent to the Parliament for approval, rejection or amendment If, within three months, Parliament approves the position (or fails to take action) then the Council will accept the act in accordance with the common position If the Parliament, by an absolute majority of its members, rejects the common position, Council unanimity is needed to act on a second reading If the Parliament, by an absolute majority of its members, amends the common position, it will be re-examined in this light by the Commission which may adopt some, all or none of the amendments, but must send all the amendments – together with their comments – to the Council The Council can either accept, by a qualified majority, the proposal amended by the Commission or it can adopt, by unanimity, the proposal with Parliament's amendments rejected by the Commission or with its own amendments.

A study has shown that, for the period from July 1987 to September 1991, some 2000 parliamentary amendments have been accepted for legislation under this procedure (Jacobs, Corbett and Shackleton, 1992, 187). The Cooperation Procedure has been included in the Maastricht Treaty as Article 189c.

The Maastricht Treaty has introduced another development of the Cooperation Procedure – known as the Co-decision Procedure – in Article 189b. The advances made in this version are: if the Council, in the second reading, does not accept all Parliament's amendments, then the matter is sent to a Conciliation Committee (similar to that mentioned on p. 120); Parliament can reject the text outright on a second reading; and Parliament's second reading amendments are to be submitted individually to Council rather than incorporated in a revised Commission proposal as under the Cooperation Procedure (op. cit., 191–2).

The Single European Act introduced an Assent Procedure whereby the European Parliament must agree a measure before it is enacted by the Council. This applied to association agreements with third countries (Article 238 EEC) and to the accession of new members (Article 237 EEC), thereby giving the Parliament a veto on the extension of the EC. To give its consent, Parliament had to act by an absolute majority of its members, not just by a simple majority of those present and voting. Until the Single European Act, Parliament only had the right to be consulted about such matters, but since 1987 it has displayed its displeasure with Turkey, Israel, Syria and Morocco (mainly over human rights issues) by delaying or refusing association agreements (op.cit., 198). The Maastricht Treaty introduces the Assent Procedure for all major international agreements agreed by the EC (new Article 228 EC) as well as for the response to applications for membership of the European Union (Article O, Treaty on European Union). Furthermore the agreement by the Parliament now has to be only a simple majority for international agreements, though assent to new members still requires an absolute majority.

Summing up the main areas where the different decision-making processes are to be used, the complexity of procedures within the EC can be seen:

Consultation Procedure: for many common policies, including agriculture, coordination of structural funds, land use, water and energy aspects of environment policy, taxation and multi-annual framework programmes; for institutional matters such as appointment of the President of the Commission, setting up the Court of First Instance, appointment to the Court of Auditors; decisions on the EC's own resources and financial regulations. (Matters with financial implications may see the *Conciliation Procedure* apply.).

Cooperation Procedure (Article 189c, Treaty on European Union): for rules prohibiting discrimination on grounds of nationality; transport; Social Fund and Regional Fund implementation; aspects of research and technological development; environment; development policy; health and safety at work.

Co-decision Procedure (Article 189b, Treaty on European Union): free movement of workers; right of establishment; recognition of diplomas; services, internal market harmonization and mutual recognition; consumer protection.

Assent Procedure: accession of new members (absolute majority of EP needed); certain international agreements; procedures for European elections; structural funds' definition; measures assisting freedom of movement.

(Adapted from Jacobs, Corbett and Shackleton, 1992, 203–5.)

The adopting of the Communities' budget is a complicated procedure different from normal decision-making (see Table 6.3).

Table 6.3	The Budget Procedure
The drafts	Each Community institution estimates its expenditure Commission consolidates these – and revenue estimate – into a preliminary draft budget Council establishes draft budget, making changes to Commission draft as it sees fit – all by qualified majority and after consulting Commission
The Parliamentary stage	Draft budget is sent to European Parliament which can accept it, amend it or reject it If it accepts it, or takes no action within 45 days, the budget is adopted Parliament, by a majority of votes cast, can propose modifications to compulsory expenditure (that made necessary by Treaty provisions or Communities' legislation) Parliament, by a majority of members, can propose amendments to non-compulsory expenditure (the rest) Parliament can reject the budget for 'important reasons' by a majority of all members and a two-thirds majority of votes cast: Council then has to place new budget before Parliament
Council deals with amendments	If Council does not change Parliament's amendment of non-compulsory expenditure within 15 days, it is adopted If Council, by qualified majority, changes Parliament's amendment of non-compulsory expenditure within 15 days, it goes back to Parliament either to accept or, by a two-thirds majority of votes and a majority of members, to reject or amend Modifications by Parliament to compulsory expenditure that do not increase total expenditure of an institution may be rejected by the Council by a qualified majority; otherwise the change is accepted Modifications by Parliament to compulsory expenditure that increases the total expenditure of an institution has to be accepted by a qualified majority; otherwise the change is deemed rejected
Return to Parliament	If Council has rejected or changed the Parliament's amendments or modifications, the budget returns to the Parliament which can uphold and thereby entrench its own changes in the non-compulsory expenditure, by three-fifths of the votes and a majority of members It cannot reject Council changes to its modification of compulsory expenditure: it has either to accept or reject the budget as a whole.

A new factor of relevance to the EC's and European Union's institutions was introduced in the Maastricht Treaty. It was that of *subsidiarity*. This vague notion was defined in the Treaty in Article 3b:

In areas that do not fall within its exclusive competence, the Community shall take action, in accordance with the principle of subsidiarity, only if and in so far as the objectives of the proposed action cannot be sufficiently achieved by the Member States and can therefore, by reason of the scale or effects of the proposed action, be better achieved by the Community (Treaty on European Union, 1992, 13–14).

It may need rulings by the EC's Court to define fully the implications of this article even though the concept of subsidarity has a considerable history (Wilke and Wallace, 1990). Though it is clear that the article was intended by some states – most notably the United Kingdom – to clip the wings of the European Union and prevent it from taking action which could just as well be undertaken by the sovereign state, the concept of subsidiarity is a two-edged sword. If decisions are, according to the Treaty's Preamble, to be 'taken as closely as possible to the citizen in accordance with the principle of subsidiarity' (Treaty on European Union, 1992, 4), then this would suggest a draining of decision-making power away from states' capitals down to their regions. The establishment by the Maastricht Treaty of a Committee of the Regions within the structure of the EC may foreshadow a more fruitful link between regional authorities and the European Union.

Achievements

Any assessment of the achievements of the European Economic Community (later joined with the Coal and Steel Community and the European Atomic Energy Community to form the European Communities) must take into consideration its aims and expectations. The Preamble of the Treaty of Rome and the activities outlined in Part One of that Treaty provide a basis for such a judgement. According to its preamble, the Treaty on European Union aimed at being a 'new stage in the process of European integration' (Treaty on European Union, 1992, 3). These activities point towards the creation of a customs union, a common market and, finally, a community with common concerns and policies. The customs union would result from an end to customs duties and quantitative restrictions between the member countries and the establishment of a common external tariff and commercial policy towards third countries. The common market would rest on the customs union together with a common agricultural policy, the abolition of obstacles to freedom of movement of persons, services and capital between member states; the non-distortion of competition and the approximation of laws between members, coordination of members' economic policies and the adoption of a common transport policy. Activities going beyond the common market were those aimed at improving employment opportunities and the living standards of workers, those which were intended to expand the Community's economy, and those with a view 'to increase trade and to promote jointly economic and social development' (Article 3.k EEC). They would also include actions leading to 'an ever closer union among the peoples of Europe'. It is not always possible to distinguish activities that contribute to the customs union from those that help build the common market and those that create a wider community – there is a good deal of overlap in each case. For the sake of clarity, the division will be made in this section and the record of the European Economic Community – later merged into the European Communities – will now be examined. The proposals contained in the Maastricht Treaty on European Union (see p. viii) will also be outlined.

The *customs union* of the European Communities was brought about earlier than required by the Treaty of Rome. By 1 July 1968, a year and a half before time, all customs duties between the then six member states of the Economic Community were removed and the Common External Tariff was established. This meant that the EEC had a uniform set of tariffs for imports from other countries and no tariffs on trade between Communities' countries. However, non-tariff barriers to trade, such as customs formalities and differing rules on safety, packaging and contents often frustrated the achievement of free movement of goods within the EEC and, since the creation of the customs union, the Commission has worked to eradicate such restrictions. They have aimed at establishing common rules of competition so that trade within the Communities may not only be free but fair. This should prevent the intentions of the customs union from being frustrated either by different governments imposing differing technical, health, safety and other standards or by firms deciding to use their monopoly or cartel powers to prevent consumers from benefiting fully from the competition that one Communities' market should bring (Articles 85 and 86 EEC). This helps take the customs union beyond a purely trading venture to a common market where goods can be traded as if there were no national barriers.

The Commission has sought to harmonize industrial standards (for example, in the electronics and automobile industries) and in 1983 a system was created whereby new national technical regulations and industrial standards would be checked by the Communities. The Commission, working with the European

Standards Committee – a technical body – can impose a standstill on such national regulations to allow Community-wide ones to be decided. Since 1985, the Communities have accepted a more active and more flexible approach to harmonization and standardization and have jettisoned the more cumbersome procedures previously used that aimed at excessive uniformity. The aims of the new policy have been to prevent new technical barriers from arising, to promote Communities' standards in the field of health, safety, protection of workers and the environment, the abolition of trade barriers within the EC, and the promotion of Europe-wide standards in the European Standardization Committee (CEN) and the European Standardization Committee for Electrical Products (CENELEC) (Pelkmans, 1987, 249–69). The Single European Act of 1986 introduced changes to the EEC Treaty (Articles 100A and 100B EEC) which allowed the Council to adopt, by a qualified majority, measures for the approximation of laws etc. of the member states aimed at the establishment and functioning of the internal market. The task of chasing up the national laws and regulations that needed harmonizing was left to the Commission, which was to submit its proposals to the Council for action before the end of 1992. The aim was to create a single European market by the end of that year, a theme that will be referred to below (see p. 140).

The European Communities have also prevented state subsidies, tax advantages or other help that would place the industry of one member state at an unfair advantage over the others (Articles 92 to 95 EEC). In industries where state aid has been permitted to help structural change (for example, to assist workers in shipbuilding to get jobs elsewhere), the Communities have tried to harmonize the rules for assistance.

The Commission can declare illegal any agreement between companies that distorts trade between members, though it could authorize agreements 'which contribute to improving the production or distribution of goods or to promoting technical or economic progress', providing that the restrictions are necessary for that purpose and do not eliminate the competition (Article 85.3 EEC). Article 86 bans companies from exploiting a dominant position in the common market 'or in a substantial part of it' and thereby affecting trade between members. It gives some idea of such improper practices:

1 unfair purchase or selling prices
2 restrictions on production, markets or technical developments

3 unequal conditions – giving special deals for particular clients
4 making a contract subject to other special conditions not related to the subject of that contract.

As the Commission's Directorate-General IV has limited resources to police the rules of competition, it has tended to tackle some of the more obvious transgressors. It has tried, with some success, to undo French and Italian state monopolies on tobacco, and salt, in so far as they affect fair trade within the Communities, and has taken on the chemical and automobile industries. One writer (Allen, 1983, 230) summed up the situation on competition policy in 1983 thus: 'in an area of relatively low political interest such as restrictive practices it has prospered, while little progress has been made with merger policy, let alone with the more sensitive question of state aids'. With the move towards a single European market, the tempo of Communities' action has increased since 1983, but the same political constraints still work.

The creation of a customs union in the European Communities has brought the necessity of an EC commercial policy. As the Communities present a unified system of tariffs to the outside world, common arrangements have to be made for this and other aspects of trade with third countries (i.e. non-Communities countries). Articles 111 and 113 gave the Commission powers to negotiate commercial arrangements with other countries, though these then have to be accepted by the Council (and some of them, under the Maastricht Treaty, by the Parliament). Under Article 116, member states proceed only by common action within international organizations of an economic character and Article 238 allows the EEC to conclude an association agreement with third countries, with 'reciprocal rights and obligations, common action and special procedures'.

From its early years, the EEC established itself as an actor in trade negotiations. It participated in the General Agreement on Tariffs and Trade (GATT) Dillon and Kennedy Rounds for tariff reductions, which ended in agreement respectively in 1962 and 1967. It also signed a number of bilateral trade agreements with states such as Iran (1963), Israel (1964) and Lebanon (1965).

Relations with third countries can be broadly divided into those with other West European states, the ex-Communist states of East and Central Europe, USA, the Lomé states and the OCTs (which will be dealt with later, pp. 152–5), and the rest of the world.

The EC's most intensive relations have been with the other West European states. Some of these have been candidates for membership during the life of the Communities and, in the case of the United Kingdom, Eire, Denmark, Greece, Spain and Portugal, have eventually joined. Individual trade agreements have been signed with the EFTA states and during 1991 the EC agreed on a European Economic Area with the EFTA states (see Chapter 7). The EC has an association agreement dating back to 1963 with Turkey. Although Turkey applied to join the Communities in April 1987, the country's backward economy, social structure and doubtful democratic record have led the Communities to postpone consideration of this case. The dilemma faced by the Communities is that while many may feel that Turkey is not properly a European country and therefore should not be allowed membership, an outright refusal could destabilize democratic elements in Turkey and lead to a self-fulfilling prophecy whereby Turkey turns more to the Middle East and Islamic fundamentalism. In July 1989 Austria applied for membership negotiations and was followed by Sweden, Finland and Norway. Discussions on these cases opened in early 1993 and there is the prospect that these states could become full members of the European Union by 1995 or 1996.

Formal relations between the Communities and Eastern Europe have been fraught in the past but entered a new phase in the 1990s. Problems arose in the early relations with members of the Council for Mutual Economic Assistance (CMEA or Comecon, see Chapter 11) as there was a basic Soviet hostility to what was seen as a capitalist club in Western Europe, the EEC, and also because EEC members had developed their own relationships – including commercial ones – with East European states and seemed reluctant to see the EEC take these over (Feld, 1967, 157). The East European states felt that, if they had to deal with the European Communities, then it should be on a bloc-to-bloc basis with CMEA facing the EC across the negotiating table. The Communities were not prepared to accept that CMEA was in any way equivalent to their organization and preferred individual trade agreements. As the national agreements with individual EC member states ran out, the new ones were negotiated by the Communities as a whole. By 1986 both Poland and Hungary had accepted invitations to trade talks with the Communities and with the 'New Thinking' introduced by Mr Gorbachev into Soviet foreign affairs, the situation started to change. The old attitude of pretending the European Communities did not exist was dropped in 1987, and in June 1988 a joint declartion was signed between the EC and Comecon that allowed for cooperation 'on matters of mutual interest'. By

October 1990 all the Comecon countries – which, except the Soviet Union, had thrown off Communist rule – had signed individual agreements with the EC (Pinder, 1991, 25). Furthermore on 3 October 1990, one of Comecon's former members, the German Democratic Republic (East Germany) became part of the European Communities when it unified with the Federal Republic of Germany. As stated above (see p. 100), the Treaty of Rome had defined inner-German trade as being 'internal' trade, thereby making adjustment to the new situation easier for the EC (Archer and Butler, 1992, 150).

The three ex-Comecon countries of Central Europe – Hungary, the CSFR and Poland – were the most obvious candidates for a closer relationship with the EC both because of their adoption of democratic practices and because their economies were the most developed within Comecon. By mid-1990 all three had non-preferential trade and cooperation 'first generation' agreements with the EC and by the end of 1991 the EC had negotiated 'Europe Agreements' with all three. These treaties of association set out full membership as the desired goal but meanwhile created a limited industrial free trade area between the EC and the associates. The outcome has been somewhat disappointing for the three countries, especially as many of their key exports such as agricultural goods, textiles and steel products have effectively been excluded from the agreement. For example, in December 1992 the EC imposed steel import quotas on each of the four Central European states (de Weydenthal, 1993, 30). A further complication to relationships was added by the division of the CSFR into a Czech and a Slovak Republic in January 1993, which increased the number of Europe Agreement states by one. By early 1993 a similar agreement had been initialled with Romania and negotiations with Bulgaria were concluded.

Other East and Central European states still only had 'first generation' agreements with the EC by 1993, but some – particularly the Baltic states and Slovenia – were hopeful of 'Europe Agreements' similar to those of the four Central European states.

Relations with the Soviet Union – later the CIS – proved difficult for the EC. An agreement on economic, political and cultural cooperation was signed with the Soviet Union in December 1989, but aid to that country was suspended as a result of the repression of the Baltic states by Soviet forces in January 1991. The EC responded to the break-up of the Soviet Union in December on four fronts. First, they recognized the new constituent republics of the

Commonwealth of Independent States (CIS) and the three Baltic states that decided not to join the CIS. Georgia was recognized after it had emerged from a civil war. Secondly, they provided emergency aid to help the citizens of the CIS survive the winter of 1991/2. Total EC aid by the end of 1991 was an estimated ECU2 billion, about the amount planned by the USA (Archer and Butler, 1992, 155). Thirdly, they planned longer-term aid, especially through the EBRD (see Chapter 3) and the EC technical aid scheme, TACIS (Technical Assistance to the Commonwealth of Independent States and Georgia). The initial TACIS funding in 1991 was ECU400 million and ECU450 million was committed in 1992. The aim of TACIS was to help the individual states to develop effectively functioning market economies and to encourage pluralistic, democratic societies. Schemes have involved energy efficiency, enterprise training and food distribution. Finally, in July 1992 the Commission proposed a new type of partnership and cooperation agreement with the CIS states and Georgia. These agreements would offer cooperation in a wide range of areas and would provide trade from these countries with most favoured nation treatment. Further trade liberalization would be considered.

An even more troubled relationship arose with Yugoslavia. As this country, despite having a Communist government, was not part of the Soviet bloc, the EC found it easy to sign a trade agreement with it in 1970, renewing this in 1973. A more advanced agreement was signed in 1980. However, when other East and Central European states were advancing towards democracy in 1990, Yugoslavia was moving to civil war and disintegration. The EC attempted to prevent this break-up by signing a loan agreement with the Yugoslav government – on the day, in June 1991, when Slovenia and Croatia declared their independence from the Yugoslav federation. The matter then became a question more for European Political Cooperation (see pp. 113–14).

United States' governments were among the early supporters of the establishment of the European Communities. More recently, the US has had doubts about the development of the EC, in particular its growing importance as a trade bloc. The Communities' relations with the US have been bitter-sweet. Member countries have looked to the US presence in Europe as a safeguard for their defence and have recognized that the Americans are a major trade partner, but the Communities have resisted transatlantic efforts to shape their development to suit US trade priorities.

Early in the life of the EEC, it found that the establishment of a Common External Tariff tested American friendship when certain US products had increased tariffs imposed on them. This led to retaliation by the US and often acrimonious trade disputes such as the 'Chicken War' of 1963-4 (Ginsberg, 1983, 174). As the American trade deficit has mounted and the EC's trade walls have become strengthened, so this pattern has continued: for example, the changes brought about by Spanish and Portuguese member-ship of the Communities affected US trade with those countries and led to threats of retaliation and counter-threats by the EC until a truce was agreed. Closer contact between the US and the EPC process resulted from the 1974 Gymnich agreement, and the 1990 Transatlantic Declaration between the two sides further institutionalized contact between the US and the EC (Krenzler and Kaiser, 1991, 363-72). The greatest area of contention is that of agricultural products where the United States believes that Com-munities' produce is unfairly subsidized and is pushing them out of their rightful markets. The whole issue has been one for nego-tiation at the Uruguay GATT round with the new Clinton administration reflecting pressures in the US to 'get tough' with the EC about the CAP and other trade matters.

The Communities' relations with the rest of the world (outside agreements such as Lomé and OCT) have been expanded over the years but still remain patchy.

It has been said that 'High-Level talks with the Japanese con-tinue to be conducted on the assumption that they respond to public bullying' (Brewin and McAllister, 1987, 350). Much of the EC's trade relationship with Japan is conducted through GATT though it should be remembered that an important link between the two is Japanese investment in the Communities, for example in automobile factories in Britain.

Relations with the Association of South-East Asian Nations (ASEAN) have been fruitful. Despite being ASEAN's third trading partner (after Japan and the US) and taking only 14 per cent of its total trade and of its inward investment, the Communities have developed an extensive network of institutions with ASEAN including the 1980 Cooperation Agreement which covered com-mercial and economic activity as well as development assistance (Drummond, 1982, 311-12). The main subject for negotiation between the two sides has been that of market access, especially for ASEAN textiles exported to Europe.

Countries on the Indian sub-continent – India, Pakistan, Bangladesh and Sri Lanka – have had a less happy relationship with the Communities as they have felt that their traditional products and those of their newly industrialized base have been unfairly treated in the Communities' markets. Commercial Agreements have been signed with Bangladesh (1976) and Sri Lanka (1975) and there are cooperation agreements with India (1981) and Pakistan (1985).

China is an emerging economic giant which, since the mid-1970s, has developed its commercial relations with the EC. A general trade agreement was signed in 1978 and renewed in 1985. A separate textile settlement was reached in 1978 and, despite some problems, this was renewed in 1984 (Redmond and Zou Lan, 1986, 133–55). As China has over a million consumers, it could provide a lucrative market for the Communities which, in their turn, could supply the sort of technology and modern equipment needed by China. However, the suppression of the student democracy movement in Beijing in June 1989 forced the EC to hold back on the expansion of economic links with China in order to show political disapproval of the government's action there.

Trade with Latin America has been adversely affected by economic crisis and the rising level of debt in the area. However, the Communities' direct investment in Latin America exceeds that of the US and the EC has cooperation agreements with Mexico (1975) and Brazil (1980) and a commercial agreement with Uruguay (1973). Argentina broke off its cooperation treaty during the Falklands conflict in 1982 but this has since been renewed. New economic cooperation agreements were signed with Chile, Mexico, Uruguay and Paraguay in 1990, and the EC has had joint meetings with the Central American states.

Links with New Zealand were tied historically to that country's trade dependence on the United Kingdom and the arrangements for New Zealand trade (especially butter and lamb exports) negotiated at the time of British entry to the EC (Archer and Butler, 1992, 166). Australia, by contrast, has reoriented its trade to the Pacific and the United States and has not established close commercial links with the Communities (Miller, 1983, 203–8).

The Communities have developed a special relationship with the Mediterranean states. As well as carrying out a dialogue with the Arab countries of the Middle East, many of which are Mediterranean littorals, the EC also have cooperation agreements with Algeria (1976), Egypt (1977), Israel (1975), Jordan (1977), Lebanon (1977), Morocco (1976), Syria (1977) and Tunisia (1976). Cyprus (1973) and Malta (1970) have free-trade agreements with the EC and both island-states applied for EC membership in 1990. Libya under Colonel Gaddafi is conspicuously missing from this list. Because of the variety in the political and economic nature of the non-Communities Mediterranean states, it is difficult for the EC to run a consistent Mediterranean policy. Spanish and Portuguese membership has heightened the Communities' interest in the area but has led to rifts between Morocco and Algeria over what the latter felt was favourable treatment of the former by the EC. Indeed, in July 1987 Morocco applied for full membership of the Communities, a move that should be seen as a way of underlining that country's links with the EC rather than as a serious quest to become the thirteenth member.

Moving from a customs union to a *common market* has involved a number of policies, the most prominent of which has been the Common Agricultural Policy (CAP). The CAP was the policy that dominated the early years of the EEC and it still takes up about two-thirds of the Communities' budget. A common policy for certain key agricultural products was agreed in January 1962 and a European Agricultural Guidance and Guarantee Fund (EAGGF, or FEOGA, using the French acronym) was established and started operating on 1 July 1964. The national arrangements originally made to finance the CAP have since been replaced by the use of the Communities' own resources raised from customs duties, agricultural levies and a share of Value Added Tax raised by national governments. This had the effect of penalizing the British during their first dozen years of membership, as the United Kingdom's agricultural sector was smaller than that of other Communities' states (and it therefore benefited less from the EC's budget) but its rate of imports was high, producing a good return for the Communities' collective coffers. Much time and trouble was spent from 1974 onwards in creating mechanisms whereby corrective payments could be made back to the United Kingdom to compensate for its high contributions (Wallace, 1980, 59).

Article 39 of the Treaty of Rome sets out the aims of the CAP (see p. 96) which are potentially contradictory. For example, assuring supplies might not mean that these products reach consumers at reasonable prices; increasing productivity may not stabilize markets; and all these could undermine the aim of a fair standard of living for farmers and workers in agriculture. These outcomes were to be achieved by the creation of a single market in agriculture whereby there would be no barriers to trade across the national frontiers within the Communities; by Communities' preference with a tariff barrier against outside produce which would bring cheaper imports up to, or over, EC prices and an export levy when EC prices were cheaper, to prevent products from being exported; and by the use of EAGGF to keep prices pegged at the level set by the Council, helping Communities' farm produce compete on the world market. One writer has succinctly described the CAP mechanism:

> It seeks to maintain prices within a certain range and protects producers under normal conditions and consumers in time of scarcity; it works on the basis of import levies and export bounties . . . normally and export levies with import subsidies in the event of a shortage; under extreme conditions there may be a straight prohibition on imports or exports as the case may be (Kerr, 1986, 80).

The CAP has two main aspects: price support and a structural policy.

The first aspect is the support price whereby the Council sets a target price each year for a product, aimed at giving the farmer a reasonable return for his effort. It can be calculated in different ways. For example, the target price for cereals would be the one representing the best price that could be obtained on the open market in the Communities. A threshold price is set for products imported into the Communities: this represents a price at which imports will not undercut EC produce and levies are placed on imports to bring them up to that price. The intervention price is some 10 to 12 per cent lower than the target price and if an excess of supply over demand brings the market price of a product down below the intervention price, then farmers can sell it at that price to the relevant intervention board which will either store it – thus the 'butter mountains' or 'wine lakes' – or dispose of it or use it for social purposes (for example to help old people, schools or poorer parts of the world) or to export it at the world market price. As this is often below the EC price, Export Restitutions are paid to make up the difference.

From 1984 to 1988 efforts were made, with British prompting, to reform the CAP. Quotas – especially for milk – were used to cut output, and real prices were reduced for many products. Co-responsibility levies were introduced, requiring farmers to pay out some of the costs of their own over-production. The various 'lakes' and 'mountains' were sold off with the amount of butter held in storage being reduced by some 1 million tonnes by 1988. Finally, farmers were encouraged to 'set aside' land from cultivation (Lintner and Mazey, 1991, 108–9).

These reforms continued into the 1990s under Commissioner MacSharry with the emphasis being placed on the second, much neglected, aspect of the CAP, structural reforms. These are meant to be undertaken with the aid of the Guidance part of the EAGGF, which on average has only received about 5 per cent of those funds. However, the MacSharry reforms met opposition from the USA in the Uruguay Round of GATT where they were seen as not being radical enough, and from farmers – especially in France – who thought that they endangered their livelihood.

The aim of an internal agricultural market within the EC has been adversely affected by currency fluctuations. The CAP system was created in a period of relatively stable currency exchanges in Europe, but since 1969 currencies have tended to move up and down in value in response to market pressures. This has made the task of fixing one price for a product throughout the Communities well nigh impossible once that price is translated into the local currency. The price in Brussels is expressed in the European Currency Unit (ECU) but the value of that price to the farmer in Italy or Denmark depends on the exchange value of the lira or kroner on any one day. In order to protect their farmers from the fluctuations of their currencies, member states started in the 1970s to use a more stable rate for calculating their farm prices – the 'green pound', 'green lira', 'green kroner' and so on. If the green rate was lower than the real value of the currency, then the farmers benefited in that country – and the consumers lost out. If the green rate was higher than the real rate – as was the case for some time for Britain during the 1970s – then food prices were kept down but farmers' incomes suffered. To combat this distortion, the Communities created a system of levies and subsidies at national frontiers – called Monetary Compensatory Amounts (MCAs) – which were aimed at making up for the differences between the real currency rates and the green rates. The intention of ending this web of green currencies and MCAs with the introduction of the single market from January 1993 was undermined by the currency crisis of September 1992 which saw several currencies – most notably the pound sterling – leave the Exchange Rate Mechanism.

Has the CAP been a success? In terms of the stated aims of the policy as laid down in Article 39 (see p. 96), the answer must be a mixed one.

There is little doubt that the CAP has helped increase the productivity of agriculture within the European Communities, purely in terms of output per man-year. In 1968 the Commissioner for Agriculture, Sicco Mansholt, produced a plan for the rationalization of agricultural production and in 1972 the Council issued three directives on this subject, aimed at modernization, structural improvement and training of the workforce. While production has risen, the percentage of the workforce in agriculture has dropped – between 1960 and 1970 it was halved or more than halved in all the then member states. The decline since then has been less dramatic and the Communities have taken steps with their Hill Farming Directive to maintain small, seemingly uneconomic farms in hill regions, whose existence has social and environmental significance.

It is difficult to decide whether the CAP has helped the farming population receive a 'fair income', partly because the concept is one which is hard to define and partly because it is not known what income farmers would have received without the CAP. Because of the Mansholt Plan and the emphasis on productivity, it does seem that the CAP has in the past favoured the larger producers in the Communities. What academic work that has been done on this subject suggests that the agricultural producers in all the EC states have benefited by a sizeable transfer of resources from the taxpayer and the consumer to them through the CAP. Because of the inefficiency involved in the process, this also means a deadweight loss of around 1 per cent of the EC's Gross Domestic Product (Demekas *et al.*, 1988, 126–7 and 140).

An important aspect of the CAP has been the stabilization of markets. Despite the reliance on political decisions which can sometimes change the financial situation of a farmer overnight, the policy has provided a certain amount of consistency and stability that might not have existed otherwise. It has guarded the Communities against some of the turbulence of the world markets.

The Communities have also guaranteed themselves a high level of security of supplies through the CAP, achieved by encouraging the self-sufficiency of the member states' agriculture and by using their economic power in the world market. A major criticism is that the EC have done this at the cost of other agricultural producers. In fact, the Communities' importation of foodstuffs has increased over the years and its imports account for about a quarter of the world's food trade. However, it is perhaps the case that the CAP has worked against the interests of other temperate-product exporters such as Australia and the United States. One study suggests that the CAP has 'a significant depressing effect on world prices', that EC exports are boosted at the expense of other countries' exports, that this distortion keeps world trade artificially low and that the effects are felt particularly in the trade in wheat, coarse grains, ruminant meat (especially beef) and dairy products (Demekas *et al.*, 1988, 132).

Much political argument in the United Kingdom has centred on whether the CAP has created reasonable prices for consumers. By excluding other products from the Communities by a system of levies and by, in most cases, keeping the prices paid to farmers at a level higher than that which the market would accept, the CAP has seemingly increased the cost of foodstuffs for the consumer. It would be cheaper, it has been argued, to buy produce on the world market. Against this, it should be pointed out that by insuring security of supply, the CAP has cut out the see-sawing of prices experienced on the free market. While it may be possible to obtain some products some of the time at a cheaper price on the world market, any gains may be wiped out by paying higher prices for other products for the rest of the time. Also, if the EC opened itself up to the world market, that in itself would change the nature of that market and would presumably increase its prices. Empirical work seems to come down against the CAP in this debate; it shows a net loss from both the consumers and the taxpayers to the producers (mainly the farmers) in all the EC member states (Demekas *et al.*, 1988, 126–7).

Further criticisms of the CAP have involved both its policy aims and administration. It has been accused of ignoring social and environmental factors by its emphasis on efficiency and by favouring the larger farms (Kerr, 1986, 80). The Commission has shown an interest in the environmental and societal aspects of agriculture but it seems that its plans for action in this area are underfunded and half-hearted (Fennell, 1987, 68–71). More recently, the various ways in which the CAP system may be abused and subsidies obtained for non-existent produce have reached public notice, as have cases of more systematic swindling (Norton, 1986, 297–312).

An evaluation of the CAP should include the fact that it has been the one central policy of the EC since the mid-1960s. As such, it represents proof that a common policy – whatever its shortcomings – can be created among the member states, but there is also the irony that this common policy directly covers such a small percentage of the Communities' working population (though the food produced affects a large number of consumers). It may be the case that in the future, when the Communities are dealing more with industrial, social and environmental policies, the CAP will decrease in importance. However, it is hard to see either the Agricultural Council of Ministers or the sizeable Agricultural Directorate of the Commission giving up their dominant position within the Communities, 'voluntary to retire to the wings where objectively they might be more properly located' (Fennell, 1987, 74). For the time being the CAP is the mainstay of the Communities and of their budget.

Associated with the CAP, insofar as it covers a form of food, is the Common Fisheries Policy (CFP). In the Treaty of Rome, fisheries products are deemed to be included in the term 'agricultural products' and are thereby covered by the requirements for a common market in such produce (Articles 38.1 and 38.4 EEC). During the first few years of the EEC, the main effect of the common market on the member states' fisheries industry was the abolition of internal tariffs and the creation of a Common External Tariff (CET), both of which disadvantaged the well-protected French industry. Fish imports into France rose from 95,000 tons in 1957 to 282,000 tons in 1966 and the response of French fishermen was to put pressure on their government to obtain a CFP that would bring them the economic advantages which they saw their farming compatriots reaping from the CAP (Wise, 1984, 87–8). In particular the French government was anxious to establish the CFP before the applicants for membership in 1970 started their negotiations, so that they would be obliged to accept the CFP as part of the existing package of the EC. There was concern that, unless this was done, the applicants – all of which were strong fishing nations – would hold up the creation of a common policy. Furthermore there were international moves, led by Iceland, toward extending fisheries limits around coasts, thereby expanding member states' fishing areas but also excluding them from some of their traditional fishing grounds. A CFP accord was reached by the end of June 1970 and had four main aspects.

First, there was to be equal access for fishing of all EC vessels to the territorial waters and exclusive fisheries zones of the member states, and this was to apply to new members. There was to be a five-year-long exception for three-mile coastal strips where a region was particularly dependent on local fisheries.

Secondly, the Communities were to provide money for structural aid to the fishing industry which would help make it more efficient.

Thirdly, there was to be a network of Producers' Organizations (POs) which would mainly be responsible for running the internal common market in fish. The POs would help run a market intervention system, similar to that of the CAP and financed by EAGGF.

Finally, a reference price for imports of major fish species would be set to ensure that these could not be imported at a price that would undercut their Communities' equivalent (Wise, 1984, 102–5).

The adoption of the CFP caused problems in the negotiations with the applicant countries – the United Kingdom, Denmark, Eire and Norway – but all except Norway managed to obtain adjustents to the 1970 accord, that satisfied their governments and people. The settlement with Norway was viewed as unsatisfactory in that country and was one of the factors that led to the rejection of membership terms by the Norwegian electorate in a referendum in September 1972.

The Treaty of Accession for the new members included four articles on fisheries (100–103). These restricted fishing in the six-mile zone around the Communities' coast to vessels based in the ports in the geographical coastal area and 'vessels which fish traditionally in those waters' (Article 100.1). This limit was extended to 12 nautical miles in certain areas, namely the Faroe Islands and Greenland and a small part of the Jutland west coast for Denmark; the Brittany coast for France; about 70 per cent of the Irish coast; the south-west and north-east of England, the east and north coast of Scotland and County Down's coast for the United Kingdom. These derogations were to last until 31 December 1982 but what would follow was left rather vague (Wise, 1984, 130–31).

The prospect of the extension of fishing limits up to 200 nautical miles as from January 1977, led to the adoption of the Hague Resolutions in November 1976 by which the Communities agreed to extend their limits in concert, to give authority to the Commission to negotiate agreements on fishing access with third countries, and to adopt common conservation measures. This led to a period of some conflict both among the members of the Communities and between the EC and third countries.

Nevertheless an agreement was reached by January 1983 for a more permanent CFP. Its five main points are:

1 All the waters within the Communities' 200-mile fisheries zone were to be open to fishing by vessels from any of the member states, except for a 12 mile coastal belt within which fishing could be restricted to the fleets of the

individual countries and those with traditional rights. These restrictions were to last until 2003 but were to be reviewed in 1993.

2   Total Allowable Catches (TACs) for species, with national quotas, were to be decided by the Council on the basis of traditional fishing patterns, the requirements of areas dependent on fishing and the need for compensation for loss of traditional fishing rights in non-EC grounds (e.g. off Iceland).

3   Measures were to be introduced to protect endangered species.

4   Other conservation measures were to be taken, including those by national governments with the permission of the Commission.

5   The member states were to enforce EC rules within their own national sectors, but on a non-discriminatory basis and under the general supervision of a group of EC inspectors.

The market organization, described above (p. 139), was strengthened, and agreements were signed with third countries such as Norway, the Faeroes and Sweden.

The whole CFP has had to adjust itself to Portuguese and Spanish membership and this has been managed by giving Spain a lengthy transitional period, restricting its access to certain waters, and helping it to restructure and reduce its fleet.

It has been mentioned above (p. 126) how the creation of a customs union with the European Communities has led to moves to make sure that trade is fair as well as free. In 1985 the Commission, in response to a request from the European Council, produced a programme for the completion of a single European market by the end of 1992. It was based on the belief – confirmed in the Cecchini Report (Commission of the European Communities, 1988) – that the cost of maintaining the panoply of restrictions and barriers to the free movement of goods, services, labour and capital ('the four freedoms') was more than ECU200 billion ('the cost of non-Europe') and that market liberalization would bring an extra 4.5 per cent benefit to the EC's Gross Domestic Product. The Single European Act, in force in 1987, was a means of streamlining Council decision-making on single European market matters, as well as allowing the EC to deal with other matters – such as social and environmental policy – that would be affected by the creation of a single market. The means to bring about the four freedoms were decisions to tackle the removal of physical, technical and fiscal barriers to a single market, and these appeared in some 289 proposals to be passed before the 31 December 1992 deadline.

The progress towards free movement of goods has been covered above (p. 125–6), and clearly the removal of any remaining physical, technical and fiscal barriers will advance that process. By far the greatest contribution has been the growing use of the single administrative document to replace the variety of import and export documents that existed before. What has been less easy to agree is the harmonization of Value Added Tax rates, though plans for single excise duties on certain alcohol, cigarette and petrol products are going ahead.

The free movement of labour, with a few exceptions, was allowed for in the EEC's Treaty and, in theory, a worker from one EC state should be able to work in another under the same conditions as a native of that country. In reality there remained bureaucratic difficulties for workers from one EC country living in another and, for most jobs, employment agencies limit their scope to the national scene. It should be noted that the largest migrations of workers across EC frontiers took place before free movement of labour was introduced (Straubhaar, 1988, 59–60). In fact, the lifting of legal barriers to migration within the Communities 'has not produced a great increase of migratory flows' (Molle and van Mourik, 1988, 336).

Free movement in the service industry and the professions had been low down on the Communities' list of priorities until the single European market proposals. Different qualifications, national systems of recognition and the close control over entry into the professions meant that any change to a Communities-wide system of professional recognition would be difficult. Certain aspects of the services industry, for example catering and tourism, have always been international in their outlook, while others, such as financial services and insurance have been rooted in national traditions. Various Communities' directives have aimed at removing unnecessary restrictions, though little can be done – or needs to be done – to abolish language qualifications, training requirements or traditions. Nevertheless, the mutual recognition of diplomas and rights for professional peoples, adopted in 1988, should open up greater movement across frontiers for the professions (Palmer, 1989, 42).

The free movement of capital has also faced a number of obstacles that could not be dealt with by a purely 'Community' approach of trying to pretend that the EC was one market without frontiers, and legislating for such at the Communities' level. The main factor that prevents the free movement of capital is not any discrimination against investors because of their nationality but national fiscal and economic policies and the lack of a common Communities' currency. As Mrs Thatcher, the British Prime Minister, pointed out, the United Kingdom abolished exchange controls in 1979 – thereby allowing British investors greater freedom to move their money internationally – but was not then followed by other EC members (Thatcher, 1989, 10). In May 1986 the Commission put forward a programme for the liberalization of capital movements within the EC by 1992, and this seems to have had some success until the currency market fluctuations of late 1992.

The section in the Treaty of Rome dealing with capital includes Article 70 which deals with the progressive coordination of the exchange policies of member states. This is an area in which the Communities have gradually advanced over the years but still remains one of contention for some countries, noticeably the United Kingdom.

After the severe disruption of the European monetary markets from 1967 to 1969, the Communities appointed the Werner Committee in 1970 to examine the question of monetary unification. The Werner Plan aimed at monetary union and the adoption of a single EC currency by 1980. This was to be attained gradually with the first steps being the narrowing of exchange bands between the currencies of the member states and the creation of a common fund to help stabilize these currencies In 1972 the EEC's six member states and the three prospective members – Denmark, Eire and the United Kingdom – agreed on a scheme to reduce the difference between the highest and lowest values of their currencies to 2.25 per cent, though the three 'new' members left this so-called 'snake-in-the-tunnel' arrangement only weeks after joining it. Another attempt was made to revive the system in March 1973, but the United Kingdom, Eire and Italy remained independent, as did France from 1974 to 1975 and after August 1977. This activity must be seen against the background of the general economic instability of the 1970s, which, however, seems to have had the effect of persuading most EC states that they could no longer continue with national exchange policies: '. . . high rates of inflation, divergent monetary policies and volatile real exchange rates provided the stimulus to the EC countries to seek monetary stability by collective, rather than national, means' (Zis, 1984, 56).

In March 1979, after a Franco-German political initiative, the EC started to operate the European Monetary System (EMS). This was aimed at creating a 'zone of monetary stability' in the Communities. To this end, each EC currency was to be given an exchange rate against the European Currency Unit (ECU – the value of which represents a basket of EC currencies). Bilateral exchange rates were to be maintained at 2.25 per cent either side of parity, with extra leeway given to the Italian lira. This Exchange-Rate Mechanism (ERM) could be adjusted by unanimous decision of the participating countries. Secondly, a European Fund for Monetary Compensation (EMF) was established in which the member states would deposit 20 per cent of their gold and dollar reserves, in exchange for which they would receive equal drawing rights in ECUs. Finally, the EMF would make available financial support to member countries (Dennis, 1980, 189–90). While the United Kingdom was a member of the EMS, it did not participate in the Exchange-Rate Mechanism (ERM) until October 1990.

An interim evaluation of the EMS in 1984 concluded that '. . . since the inception of the system, member countries have enjoyed the benefits of greater exchange-rate stability, less divergent monetary policies, more convergent inflation rates and the emergence of the ECU as a major international currency' (Zis, 1984, 65). The move towards an economic and monetary union was covered in the Single European Act, and in the Commission's Delors Report.

The Delors Report, issued in 1989, recognized that one of the major roadblocks to a single market in the EC was the existence of 11 national currencies (Luxembourg uses that of Belgium), and proposed the achievement of EMU in three stages. Stage I would be completed with all the EC states joining in the ERM and with greater coordination and cooperation between central banks. This was considered to be substantially achieved by end-1990. Stage II would see a limitation in the changes allowed in the ERM and the establishment of central EC banking institutions, while Stage III would see the permanent fixing of exchange rates, the creation of a single European currency and the assumption of important monetary and economic powers. It was to agree on the method of and timetable for the creation of EMU that an Intergovernmental Conference (IGC) was held from December 1990 to December 1991, culminating in the Maastricht Treaty. A parallel IGC was held to discuss the political aspects of the Treaty on European Union, but it was the necessity to agree on EMU that drove the process. In the final document the title covering EMU runs to 20 of the 80 pages devoted to amendments to the EEC treaty.

What was agreed on EMU? Ministers at Maastricht amended a number of articles in the Treaty of Rome covering economic and monetary policy; they attached seven Protocols concerning EMU to the Treaty; and made five Declarations on the subject. All this was aimed at creating EMU with the European Union by, at the latest, 1 January 1999. Article 2 of the EC was to be revised so that the principles of the European Economic Community (to be renamed the European Community) are to establish a common market and an economic and monetary union and to promote a harmonious and balanced development of economic activities, sustainable and non-inflationary growth respecting the environment, convergence of economic performance, a high level of employment and social protection, economic and social cohesion and solidarity, and an increase in the standard of living and quality of life. Article 3a laid down that an economic policy would be adopted which would include:

– the irrevocable fixing of exchange rates leading to a single currency, the ECU;
– a single monetary and exchange-rate policy, the primary aim of which shall be price stability and – without prejudice to that objectives – support of the general EC economic policies, in line with the principle of an open market and free competition;
– compliance with the guiding principles of stable prices, sound public finances and a sustainable balance of payments.

Articles 73a–h replaced the section in the Treaty of Rome on capital and payments and basically prepared for Stage II of EMU by ending most of the restrictions on the movement of capital and of payments between EC states and between the EC members and third countries.

A new Title VI dealt with EMU and is a central column of the Maastricht Treaty. Chapter 1 deals with economic policy. As the economic policies of the member states are accepted as being a matter for common concern, Article 103 establishes a system whereby the Council of Ministers and the European Council can monitor performance and make recommendations. From the beginning of Stage II – which, according to Article 109e.1, is to begin on 1 January 1994 – 'Member States shall endeavour to avoid excessive government deficits' (109e.5) and the budgetary discipline of governments is to be monitored according to Article 104c.2–8. Compliance with two criteria is required:

i the ratio of planned or actual government deficit to GDP should not exceed a ceiling of 3 per cent, unless this figure is declining and closing in on the ceiling or the excess is temporary and exceptional;
ii the ratio of government debt to GDP should be sufficiently diminishing and approaching a reference value of 60 per cent at a satisfactory pace.

From Stage III of EMU (starting no later than 1 January 1999), member states 'shall avoid excessive government deficits' (Article

104c, emphasis added), and any state failing to fulfil the above two criteria would have to undertake a programme of measures decided by the Council on a two-thirds majority, excluding the state concerned. Failure to do so could lead to measures such as the European Investment Bank reconsidering its lending policy to that country, the requirement that the states makes a non-interest-bearing deposit 'of an appropriate size' with the EC until the deficit is corrected, or the imposition of fines (104c.11).

Chapter 4 of Title VI covers the transitional arrangements leading up to the creation of EMU. Before Stage II member states are supposed to allow free movement of capital and adopt measures to ensure the lasting convergence necessary for EMU, especially with regard to price stability and sound public finances. During Stage II (beginning on 1 January 1994), member states – apart from endeavouring to avoid excessive government deficits – should start the process leading to the independence of their central banks (109e.5). A European Monetary Institute (EMI) is to be set up to strengthen cooperation between central banks and coordination of states' monetary policies, with the aim of ensuring price stability; to monitor the EMS; to take over the tasks of the European Monetary Cooperation fund; facilitate the use of the ECU; and prepare for Stage III of EMU. The EMI is to consist of the governors of the central banks of the member states.

Under Article 109j.1, the Commission and the EMI shall report to the Council on the progress of the member states towards the achievement of EMU. Such reports should especially examine convergence with reference to the following criteria:

  i the achievement of a high degree of price stability, being a rate of inflation not more than 1.5 per cent above the average of the three best performing member states;
 ii the government deficit should not be above 60 per cent of the GDP;
iii the currency should stay within the fluctuation margins of the ERM for at least two years, without devaluing against the currency of other members;
iv the durability of convergence in the ERM reflected in long-term interest rate levels.

Not later than 31 December 1996, the European Council – acting by a qualified majority – shall decide whether a majority of member states fulfil the necessary conditions for the adoption of a single currency, that is Stage III of EMU; whether it is appropriate for the EC to go ahead to Stage III; and – if the answer to the previous two questions is positive – on the date for the start of Stage III.

If, by the end of 1997, the date for Stage III has not been set, then it shall start on 1 January 1999. Before 1 July 1998, the European Council, after examining the situation – and acting by a qualified majority – will confirm which member states fulfil the necessary conditions for Stage III. Under Article 109k, states that the Council had decided do not fulfil the conditions for Stage III, are referred to as 'Member States with a derogation' and are excluded from Stage III and the decision-making connected with it, though they could join at a later stage should they fulfil the conditions. This deals with states not *able* to join Stage III.

What about states not *wishing* to join that stage? Two protocols are of relevance here. The one concerning the United Kingdom recognizes that Britain will not be obliged to move to Stage III of EMU 'without a separate decision to do so by its government and Parliament'. Indeed, the United Kingdom will not be obliged to move to Stage III unless it notifies the Council of its intention to do so. The United Kingdom would thus have an exemption from Stage III. If they notify the Council that they do not intend to go ahead, they will not be allowed to participate in the decision on whether a majority of the member states fulfil the conditions for Stage III. Likewise the United Kingdom would not be able to participate in the European Central Bank (ECB – see p. 147) and the European System of Central Banks (ESCB – see p. 147). Should the UK government change its mind and decide to join Stage III once it had started, it could only join if it fulfils the Article 109j.1 conditions, mentioned above. Once the Council has decided positively on this, then the United Kingdom will have the same rights as other states that have moved to Stage III. The Danes obtained a somewhat weaker chance of exemption in the Maastricht Treaty, but at the Edinburgh European Council, held in December 1992, they were able to extract exemption similar to that of the United Kingdom.

It could be the case that, when the final decision is made to go ahead to Stage III, all EC states (including any new members) will be able and willing to adopt a single European currency. However, it is perhaps more likely that both the United Kingdom and Denmark will not participate and that a number of states, including Spain, Portugal, Italy and Greece ('the Club Med') and Ireland will be unable to take part. This could leave a core membership – France, Germany and the Benelux states – to form a monetary union.

What does Stage III entail? The ESCB – comprising of the ECB and the national central banks (Article 106) – will be established before Stage III and will be governed by the decision-making bodies of the ECB, its Governing Council and Executive Board. The ECB's Executive Board is to be an independent body of bankers chosen in a fashion similar to the Commission, and the Governing Board consists of the Executive Board and the governors of the national banks (Article 109a). The ESCB will take over from the EMI for Stage III.

The tasks of the ESCB are to be, according to Article 105:

  i to define and implement monetary policy;
  ii to conduct foreign exchange operations;
  iii to hold and manage member states' official reserves;
  iv to promote the smooth operation of the payments system.

Once Stage III begins, all the participating states will agree the conversion rates at which their currencies will be irrevocably fixed and exchanged for ECUs. The ECU will then be substituted for these currencies and become a currency in its own right (Article 109 1.4). The ECB will have the exclusive right to authorize the issue of ECU banknotes in the EC either by European or national banks. Member states will only be able to issue coins subject to ECB approval. The Council will unanimously agree on an exchange rate system for the ECU towards non-EC currencies, and the EC will speak as one in international monetary negotiations.

The above are the plans for EMU that form a central part of the Maastricht Treaty. Since its signing in February 1992, the ERM has been seriously undermined by the exchange rate chaos of the latter part of 1992, during which the pound sterling left the mechanism and a number of other currencies – those of the 'Club Med' states and of Eire – were devalued. This does not bode well for Stage II of EMU starting on 1 January 1994. Furthermore, high German interest, offsetting the costs of German unification, has made other EC countries even more reluctant to tie their futures inextricably to the German mark through monetary union, and there are some in Germany who doubt the wisdom of watering down the mark through participation in EMU (see 'German economists attack EMU policy' *Financial Times*, 11 June 1992, 2). The most likely outcome seems to be a closer liaison between the currencies of the original six members of the EC, with perhaps Italy removed and Denmark and the other Nordic states included – a sort of extended Deutschmark zone.

Although the Treaty of Rome had 11 articles covering transport, comparatively little has been achieved in that area. So far, the

Commission has attempted limiting some government subsidies to rail transport, controlling working conditions for long-distance lorry drivers, creating uniform qualifications for drivers and operators, and ending price-fixing for air traffic. Over the years, the EC has failed to provide for a common shipping policy of any worth but, faced with the creation of an internal market after 1992, the Council adopted proposals in 1986 that should lead to a greater freedom to run services between member states or between members and third countries and should cut down on unfair pricing and on obstacles to competition (*European Yearbook*, 1988, EC29).

Turning a common market into a *community* that has more binding it together than just trade and economic factors requires the development of policies that emphasize common need and the social element. Title III of Part Three of the Treaty of Rome covers social provisions and includes a chapter on the European Social Fund (ESF), which has been the main conduit for EC assistance in increasing employment opportunities for workers.

The first regulations of the ESF were adopted by the Community of the Six in 1960 and were aimed at providing help to workers and firms to adapt themselves to changes in economic circumstances. This followed on the work of the European Coal and Steel Community which had helped thousands of workers redeploy from those ageing industries (see above Chapter 5, pp. 81). In 1971 the Fund was reformed and widened in scope and in 1974, after the first extension of the Communities, the Council agreed to undertake a programme of social action aimed at full and improved employment, better working and living conditions, and more involvement of workers in their firms and of labour and management in the social policy of the Communities. However, the ravages of the 1974 Oil Crisis and of growing unemployment throughout the 1980s and early 1990s seemed to overwhelm this programme.

The Fund can intervene in two main areas: where the employment situation is affected by decisions of the Council; where unemployment in certain regions, branches of the economy or groups of undertakings is threatened. Examples of action taken under the first heading is the assistance given to those leaving agriculture, help for migrant workers and for young people and women. Under the second heading, money can go to the regions, specific groups and to the handicapped (Laffan, 1983, 392–3). It should be remembered that social policy is still predominantly run at the national level and even the ESF, which takes less than 10 per cent of the EC budget, normally only provides matching money to that given by national authorities.

The Single European Act supplemented the EEC Treaty with two articles under the heading of 'Social policy'. Article 118A required member states to pay particular attention to encouraging improvements in health and safety, especially in the working environment, by harmonization of conditions, while maintaining existing improvements. Article 118B requested the Commission to develop a dialogue between management and labour at a European level which, if both sides so wished, could lead to 'relations based on agreement'.

The response, in 1989, of the Commission and the European Parliament to this section of the Single European Act and to the prospect of the creation of a Single European Market by the end of 1992, has been to raise again the notion of a People's Europe with a European Social Charter (Lodge, 1989a, 312–16). This included sections on social security rights, industrial democracy, health and safety measures and on wages, and was opposed by the British Conservative Government under Mrs Thatcher as being a 'Socialist Charter' that would stifle the free enterprise which the Conservatives wished to encourage. Nevertheless, the other 11 countries adopted the Social Charter in 1989 in spite of this opposition. During the Maastricht negotiations a version was attached to the Treaty in the form of two protocols. A protocol concluded by the EC member states minus the United Kingdom covered matters such as the work environment, workers' consultation, gender equality in the labour market, social security and protection of workers, co-determination and the employment of third-country nationals. Excluded from the article were pay, the right of assocation (that is, to join a trade union) and the right to strike or to impose a lock-out. Despite these exceptions, the United Kingdom government felt unable to agree to the protocol and was allowed to opt out. It may yet be that such unequal treatment for British workers will be challenged before the EC Court.

While a specific regional policy was not a subject of the Treaty of Rome, both the European Social Fund and the European Investment Bank had a regional element to their work, insofar as they aided the less-well-off areas in the Communities. When the Communities were expanded in 1973, a European Regional Development Fund was established, partly in response to the fears of the outer areas of the United Kingdom and of Eire that they would be excluded from the benefits of a market very much centred on a 'golden triangle' stretching from Bonn to London and Paris. By 1975 the EC had worked out a Regional Policy which broadly required local authorities to submit schemes for support to their national governments which, in turn, would send them to the Communities for consideration. The Regional Development Fund would help a number of cases – decided within a national quota – that countered agricultural poverty, brought about industrial change or provided infrastructure. The national governments would at least match the money from the Fund for each scheme.

The EC was concerned about indiscriminate national aid to regions as this could lead to areas that might be 'poor' in their national context receiving grants whereas an objectively more deprived zone in another member country would not get any aid because its government had not defined it as a subject of regional policy. Furthermore, there could be competitive bidding in the amount of aid given to industry going into different regions.

As a result of shortcomings in the regional policy, the regulations governing the ERDF were revised as from January 1985. The pre-1985 quota system had guaranteed even the richest EC countries a certain share of the Fund and meant that the bidding was uncompetitive and inflexible, and the expenditure uncoordinated (Croxford *et al.*, 1987, 27). In essence, the ERDF was not a true Community fund but a 'topping-up' scheme for some national projects. The 1985 revisions introduced 'indicative ranges' whereby maximum and minimum percentage allocations to the member states over a period of three years was fixed. If, during that period, a state did not submit eligible applications, it would not get its minimum share. The minimum shares added up to 88 per cent, leaving a maximum of 12 per cent of the Fund to be allocated by the Commission on a basis of need. The major beneficiaries of the new system were Italy (21.6 per cent of the minimum), Spain (18 per cent), the United Kingdom (14.5 per cent) and Portugal (10.6 per cent). The rules were tightened so that consistency with Communities' objectives were included in the evaluation criteria; also a greater share of finance was to be given to fewer projects. The regulations introduced National Programmes of Community Interest, put forward by authorities within the states, and Community Programmes, initiated by the Commission and normally covering the territory of more than one member state. Greater coordination with the European Investment Bank was encouraged with the formation of inter-agency 'Integrated Development

Operations'. Since the reform of the ERDF, there has been more competition for the money available and more resources seem to have gone to the poorest regions. The coordinated programmes took some time to get launched but may provide useful initiatives in the long run (Croxford *et al.*, 1987, 28–35).

The European Investment Bank (EIB) has proved a useful agent for capital investment in projects in the economically less favoured regions or in those serving the common interest of several member states and those creating new activities called for by the establishment of a common market. The EIB is a complementary source of finance, normally providing only up to 50 per cent of the investment needed for a project, but it lends more to countries with the greatest regional problems. In 1992 it provided loans worth ECU16.8 billion. From 1958 to 1972 Italy received about a half of EIB's financing, thereafter its share (within an expanded Community) settled down to just over a quarter (EIB, 1993, 98).

The Single European Act inserted regional policy into the Treaty of Rome under the heading of 'Economic and social cohesion'. The aim of new Article 130A was to strengthen this cohesion and to promote 'overall harmonious development', in particular by reducing disparities between the various regions and the backwardness of least-favoured regions. Member states were to conduct their economic policies to this end and the achievement of the Single European Market was to take into account the needs of economic and social cohesion. The structural funds – the Guidance Fund of EAGGF, the European Social Fund and the Regional Development Fund – and the European Investment Bank were also to be used to achieve these objectives (new Article 130B EEC). The ERDF was to be used to adjust regional imbalances within the EC and plans were to be made to rationalize the various structural funds so that they may more efficiently achieve economic and social cohesion within the Communities.

The Maastricht Treaty contains a section (Article XIV) on economic and social cohesion, which was very much the work of Spain and the Club Med states. The EC should aim at 'reducing disparities between the levels of development of the various regions and the backwardness of the least favoured regions, including rural areas' (Article 130a). This aim is to be supported through the use of the structural funds, the EIB and other financial means. Also a new Cohension Fund was to be established before the end of 1993 and it was agreed at the Edinburgh European

Council in December 1992 that this fund should be established and have an ECU2.6 billion balance by 1999. At the same meeting an increase in the structural funds was accepted, allowing them to grow from their 1992 figure of ECU18.6 billion to ECU27.4 billion in 1999. The Cohesion Fund is to benefit Greece, Ireland, Portugal and Spain.

From the beginning, the European Economic Community has been interested in trade with and the development of the Third World. When the Treaty of Rome was signed in 1957, much of this area was still colonized. Of the original six EEC states, three – Belgium, France and the Netherlands – had colonies and Italy administered the Trust Territory of Somalia. Part Four of the Treaty dealt with Association of Overseas Countries and Territories and covered the non-European areas with which the Six had special relations. It allowed these territories free access to the Community market and aimed at transforming their trade relations with the EEC from one of dependence on one state – their colonial power – to a non-discriminatory relationship with the EEC as a whole. At the same time a European Development Fund was established to promote the social and economic development of the Part Four territories.

At the time of the signing of the Treaty of Rome many of the areas covered by Part Four were moving towards greater political autonomy and from 1960 a majority had obtained independence. The provisions of the agreement were anyhow up for reconsideration after five years, but it was no longer possible for the EEC Council to decide on terms by themselves. They had to negotiate with sovereign states, most of which were sub-Saharan African countries belonging to the French franc area. An agreement was reached in 1962 and signed in July 1963 in Yaoundé, Cameroon, between the Six and 18 African associates. The Yaoundé Convention broadly continued the free trade arrangement of Part Four of the Treaty of Rome. Customs duties on leading tropical products from the associates were abolished and the associates introduced non-discriminatory tariffs whereby, say, West German trade could not be treated less favourably than that from France. Community aid was to be continued through the European Development Fund (EDF) and, to a lesser extent, the European Investment Bank. An Association Council was established with membership drawn from the EEC's Council and Commission and ministers or ambassadors from the associates. It was to deliberate and to supervise the implementation of the Convention, and decisions were made by consensus between the two sides. There was also a meeting of parliamentarians which had a consultative role.

The African associates were not satisfied with their trade with the Community, which did not seem to grow substantially in the 1960s; they were concerned about high internal taxes on their products; and the ability of other EEC businesses to establish themselves in the former French colonies that made up most of the associates was scarcely improved by the non-discriminatory clauses (Feld, 1967, 124–6). Nevertheless, the associates seemed to appreciate the institutional aspects of the Yaoundé Convention and looked to long-term trade benefits. In 1967, the Six and the associates signed Yaoundé II which continued the work of the 1963 agreement.

After negotiations for British membership broke down in January 1963, other African countries with similar economic structures to those of the Yaoundé states were invited to negotiate with the EEC for equivalent arrangements. Nigeria applied for association separate from the Yaoundé Convention. After delicate negotiations which had to consider Nigeria's position in the Commonwealth and the effect of an agreement on other Yaoundé countries, as well as Nigerian and EEC interests, an association treaty was signed in July 1966, which allowed Nigeria duty-free access to the EEC for most of its products. The three East African states of Kenya, Tanzania and Uganda signed a similar agreement with the EEC at Arusha in 1969.

The 1972 Treaty of Accession, by which the United Kingdom joined the Communities, extended the terms of Yaoundé II to British Commonwealth countries of a similar standing in Africa, the Caribbean and the Pacific, but it was clear that a new agreement had to be worked out as the newcomers changed the outlook and trade balance of the associates. In February 1975, 46 countries, including African francophone states and Commonwealth nations, and the European Communities signed the Lomé Convention in Togo. The 46 were known as the ACP (African, Caribbean and Pacific) states and were joined by other states from these regions so that they numbered 66 by 1989. Lomé II ran from 1980–5, Lomé III from 1985–90 and Lomé IV from 1990–2000. Negotiations for a fourth Lomé Convention brought to the surface ACP complaints about the working of Lomé III: the share of the EC's imports taken by the ACP had sunk to 3.8 per cent by 1988.

The EC replied by advising the ACP to rely more on competitiveness rather than on preferences (*Financial Times*, 21 July 1989, 3).

The trade arrangements of Lomé I have been summarized thus: '... a measure of preferential access to the EC market, without formal tariff or non-tariff reciprocity, but with important exclusions and some quota arrangements ...' (Hewitt, 1984, 101). Complete duty-free access for all ACP exports was not offered and during the course of Lomé I, the ACP share of the Communities external trade actually fell (op. cit., 102). It may well be that this adverse development was more the result of the economic conditions in the ACP states rather than the fault of the Lomé system. Indeed, Lomé I introduced an innovation that has been developed in the subsequent agreements, that of Stabex, the export earnings stabilization scheme. It is a product-by-product arrangement whereby the EC provides a fund to guarantee ACP states against adverse fluctuations in the export earnings of these products over a period of time. Aid from the EDF was also continued under Lomé I, with a quite generous fund of some ECU3 billion.

Lomé II was signed by 48 ACP states and the European Communities. It increased the number of products in the Stabex scheme and liberalized its operations. A similar, more limited, arrangement was established for minerals. ACP citizens working in the EC were guaranteed equal treatment as EC nationals for their employment conditions. Agreements were made on fishing and transport and the ACP states were to participate in the administration of EC aid.

Lomé III increased the funding for Stabex and its mining equivalent, Sysmin. Special treatment was afforded the least-developed, landlocked and island states, concern was expressed over the control of drought and desertification (Articles 38–43, *passim*) and development problems were covered in some detail and with sensitivity (Kerr, 1986, 218–25). The treaty also encouraged regional cooperation between ACP countries (Articles 101–113) and allowed for social and cultural factors to be taken into account in all projects and programmes (Article 117). The EDF was to receive ECU7.4 billion, some of which was earmarked for Stabex and Sysmin. Lomé III is one of the new North–South agreements that reads as though it not only had the interests of the Third World in mind but had been drafted by those countries.

Lomé IV left the pattern set by the previous agreement substantially unchanged and it now applies to some 70 ACP countries. The

Stabex system was reformed to encourage diversification of the ACP economies and money was made available to match the IMF's Structural Adjustment Loans. The convention attempted to stress environmental matters, banning all export of toxic and radioactive waste from the EC to ACP states.

Concern has been expressed that the ACP relationship is becoming less important for the EC. Not only does the ACP exclude some of the most important 'Third World' countries (such as India, China, the ASEAN states and much of Latin America), its position is also being challenged by the growing importance for the Communities of what used to be the 'Second World' – the former Soviet bloc. As demands are being made on EC coffers for aid to East and Central Europe, so the comparative position of the ACP states deteriorates in the Communities' hierarchy.

The Maastricht Treaty has a section (Title XVII) on development cooperation but this adds little to current EC policy except to say that, in this area, it should contribute to the general objective of 'developing and consolidating democracy and the rule of law, and to that of respecting human rights and fundamental freedoms' (Article 130u).

Since its inception the Economic Community has tried to develop its competence in a number of areas not always specifically mentioned in the Treaty of Rome but where a common policy might help to 'establish the foundations of an ever closer union among the peoples of Europe'.

The Treaty of Rome referred to certain aspects of education and training. Article 57 opened up the prospect for the mutual recognition of diplomas, certificates and other qualifications; Article 118 called for close collaboration in matters relating to basic and advanced vocational training; and Article 128 foresaw a common policy on such training. It was 1976 before Education Ministers started to make common decisions affecting education and most of these were either very general – 'promotion of closer relations between educational systems in Europe', pious hopes – a standard school record card, or modest first steps – the establishment of European schools in cities with a large Communities' staff (Kerr, 1986, 188–90). In the 1980s attention turned to higher education with the ERASMUS programme aimed at allowing students from centres of advanced learning in one EC country to undertake part of their studies in a college or university in another member state and at encouraging cooperative research between staff members from a number of centres of higher education.

The Communities have also established a number of research schemes. Most noticeable among these is the European Strategic Programme of Research and Development in Information Technology (ESPRIT) which was established between 1980 and 1982 with the participation of industry and national governments and with the aim of establishing the Communities' position in the technological sphere (Woolcock, 1984, 328; Sharp, 1989, 206–10). Cooperation between universities and industry was encouraged by the Community in Education and Training for Technology (COMETT) programme; Research and Development in Advanced Communication Technology for Europe (RACE) developed telecommunications; Basic Research in Industrial Technologies in Europe (BRITE) applied technology to older industries; Strategic Programme for Innovation and Technology Transfer (SPRINT), Biotechnology Action Programme (BAP) and the European Collaborative Linkage of Agriculture and Industry through Research (ECLAIR) are further programmes run by the Communities. The Commission has promoted a new information network called DIANE, consisting of computer centres with access to information databases (Kerr, 1986, 126).

Two research projects are connected with Euratom's work: those of the Joint Research Centre, which also examines non-nuclear sources of energy, and the Joint European Torus at Culham, near Oxford. This aims at developing nuclear fusion, with its promise – as yet unfulfilled – of an endless pollution-free source of energy.

The Single European Act included 11 articles under the title of research and technological development. The aim was 'to strengthen the scientific and technological basis of European industry', encouraging it to become more competitive internationally. The object was to complement the activities of the member states (Article 130G), coordinate these policies and to adopt a framework programme which would lay down scientific and technical objectives, define priorities and set out the main lines of activities (Article 130I).

The Maastricht Treaty on European Union covers education, vocational policy, and research and technological development. The EC's role is to that of encouragement of cooperation in these areas that are dominated by national policies and the implementation of framework programmes in research and technology (Article 130i). The Treaty also allows for the establishment of trans-European networks in the areas of transport, telecommunications and energy infrastructures that will help to link regions across national frontiers. Support for such projects can be obtained from the Cohesion Fund (see p. 152).

In 1972 the Commission was asked to draw up an environmental programme. This emphasized the need to prevent, reduce or abolish pollution of the environment, to manage natural resources soundly, and to improve human health. The Commission has tried to establish environmental standards at a Community level, for example in relation to particularly harmful substances (such as lead) and also with respect to commercial processes where national standards could represent a hidden barrier to trade.

The Single European Act introduced the environmental theme into the Treaty of Rome under new Title VII, Articles 130R to 130T. EC action has as its aims the three basic points of the Commission's earlier report mentioned in the above paragraph. Action was to be based on the principles that preventive action should be taken, that environmental damage should be rectified at source and that the polluter should pay. Furthermore, there would be an environmental component in the EC's other policies and action would be taken at that level when the objectives could be best achieved at Community rather than member-state level. An important Article was 130T which laid down that EC environmental action in the form of protective measures 'shall not prevent any Member State from maintaining or introducing more stringent protective measures' compatible with the Treaty. This was insisted on by countries such as Denmark that were afraid that environmental standards adopted by the EC would represent a compromise between their high level of activity and that of the southern European states that had not advanced so far. This could have meant that the Danes would have had to drop their environmental standards, something that would benefit neither them nor, in the long run, other members of the Communities. The Maastricht Treaty's Title XVII mirrors substantially the SEA's section on the environment, though financial support for environmental measures will be available through the Cohesion Fund for the states benefitting from that fund.

The European Communities' interior ministers and ministers of justice have increasingly cooperated over matters of law and order. Whilst this is a national concern, there is clearly an EC dimension, especially as the single European market meant reducing customs and immigration posts between countries. Interior ministers have some reservations about such a move as it could allow criminals and terrorists easier access throughout the Communities. These meetings have also allowed closer cooperation in the fight against terrorism.

In making changes to the EC's treaties, the Maastricht Treaty also established citizenship of the European Union for every person holding the nationality of a member state. Subject to the limits and conditions in the Treaty, and the subsequent measures to give them effect, every citizen of the Union is to have the right 'to move and reside freely' within the territory of the member states (Article 8a). Union citizens residing in member states of which they are not nationals will have the right to vote and stand at municipal and European Parliament elections there, once the EC has decided on detailed arrangements (Article 8b). Union citizens will also have the right to petition the European Parliament and apply for assistance from the Ombudsman.

As well as developing the European Communities, the Maastricht Treaty provided for cooperation in the fields of justice and home affairs on an intergovernmental basis. To achieve the aims of the Union, especially the free movement of persons, the member states agreed to inform and consult each other, with a view to coordinating action on asylum policy, control of people entering the Union, immigration policy, combating fraud and drug addiction, and to cooperating in civil and criminal judicial matters, and customs and police actions to prevent serious forms of international crime. The latter is to be undertaken through a Union-wide system of information exchange within a European Police Office (Europol).

The third pillar of the Treaty on European Union – the other two being changes to the European Communities and intergovernmental cooperation on justice and home affairs – was that of a common foreign and security policy (CFSP). The institutions of and background to EPC have been dealt with (pp. 112–4), and the Maastricht Treaty followed up the pattern set down by the Single European Act.

The record of attempts by the EC member states to forge a CFSP to date has not been good. The 1980 Venice Declaration on the Middle East was ignored by both sides in the Arab–Israel dispute. The process of European Political Cooperation between the EC states did work in the CSCE negotiations and was seen by a US diplomat as 'a particularly successful example of foreign policy coordination' (Maresca, 1987, 19). However, the response to the invasion of Kuwait by Saddam Hussein's Iraq in August 1990 'provided an object lesson – if one were needed – on the limitations of the European Community. The response to the break-up of Yugoslavia from the summer of 1991 was not a good advertisement for a CFSP (Archer and Butler, 1992, 176).

In the Maastricht Treaty, the common foreign and security policy is to be defined by the Union and the member states, though the decision-making process is not the Communities' one and is more intergovernmental. Article J.2 places the emphasis on information and consultation between the member states concerning their foreign and security policies more generally. The principles and guidelines for the common foreign and security policy are to be decided by the European Council. Where necessary a common position will be defined by the Council, and the Council will decide that a matter 'should be the subject of joint action' (Article J.3). Article J.4 states that the common policy 'shall include all matters related to the security of the Union, including the eventual framing of a common defence policy, which might in time lead to a common defence'. The Western European Union (see Chapter 10) is to be brought in as 'an integral part of the development of the Union' (Article J.4.2) to help elaborate decisions and actions with defence implications. This was not to prejudice either 'the specific character of the security and defence policy' of certain member states or obligation under the North Atlantic Treaty (Article J.4.4).

A note should be added here on the European Atomic Energy Community, Euratom, which was established by the second Treaty of Rome signed in March 1957. At the time, hopes were high that atomic energy would provide a clean and cheap source of energy, though the idea that this might be developed through Euratom was tempered by the non-membership of the then leading West European state in the development of nuclear power, the United Kingdom.

The aims of the Atomic Energy Community were to establish the 'conditions necessary for the speedy establishment and growth of nuclear industries' (Article 1 EAEC). On the whole, the organization was to promote research, establish standards, help investment, ensure the supply and the outlet for nuclear fuels, prevent improper use of materials, and to deal with relations with third countries. However, Euratom was given two very important powers: the right of ownership of fissionable materials and the option of ownership of nuclear materials and ores. The former right does not extend to materials intended or prepared for defence and those stored in military establishments (Articles 84 and 86 EAEC), which substantially reduced the potential for control. Also, within a few years of Euratom's existence, it became clear that the French government of President de Gaulle opposed its control over nuclear supplies (Polach, 1964, 129). The principle of Euratom ownership of special fissionable material has meant that, within the Community, it should be bought and sold through the Euratom Supply Agency, established to supervise supply policy. In reality, this has been downgraded to an Agency officer countersigning the paperwork for such sales.

The main activities of Euratom are in the research field, a factor recognized in the organization's annual reports as early as 1961 (Polach, 1964, 139). Euratom's Joint Research Centre consists of four establishments that concentrate mainly, but no longer exclusively, on nuclear research and development. The largest is at Ispra, North Italy, and it works on fissile materials, the use of metals in reactors and reactor safety. Other centres are in Petten, the Netherlands, dealing with high-flux reactors; Karlsruhe, Germany, which experiments on high-temperature behaviour of transuranium elements; and Geel, Belgium, which works on nuclear standards and measurements. A more recent project is that of the Joint European Torus (JET) at Culham, Oxford, which works on nuclear fusion with, once more, the dream of cheap and clean energy. Other non-Community states, such as Sweden, have involved themselves in some of these projects (Kerr, 1986, 194–5).

The institutions of Euratom were the same as those of the European Economic Community. In fact, apart from specialized agencies such as the Euratom Supply Agency and having their own Commission, Euratom shared the institutions created by the EEC Treaty of Rome and thus the process of merging the Communities' institutions undertaken from 1965 to 1967 created few problems. Increasingly, the work of Euratom has become integrated into the wider energy and research policies of the EC. The Maastricht Treaty made the same institutional changes to Euratom as to the European Economic Community.

How is the new activity presaged by the Maastricht Treaty to be financed? The actions arising from the 1987 Single European Act were paid for by the 'Delors I' package which covered the years from 1988 to 1992. In 1988 the EC's finances were placed on a more regular basis than before, allowing its own resources to expand by up to 1.2 per cent of the EC's Gross National Product (GNP) and its commitments to go up to a ceiling of 1.3 per cent of

EC GNP (Shackleton, 1990, 14). The Guarantee side of the CAP's EAGGF was to be capped so that, during the five-year period, it was not allowed to increase to more than three-quarters of the growth in EC GNP. Expenditure from the structural funds (see earlier, pp.151–2) were to be doubled between 1988 and 1993. Until 1988, the EC budget was financed in three main ways: by customs duties and tariffs and levies on agricultural imports; by paying 1 per cent (up to 1984) then 1.4 per cent (from 1984–8) of the VAT base (not the VAT revenues) to the EC; and direct contributions by member states, which were discontinued in 1980. In 1988 a 'fourth resource' was added to the EC's income. The difference between EC expenditure and its 'own resources' received through the first two financing methods is to be made up from member states 'in proportion to their national income' (Lintner and Mazey, 1991, 75–6).

In February 1992 the Commission announced its plans to finance the results of Maastricht – 'Delors II'. The intention was that there should be a real budget growth of some 5 per cent in real terms from 1992 to 1997 and that this should be financed by raising the EC's 'own resources' ceiling from 1.2 to 1.37 per cent of EC GNP.

The compromise reached between the EC members and the Commission at the December 1992 summit set budget terms for the period up to 1999. The budgetary ceiling will be 1.27 per cent of the EC GNP. Structural expenditure, including that for the Cohesion Fund, will rise from ECU18.6 billion to ECU30 billion in 1999. Farm spending will increase form ECU35.3 billion to ECU38.4 billion in 1999, less than that planned in the Delors II package, though the way is left open for extra expenditure to meet exchange rate turbulence (*Financial Times*, 14 December 1992, 2).

Contribution

The European Communities have clearly made a major contribution to the functioning of the European political system. They have provided a focus for the economic rebuilding of Western Europe, a medium for the rapprochement between France and West Germany, an attraction for other non-Communities West European states and a source of envy for the nations of East and Central Europe. Chapter 13 will discuss the wider implications of the development of the European Communities and, later, the European Union within the European political system. This section will evaluate the contribution of the EC as a transformation system.

More than any other European organization, the European Communities have shown an ability to transform political inputs into their system into outputs such as rules, information and activities.

The Communities have developed a fairly sophisticated network for articulating and aggregating supports for and demands on their political system. The Council of Ministers advances the standpoint of the member states' governments and aims at trying to bring together sometimes disparate views to produce an agreed position. The stance of various interest groups is expressed and brought together in the Economic and Social Committee, and to a lesser extent by the Commission, in the early stages of decision-making. The European Parliament provides a democratic input into the system, expressing the interests of regional-based constituencies and of political groupings.

The Communities system also has certain resources which reflect its ability to maintain and adapt itself and its capabilities. It has norms – values – that help to underpin the EC structure. These can be seen in the Preamble to the Rome Treaty which expressed a determination 'to lay the foundations of an ever closer union among the peoples of Europe', in the commitment to a European Union in the Solemn Declaration of Stuttgart of 19 June 1983 by the Heads of State and of Government, in the Single European Act's Preamble which confirmed the resolve 'to implement this European Union' and in the Maastricht Treaty's establishment of a European Union. This particular value has sometimes had to compete against demands of member states that have tried to curb the 'Europeanist' ideology. This was most noticeably the case with the government of France under President de Gaulle from 1958 to 1969 and that of the United Kingdom under Mrs Thatcher from 1979 to 1990.

The Communities have also managed to uphold their activities by the means of socialization whereby citizens and groups within the member states have their system of beliefs and patterns of behaviour affected. The institutions of the Communities, especially the Commission, the European Parliament, the Economic and Social Committee and the Court of Justice have tried to foster a 'Community spirit' among the citizens of the member states which would mean that they would have a loyalty towards 'Europe' as well as to their nation-state and localities. Opinion polls have shown that they have been quite successful in this, although Community-mindedness has been less evident among the population of Denmark and the United Kingdom. The institutions of the EC have also socialized the governments in their activities, insofar that they now must consider the 'Community dimension' to many of their policies and automatically consult with other EC states over a wide range of subjects from the environment to foreign policy. The Maastricht Treaty created a European Union citizenship.

The working of the Communities has been considerably assisted by their ability to recruit new members. The original core membership of the Six has been doubled to include a section of Europe stretching from Eire in the west to Greece in the east and from the Shetlands in the north to Sicily in the south. The Communities have also been able to recruit non-governmental organizations to participate in the Communities' institutions, especially in the Economic and Social Committee. This has meant that over the years a number of interest groups, especially those in agriculture and business, have increasingly shifted 'their loyalties, expectations and political activities toward a new centre, whose institutions possess or demand jurisdiction over the pre-existing national states' (Haas, 1968, 16). As the Communities' capability increases in other functional areas, so interest groups will look more to the EC institutions in Brussels or Strasbourg than to their national governmental structure.

The European Communities have become a system which has demands regularly made on it and which is fairly resilient because of its innate political resources. It can respond to its environment, adapt itself and produce outputs in the form of authoritative allocation of resources that can be implemented.

These outputs can be seen in five main forms, following Almond and Powell (1966, 28–9). First, there is rule-making and the European Communities have developed a noticeable capacity here which has been described earlier (pp. 118–24). The importance of Communities' legislation has been accepted by the member states, though they have preferred to keep greater national control of this process in a wide range of areas, especially those affecting security matters and foreign affairs. Thus in the latter case they have developed European Political Cooperation parallel to the European Communities. Secondly, the European Communities have to make sure that their rules and laws are applied. In most cases, the EC depends on national agencies for this task, but the Commission scrutinizes this process to make sure that EC law is applied and is done so fairly. In the case of rule-adjudication the

European Communities have the Court of Justice (and, to a lesser extent, the Commission) which can make authoritative judgements on cases within the areas covered by the treaties establishing and developing the Communities. Furthermore, the Court's rulings in these cases are superior to those of the national courts. The EC also has a well-developed information network that attempts to reach down to the ordinary citizen and to interest groups, and also undertakes a number of operations, the most important of which are running the Common Agricultural Policy, the Common External Tariff and the EC's commercial policy.

This output of the Communities' system may not be as intrusive in everyday life as that of the sovereign state, but it is now growing in its effect on the citizen. The signing of the Single European Act in 1986 laid the basis for the creation of a Single European Market within the Communities, though this will be circumscribed for the time being by the continuation of national currencies. The Act also brought into the EC's remit research and technological development and environmental policy, two vital areas of governmental policy for the 1990s. These were entrenched in and to by the Maastricht Treaty which also included plans for a common foreign and security policy and Union citizenship, thereby reaching to the heart of sovereign state activity. The reality is that the Communities have now developed a functioning political system covering, in varying intensity, a wide range of policies for the most important countries of Western Europe.

References

Allen, D. 1983: Managing the Common Market: the Community's competition policy. In Wallace, H., Wallace, W. and Webb, C. (eds.) *Policy-making in the European Community*, 2nd edn (Chichester: John Wiley & Sons), 209–36.

Almond, G. and Powell, G.B. 1966: *Comparative Politics: A Development Approach*. Boston: Little, Brown.

Archer, C. 1992: *International Organization*. London: Routledge.

—— and Butler, F. 1992: *The European Community Structure and Process*. London: Pinter.

Brewin, C. and McAllister, R. 1987: Annual review of the activities of the European Communities. *Journal of Common Market Studies* XXV, 4, 337–72.

Camps, M. 1964: *Britain and the European Community 1955–1963*. London: Oxford University Press.

Charlton, M. 1983: *The Price of Victory*. London: British Broadcasting Corporation.

Commission of the European Communities 1988: *Research on the 'Cost of*

Non-Europe'. *Volume 1 Basic Studies: Executive Summaries*. Luxembourg: Office for Official Publications of the European Communities.

Croxford, G.J., Wise, M. and Chalkley, B.S. 1987: The reform of the European Regional Development Fund: a preliminary assessment. *Journal of Common Market Studies* XXVI, 1, 25–38.

Demekas, D., Bartholdy, K., Gupta, S., Lipschitz, L. and Mayer, T. 1988: The effects of the Common Agricultural Policy of the European Community: a survey of the literature. *Journal of Common Market Studies* XXVII, 2, 113–45.

Dennis, G. 1980: European monetary co-operation. In Twitchett, K.J., *European Co-operation Today* (London: Europa), 172–96.

De Weydenthal, J.B. 1993: EC Keeps Central Europe at Arm's Length. RFE/RL Research Report 2:5, 29–31.

Drummond, S. 1982: Fifteen years of ASEAN. *Journal of Common Market Studies* XX, 4, 301–19.

ECSC EEC EAEC 1987: *Treaties Establishing the European Communities*. Luxembourg: European Communities.

EIB European Investment Bank 1993: *Annual Report*. Luxembourg: EIB.

European Yearbook 1988: European Communities. *European Yearbook 1986*. Dordrecht: Nijhoff.

Feld, W. 1967: *The European Common Market and the World*. Englewood Cliffs: Prentice-Hall.

Fennell, R. 1987: Reform of the CAP: shadow or substance. *Journal of Common Market Studies* XXVI, 1, 61–77.

Foster, N. (ed.) 1992: *Blackstone's EEC Legislation*, 3rd edn. London: Blackstone Press Ltd.

Fursdon, E. 1980: *The European Defence Community: A History*. London: St Martin.

Ginsberg, R.H. 1983: The European Community and the United States of America. In Lodge, J. (ed.), 1983b, 168–89.

Haas, E.B. 1968: *The Uniting of Europe. Political, Social, and Economic Forces 1950–1957*. Stanford: Stanford University Press.

Hallstein, W. 1962: *United Europe. Challenge and Opportunity*. London: Oxford University Press.

Hartley, T.C. 1988: *The Foundations of European Community Law*. Oxford: Clarendon Press.

Hewitt, A. 1984: The Lomé Convention: entering a second decade. *Journal of Common Market Studies* XXIII, 2, 95–115.

Jacobs, F., Corbett, R., and Shackleton, M. 1992: *The European Parliament*, 2nd edn. Harlow: Longman.

Kerr, A.J.C. 1986: *The Common Market and How it Works*, 3rd edn. Oxford: Pergamon Press.

Krenzler, H. and Kaiser, W. 1991: 'The transatlantic declaration: a new basis for relations between the EC and the USA', *Aussenpolitik*, 42(2), 363–72.

Laffan, B. 1983: The European Social Fund, *Journal of Common Market Studies* XXI, 4, 389–408.

Lintner, V. and Mazey, S. 1991: *The European Community: Economic and Political Aspects*. London and New York: McGraw-Hill Book Company.

Lipgens, W. 1982: *A History of European Integration. Volume 1 1945-1947.* Oxford: Oxford University Press.

Lodge, J. 1983a: The European Community and New Zealand. In Lodge, J. 1983b, 209-16.

—— (ed.) 1983b: *Institutions and Policies of the European Community* London: Frances Pinter.

—— 1989a: Social Europe: fostering a People's Europe. In Lodge, J. 1989b, 303-18.

—— (ed.) 1989b: *The European Community and the Challenge of the Future.* London: Pinter.

Maresca, J.J. 1987: *To Helsinki.* Durham and London: Duke University Press.

Miller, J.D.B. 1983: The European Community and Australia. In Lodge, J., 1983b, 203-8.

Molle, W. and Van Mourik, A. 1988: International movements of labour under conditions of economic integration: the case of Western Europe. *Journal of Common Market Studies* XXVI, 3, 317-42.

Nicoll, W. 1984: The Luxembourg compromise. *Journal of Common Market Studies* XXIII, 1, 35-44.

Norton, D. 1986: Smuggling under the common agricultural policy: Northern Ireland and the Republic of Ireland. *Journal of Common Market Studies* XXIV, 4, 297-312.

Palmer, J. 1989: *1992 and Beyond.* Luxembourg: Office for Official Publications of the European Communities.

Pelkmans, J. 1987: The new approach to technical harmonization and standardization. *Journal of Common Market Studies* XXV, 3, 249-69.

Pinder, J. 1991: *The European Community and Eastern Europe.* London: Pinter.

Polach, J.G. 1964: *Euratom. Its Background, Issues and Economic Implications.* Dobbs Ferry, NY: Oceana.

Redmond, J. and Zou Lan 1986: The European Community and China: new horizons, *Journal of Common Market Studies* XXV, 2, 133-55.

Shackleton, M. 1990: *Financing the EC.* London: Pinter.

Sharp, M. 1989: The Community and new technologies. In Lodge, J., 1989b, 202-20.

Straubhaar, T, 1988: International labour migration within a common market: some aspects of EC experience. *Journal of Common Market Studies* XXVII, 1, 55-62.

Thatcher, M. 1989: Speech given by the Rt Hon. Margaret Thatcher FRS MP at the opening ceremony of the 39th academic year of the College of Europe. *College of Europe Information January 1989.* Bruges: College of Europe.

Thygesen, N. 1989: The Delors Report and European economic and monetary union. *International Affairs* Autumn, 637-52.

Treaty on European Union 1992: Luxembourg: Office for Official Publications of the European Communities.

Wallace, H. 1980: *Budgetary Politics: The Finances of the European Community.* London: George Allen & Unwin.

Wilke, M. and Wallace, H. 1990: *Subsidiarity: Approaches to Power-*

sharing in the European Community. London: Royal Institute of International Affairs.

Wise, M. 1984: The Common Fisheries Policy of the European Community. London: Methuen.

Woolcock, S. 1984: Information technology: the challenge to Europe. Journal of Common Market Studies xxii:4, 315–31.

Zis, G. 1984: The European monetary system 1979–84: an assessment. Journal of Common Market Studies XXIII, 1, 45–72.

7

The European Free Trade Association

Establishment

The reasons for the creation of the European Free Trade Association (EFTA) can be found in the post-war drive by certain West European governments towards the liberalization of trade and in the desire of the British, the Scandinavians and the Swiss to counter-balance the emerging EEC.

Having decided not to participate in the Messina discussions (see pp. 90), the British government had to find a strategy that would suit their trade requirements in Western Europe. In contrast to the customs union for industrial and agricultural goods run by a supranational authority, which was being planned by the Six at Messina, the British proposed an industrial free trade area with intergovernmental institutions. From 1956 until November 1958 the Six and other West European states led by the United Kingdom, attempted to reconcile these two sets of views in OEEC working parties and committees. The hope was that a customs union of the Six could be enveloped within a wider OEEC free trade area, thus avoiding a split in Western Europe over trading matters.

The nature of these negotiations changed with the signing of the Treaty of Rome by the Six in March 1957. The prospect of EEC tariff reductions on 1 January 1959 gave a sense of urgency to the talks but at the same time allowed the Six – especially the French – to set their pace. It was the French government which was most insistent that any wide free trade agreement could only be reached on the basis of clearly determined obligations and benefits, that agricultural goods should be included in the arrangement and that there should be tight institutional control. During the 'Maudling Committee' negotiations about the details of a free trade settlement, the British government gradually gave way on a number of points but, by the end of 1958, the discussions had broken down amidst Franco-British recriminations. The start of tariff-cutting within the EEC from 1 January 1959 in effect placed imports from non-EEC West European countries at a disadvantage to similar products from within the EEC area. The OEEC countries outside the EEC were a motley crew dominated by the presence of the British. Not all of them agreed with the British line: the Danes, for example, were eager to include agricultural goods in any settlement (Griffiths, 1992, 34–40).

Even by mid-1958 the Swiss were thinking about a 'small' free trade area based on some of the plans advanced in the Maudling Committee and including the OEEC states outside the EEC (Truninger, 1976, 171). After the breakdown of the Maudling Committee negotiations, officials from Austria, Denmark, Norway, Portugal, Sweden, Switzerland and the United Kingdom – the 'Outer Seven' – met in Geneva. More detailed plans for a free trade area were discussed at meetings of business and farming interests in January and at a delegates' meeting in Oslo in February 1959. After a further official meeting in March, negotiators from the Outer Seven were called to a meeting for 1 June 1959 in Saltsjöbaden, near Stockholm, to draw up a free trade agreement.

For the United Kingdom these negotiations provided two opportunities: to create freer access to the markets of the 'Outer Seven' countries and, by accepting a 'small free trade area' which could then negotiate with the Six, to work towards 'a multilateral association embracing all members of the OEEC' (Board of Trade Journal, 5 June 1959, 1297). The strategy was to prevent the smaller 'Outer Seven' states being offered inferior bilateral trade agreements by the Six and to bring the EEC back to the negotiating table to get a wider West European trade settlement for fear of losing their valuable markets in Scandinavia, Switzerland and the United Kingdom. A decent outcome in Saltsjöbaden was to provide Britain with an interim economic benefit and a long-term political solution to the trade division of Western Europe.

The Swedish, Swiss and Austrian governments saw a limited free trade area as the second-best alternative to the West European-wide counterpart. However, they were frightened that, in a position of weakness, they may have to choose between losing trade advantage or accepting an agreement with the Six controlled by the Community's supranational institutions, thereby compromising their ability to pursue their neutrality. An 'Outer

Seven' arrangement lifted the free trade spirit of these countries without compromising their political integrity. For Sweden there was the added advantage that this arrangement offered a practical alternative to the idea of a Nordic Customs Union with Norway and Denmark, negotiations for which had dragged on unsuccessfully for almost a decade.

Portugal's aim at Saltsjöbaden was to secure their processed agricultural and fishing exports in the British market and to obtain help for industrial development from the richer 'Outer Seven' members.

The Danes had considerable doubts about the whole Saltsjöbaden process and until well into the negotiations were still trying to get a solution including all West European countries. In the end they retreated from this hope and satisfied themselves with keeping their markets in Britain and Scandinavia though, as their exports were then predominantly agricultural, they wanted that side of their trade covered by any agreement. Furthermore, they did not wish to be cut off from their important West German market and thus required that any small free trade area should very soon start negotiations with the Six.

The Norwegians were more concerned with protecting their home industries, which had been carefully nurtured after wartime destruction, and also wanted their fish exports safeguarded in any deal (Griffiths, 1992, 39–40).

These diverse demands were sufficiently overlapping to produce a quick agreement at Saltsjöbaden. After all, the negotiators there had the extensive work of the Maudling Committee on which to build. A treaty was drafted in June, accepted with a few changes by Ministers in July, finalized in November 1959 and signed on 4 January 1960 to come into force in May that year.

What emerged from Saltsjöbaden was a treaty that balanced the demands of those wanting 'trade security' – Austria, Denmark, Norway and Portugal – and those countries, such as Britain, Sweden and Switzerland, that could provide it in the form of special concessions in the area of agriculture, fisheries and development aid. However, the nature of these arrangements was a constant source of argument during EFTA's first decade.

The *Stockholm Convention* was built on the twin pillars of free and fair trade. The objectives of the convention stated that economic advantages had to be promoted not only throughout the Area but also in each member state, thereby ensuring that advancement was not achieved to the detriment of the poorer members. As well as creating an industrial free trade area the Convention aimed at bringing out 'conditions of fair competition' (Article 2b) for trade between member states. It was also an aim of the Convention to contribute to 'the harmonious development and expansion of world trade and to the progressive removal of barriers to it' (Article 2d). The Preamble specifically mentioned the OEEC and closer economic cooperation with the EEC, indicating that the members still hoped for a *modus vivendi* with the Six.

The heart of the Convention concerned the elimination of barriers to trade in industrial goods between members. Article 3 set out a timetable for the abolition of import duties among states in a series of eight steps from July 1960 to January 1970. In order that only goods made completely or substantially in the member states would benefit, Article 4 set out the conditions for Area tariff treatment and, as the basis for designating such goods, an EFTA 'Certificate of Origin' was created in Annex B, rule 8. Export duties and quantitative restrictions (QRs) on trade were also to be eliminated along similar lines as import tariffs.

The notion of encouraging fair trade was encapsulated in Articles 13 to 17. The Convention required that the benefits an EFTA state might expect from the freeing of trade should not be frustrated by government aids to exports by other members (Article 13), by the purchasing action of public undertakings (Article 14), by restrictive business practices (Articles 14 and 15) or by restrictions on the establishment and operating of firms by nationals of one member state in another EFTA country (Article 16). Under Article 17 members were allowed to act against the import of dumped or subsidized products from other EFTA states.

There were exceptions to EFTA's trading rules but they were worded in order not to be too wide-ranging. Article 18 laid down that nothing in the Convention affected the safeguarding of information, trade in arms and defence materials, the limiting of nuclear materials to peaceful uses, measures taken in times of war or emergency or undertakings aimed at maintaining international peace and security. Article 19 allowed a member state to introduce QRs on imports to safeguard its balance of payments, though the EFTA Council could make counter-recommendations by a majority vote. On the whole the emphasis was on helping rather than punishing a state with balance of payments problems. Article 20 had a complicated formula to deal with difficulties in particular sectors. If the removal of trade protection led to a rise in

EFTA imports into a member state and this in turn created a decrease in demand for the equivalent home industry's products, thereby producing an appreciable rise in unemployment in a sector of industry or a region, then QRs could be reimposed to freeze, but not reduce, the level of offending imports.

In order to maintain the balance of advantage between members, the Convention also covered trade in agriculture and fisheries goods, which, except for Article 17 on dumping, was not otherwise dealt with by the core of the Stockholm Convention (Articles 2 to 20). In Article 22 the members recognized that the aim of their agricultural policies was to promote rational productivity, market stability, adequate supplies at reasonable prices and a satisfactory standard of living for those working in agriculture. The objective of the Association was to help the expansion of trade in order to provide 'reasonable reciprocity to Member States whose economies depend to a great extent on exports of agricultural goods' (Article 22, para 2). To achieve this, agreements between members ending restrictions on agricultural trade were encouraged (Article 23), agricultural export subsidies discouraged (Article 24). The special provisions for fish products, set out in Articles 27 and 28, generally accepted that trade in fish and other marine products should be expanded but left the whole question to be examined by the EFTA Council. What were to be regarded in EFTA terms as agricultural and fishery products were defined, respectively, in Annex D and Annex E of the Convention thus allowing the EFTA Council to exclude certain products from these lists, thereby making them eligible for free trade treatment as 'industrial products'.

It can be seen that, despite these special arrangements, the balance of advantages in the Stockholm Convention was still very much in favour of the industrialized members, thus reflecting the power and interests of Sweden, Switzerland and the United Kingdom. While arrangements for industrial free trade were definite and extensive, those for fish and agricultural produce were vague and conditional.

The balanced agreement negotiated at Saltsjöbaden was finally acceptable to all the Outer Seven. It applied to Greenland from July 1961 and to the Faeroe Islands from January 1968 until 31 December 1972 when the Danish Kingdom, to which they belong, left EFTA. The Convention also covered Liechtenstein which, since 1923, has formed a customs union with Switzerland which, for practical purposes, represented the principality within the Association until 1991 when it became a full member in its own right.

Any state accepted by the existing membership could accede to the Stockholm Convention, as did Iceland in 1970, Finland in 1986 and Liechtenstein in 1991. The Council could 'negotiate an agreement between the Member States and other states, union of states or international organization, creating an association' with reciprocal rights and obligations (Article 41 (2)). In 1961 Finland signed an agreement aimed at creating a free trade area with the seven EFTA members. This arrangement helped safeguard Finland's special relationship with the USSR. The institution created in 1961 – commonly called FINEFTA – differed only in small details from EFTA and in 1986 Finland formally became a full member of EFTA (*EFTA Bulletin*, 4/85, 3). EFTA has also signed treaties of cooperation with Yugoslavia establishing a joint EFTA–Yugoslavia Committee in 1978, and with Spain, setting up a similar committee in 1980. The link with Yugoslavia was suspended in December 1991 because of the conflict in that divided country, but new links were made with the ex-Communist countries of East and Central Europe. Cooperation agreements were signed with the Czech Slovak Federal Republic (the CSFR), Hungary and Poland in June 1990, with Bulgaria, Romania, Estonia, Latvia and Lithunia in December 1991 (*EFTA Bulletin*, 1.92, 17–30) and with Slovenia in May 1992 (*EFTA Bulletin*, 2.92, 9–10). A free trade agreement was signed with Turkey in December 1991, entering into force in May 1992 (*EFTA Bulletin*, 3–4. 91, 25), and with the CSFR in March 1992. Other free trade agreements are expected with Hungary and Poland and cooperation agreements with Israel and the Gulf Cooperation Council are being discussed (EFTA Secretariat, 1992).

Institutions

The nature of EFTA's institutions was determined by the genesis of the organization: they were to supervise the creation of a free trade area and had to match the reservations of founding governments about any supranational authority. They are thus simple and unpretentious. The major institution is the EFTA Council in which each member state has one vote and which may meet at ministerial or official level to make recommendations and take decisions.

The Council supervises and reviews the operation of the Stockholm Convention and considers whether further action should be taken to promote the aims of the Association. In exercising the powers and functions conferred on it by the Convention, the Council takes its decisions by unanimity except where a majority decision is allowed for – Articles 5(3), 5(6), 10(8), 13(2), 19, 20, 21 and 31. On the whole these prevent the use of the veto by members to avoid their responsibilities but, in turn, agreements cannot be thrust upon unwilling members.

The Council, under Article 32(3), can establish 'such organs, committees and other bodies' to help accomplish its task. Indeed, the Customs Committee, the Committee of Trade Experts, the Budget Committee and the Consultative Committee were established in 1960, the Agricultural Review Committee and the Economic Committee in 1964 and the Committee of Members of Parliament – made up of a representative group of parliamentarians – in 1977. The Consultative Committee consists of non-governmental representatives with interests in the functioning of the free trade area – business, agricultural and trade union spokesmen. It meets only occasionally and discusses general EFTA questions and current topics of interest but does not have the treaty status of the Economic and Social Committee of the European Communities. EFTA parliamentarians had a number of meetings during the first 17 years of EFTA's lifetime, then this tradition was formalized in the Committee of Members of Parliament to make dialogue with the representatives of the European Parliament of the EC easier.

Under Article 34(b) the Council was obliged 'to make arrangements for the secretariat services' and this it did in 1960 by establishing a small Secretariat in Geneva under a Secretary-General. For practically the whole period of British membership of EFTA, the post of Secretary-General was held by British civil servants – Sir Frank Figures from 1960 to 1965 and Sir John Coulson from 1965 to 1972. Bengt Rabaeus of Sweden took over in 1972, to be followed by a Swiss, Charles Muller, in 1976, Per Kleppe from Norway in December 1981 and Georg Reisch of Austria from 1988. The EFTA Secretariat has always been kept small – with scarcely a hundred people working for it at its height – and its main duties have been to provide information, encourage consultation and administer the daily work of the Association. The Secretaries-General have obviously been chosen by the Council for their experience and, on that basis, could exercise a certain influence. However, they have no charter rights and duties and have therefore been careful not to alienate the EFTA members. At the same time it has been expected that the Secretariat would in particular help the smaller member countries – with the full knowledge of the larger states (Archer, 1976, 16).

EFTA had no court, but Article 31 empowers the Council to deal with complaints arising from members considering that EFTA benefits are being frustrated. It can make recommendations by a majority vote and could authorize – again by a majority vote – other members to suspend obligations toward a defaulter if it was decided that an obligation under the convention had not been fulfilled. This semi-judicial function has never been used by the Council – it would, after all, involve admitting the failure of political procedures.

Changes in EFTA's institutions were necessitated by the signing of the European Economic Area (EEA) agreement (see p. 180). In anticipating of the agreement coming into force, the EFTA states agreed to establish the EFTA Standing Committee, the EFTA Surveillance Authority (ESA) and the EFTA Court that would be able respectively to coordinate EFTA states' actions, and to survey and to adjudicate on the application of EEA rules within the EFTA area. (For other EEA institutions, see p. 183.)

Achievements

Any assessment of EFTA's achievements must take into account the dual purpose for which the Association was established – to create an industrial free trade area among its members and to procure a wider settlement of trade differences between all the West European countries. Both ends have been achieved though the role of EFTA as an organization in bringing about the latter is disputed.

Industrial free trade within EFTA was achieved three years earlier than planned – in December 1966. During 1960–1 the EFTA Council agreed to an acceleration of tariff cuts in order to keep pace with those introduced within the EEC and thereby make an overall EEC–EFTA trade settlement easier. After it became clear in January 1963 that any such agreement was not on the horizon, the Lisbon EFTA Council Meeting of May 1963 decided to rearrange the tariff-cutting timetable once and for all, thereby allowing industry to plan its future.

This quickened pace created problems for EFTA states wishing to protect certain home industries – Austria, Finland, Norway, Portugal and, to a much lesser extent, Denmark. They were given *decalage* arrangements allowing them to 'get out of step' from tariff reductions for some or all of their industrial imports. The creation of a free trade area was also eased for some countries – notably Austria, Portugal, Switzerland and the United Kingdom – by a system of 'drawback' being permitted until December 1966. This allowed an EFTA producer a refund of duties on imported components for products which were then exported. Thus 'drawback' was not allowed for products on the home market and the ending of tariffs within EFTA made the area an extended home market. It was thus abolished after the creation of the free trade area (Curzon, 1974, 48–50).

In order to balance the advantages of industrial free trade expected by Sweden, Switzerland and the United Kingdom, the other members were promised 'reasonable reciprocity' in their agricultural and fisheries trade. In partial fulfilment of this promise, a number of bilateral agreements were signed at the time of Saltsjöbaden, mainly between Britain and Denmark and Britain and Portugal for agricultural products and between Britain and Norway on frozen fish fillets.

The Danes in particular attempted to press the United Kingdom for a better deal through the Agricultural Review Committee, established in 1963 to persuade Denmark not to oppose the new tariff-cutting timetable for industrial goods. With the acceptance of the Lisbon Council decision, Denmark's bargaining position was undermined. When the Norwegian quota of fish fillets to be treated as 'industrial goods' was exceeded in 1968, the British government placed a tariff on the excess amount. After delicate negotiations the tariff was abolished and a minimum price adopted by Britain for home, Norwegian and Danish frozen fish fillets. This case demonstrates a general point that, in the end, it was improved prices and market conditions that most benefited the agricultural and fisheries exporters rather than special arrangements with the more industrialized EFTA members. With the British and Danes leaving EFTA, the possibility of such arrangements became more limited. However there have been two noteworthy efforts to balance the advantages in post-1972 EFTA: the agreement, in March 1989, to liberalize intra-EFTA trade in fish from 1990; and the establishment in 1975 of the Industrial Development Fund for Portugal. This Fund will operate until 2002, although Portugal is now a member of the EC.

A crisis arose within EFTA in October 1964 when the incoming Labour Government in Britain imposed a 15 per cent surcharge on the value of most industrial imports to help overcome balance of payments difficulties. The other EFTA members pointed out that Article 19 only allowed QRs and that the surcharge had been applied without prior consultation. During the debate that followed within EFTA, the emphasis was on improving the British economy rather than on any retribution. An Economic Committee was established for mutual consultation on economic and financial policies and the first reduction in the surcharge was announced by the British at the EFTA Ministerial Council of 22 February 1965. The rest of the surcharge was allowed to lapse in November 1966 thereby not interrupting the creation of the EFTA industrial free trade area in December 1966.

Non-tariff barriers were not covered by the EFTA Convention in the same way as tariffs. 'Rules of Competition' were established preventing governments from giving their home industries hidden protection. From 1966 to 1968 attempts were made to tackle these barriers to trade: government aids, public procurement policy, restrictive business practices, rights of establishing businesses, and dumped and subsidized imports. The 1968 London Council meeting agreed on an 'action programme' and, overall up to 1973, 'work on dumping was disappointing while work on government aids, restrictive business practices and establishment was probably quite effective' (Curzon, 1974, 146). Since their Vienna summit of May 1977 the EFTA states have given greater consideration to non-tariff barriers within EFTA. Since the 1984 Luxembourg Summit of EFTA and the EC some progress has been made between the two organizations, for example, in the registration of pharmaceutical products and on hallmarking.

How has EFTA fared in its *relations with the European Communities*? The original hope in 1960 that the EC would deal with EFTA as an equal trade bloc was not then realized as the Community countries did not accept that the issues to be discussed were just ones of trade. The nature of the future of Western Europe was at stake.

EFTA countries, on the other hand, pressed for tariff reciprocity. They hoped that the EEC would agree with them a mutual extension of the July 1960 tariff cuts and that the creation of the OECD (see Chapter 3) would bring about a unification of the West European trade divide: the 'Outer Seven', the 'Inner Six' and the 'Forgotten Five' (Greece, Eire, Iceland, Spain and Turkey) would unite into one market. The EEC's response was to accelerate their tariff cuts in May 1960 causing the EFTA states to announce an acceleration in their cuts in February 1961.

In May 1961 the United Kingdom government decided to apply for full membership of the EEC. It had first to square this move with the Stockholm Convention's aim of creating a multilateral trade association for all Western Europe. At the EFTA London Ministerial Council, 27–28 June 1961, the British were persuaded to adopt a 'convoy' strategy: their application would place them to the fore of the EFTA fleet but all members would coordinate their actions and 'remain united throughout the negotiations'. The Association was to be kept intact until arrangements had been made with the EEC to meet 'the various legitimate interests of all members of EFTA, and thus enable them all to participate from the same date in an integrated European market' (*EFTA Bulletin*, August/September 1961, 1). Britain thus went ahead with its application to the EEC leaving other EFTA states to make their own arrangements. However it did mean that any agreement between Britain and the EEC could have been held up by the slowest negotiations between an EFTA state and the EEC. From July 1961 to the end of 1962, Denmark and Norway joined Britain in the queue for full EEC membership whilst Austria, Sweden, Switzerland and Portugal applied for association under Article 238 of the Treaty of Rome: the first three ruled out full membership because of their neutrality and Portugal because of its low level of development (and its undemocratic political system).

The attempts by the EFTA states to negotiate a settlement with the EEC came to an end with President de Gaulle's veto on British entry in January 1963. Only the Austrians continued negotiations, though these were vetoed by the Italians over disputed territory. The May 1965 meeting of EFTA prime ministers called for greater EFTA–EEC cooperation but this call brought no response from the EEC.

A second attempt was made by Britain to open membership negotiations with the Community in May 1967. The British Prime Minister, Harold Wilson, said the British would 'do our best' to ensure satisfactory arrangements for other EFTA states but this promise was never put to the test: de Gaulle again vetoed British entry in November 1967. Once more overtures from EFTA to the EEC to reduce differences between the two groupings were rebuffed.

The Hague Summit of the EEC in December 1969 opened the

door for eventual British membership. The United Kingdom, Denmark, Norway and a non-EFTA country, Eire, applied for full membership and the EEC accepted that 'satisfactory arrangements' should be negotiated for all EFTA members. The outcome of the 1970-2 negotiations was that the United Kingdom and Denmark (together with Eire) joined the European Communities as full members from 1 January 1973. Austria, Finland, Ireland, Norway (whose people had rejected full membership in a referendum), Portugal, Sweden and Switzerland each signed separate, though similar, free trade agreements with the new enlarged European Communities. These treaties created an industrial free trade area in most goods between EFTA states and the Communities of the Nine by July 1977. The proper implementation of the agreements was overseen by joint committees of the EC and each of the EFTA states – there was no grand EFTA–EC settlement. All the treaties – except that of Finland – had an 'evolutionary' clause which allowed matters not covered by the free trade arrangement to be discussed.

At the Vienna Summit of EFTA leaders in May 1977 they agreed to explore closer cooperation with the EC, especially on economic policy. After the remaining few tariffs between EFTA and the EC were dismantled on 1 January 1984, a 'Jumbo' meeting between ministers of the two blocs – the first – took place in April 1984 and discussed a wide range of topics including non-tariff barriers, 'flexible cooperation' outside the free trade agreements, intensification of contacts on transport, agriculture, fisheries and energy and common action in international forums (*EFTA Bulletin*, 2.84, 7). Thus began a period of 'combined bilateralism and multilateralism' (Pedersen, 1991, 13). The idea was to create a European Economic Area enveloping the EC and EFTA (Curzon Price, 1985, 124–35).

In January 1989, the President of the EC Commission, Jacques Delors, advanced two alternative strategies for future EC–EFTA relations: the first involved the ultimate creation of a free trade area between the two; and the second was a 'more structured partnership with common decision-making and administrative institutions to make our activities more effective and to highlight the political dimension of our cooperation in the economic, social, financial and cultural spheres' (*EFTA Bulletin*, 1.89, 1).

The heads of government of the EFTA states met in Oslo in March 1989 to discuss their relations with the EC, especially in light of the proposed creation of the single European market by the start of 1993 (see p.140). The notion of an European Economic Area showed that the EFTA states desired their relations with the EC to go beyond those of trade (Reisch, 1989, 6), but there was disagreement within EFTA as to where the line should be drawn. Norway wished links that included discussion of foreign policy issues, whereas Sweden, Switzerland and Austria wanted a wide coverage of all aspects of EC activity as long as this did not impinge on their neutrality. At Oslo the EFTA governments recognized the need to negotiate with the EC over the free movement of goods, services, capital and labour between the two blocs – EFTA and the EC – and the necessity for 'additional instruments' to aid this process (EFTA Bulletin, 2.89, 5). This common approach did not rule out individual action: in July 1989 the Austrian government applied for membership of the EC. However, the EEA proposal seemed to offer the best of both worlds for the EFTA states. It provided a half-way house for those considering EC membership, and ameliotated the costs of non-membership for those wishing to stay out.

The achievement of the EEA has however been fraught with difficulties. The EFTA and EC ministers, meeting in December 1990, decided that negotiations to create an EEA should be completed by the summer of 1991, and set down the political guide-lines for such an agreement. Throughout the summer of 1991 negotiations seemed to stall on the questions of fisheries and the transit of EFTA states by EC vehicles. On 22 October 1991 an agreement was initialled. However, all this work was placed in jeopardy when the EC's Court of Justice – to which the EC Commission had referred the plans for the EEA judicial machinery for an opinion – criticized the idea of an independent EEA Court as being inconsistent with the autonomy of the EC legal order which the EC's Court was meant to protect (Court of Justice, 1991, 3–5). The institutional arrangements were hurriedly renegotiated and the EEA agreement was signed in Oporto on 2 May 1992. The agreement then had to be ratified by the 12 EC and seven EFTA states and the European Parliament to put the EEA in place for 1 January 1993. In December 1992 the process again faltered when a majority of the Swiss electorate voting in a referendum rejected their country's membership of the EEA. Its achievement was postponed until the two sides – the EC and EFTA minus Switzerland – could decide on whether and how the EEA can still be achieved. Meanwhile, Austria has been joined by Sweden (in 1991) and Finland and Norway (in 1992) in applying for membership negotiations with the EC.

What then is the EEA, the attempted creation of which has caused so much anguish? The idea of the European Economic Area was that on 1 January 1993, when the single European market was planned for the EC (see pp. 140–2), the basic elements of that market should be extended to the EFTA countries, thereby creating an economic area of some 376 million people. The Oporto agreement between the EC and the EFTA states included three main elements to this end.

First, the four freedoms of movement of goods, services, capital and persons were to cover the 19 countries. The individual free trade agreements that each EFTA state had with the EC had done much to ensure free trade between the two sides. Almost all remaining restrictions were to be abolished in the EEA and about 800 pieces of EC legislation integrated into the Agreement to that end. State aid that distorts trade, for example, would generally be prohibited for the whole Area (as it is within the EC) and certainly EFTA countries would have to provide information about such aid schemes to the EFTA Surveillance Authority (see p. 183). Free movement of agricultural and fisheries goods was not included in the Agreement, though both sides promised to liberalize trade in such goods in the GATT negotiations. However, bilateral agreements between EFTA states and the EC will allow some of those products – 'cohesion products' – from less-developed parts of the EC into the EFTA market. Also the EC negotiated separate deals with both Iceland and Norway which would allow some of their fish products full access to the EC market from 1 January 1993 (with duties on other types of fish being reduced in the period to January 1997) in exchange for greater EC catches in Norwegian waters and a share in Icelandic waters. Although 'free movement of goods' is an aim of the EEA, it would not create a customs union between the EC and EFTA states: the EFTA countries can retain their tariffs towards third countries and, as noted, agricultural goods are not included.

Free movement of persons means that the EEA workers (excepting those in some government jobs) should face no discrimination on the basic of nationality 'with regard to employment, pay or other working conditions' (EFTA Secretariat, 1992a, 7). Thus EEA citizens will have the right to seek and hold a job anywhere in the Area and will be able to 'export and import' their social security benefits. Diplomas and other professional qualifications attained in one member state would be also become valid throughout the Area. Switzerland and Liechtenstein, which have tightly controlled labour markets, would have five years to adopt the free movement of EEA labour.

Free movement of services would allow them to be provided on a non-discriminatory basis throughout the Area, meaning that service entrepreneurs could set up businesses or practise their profession outside their home country. A bank based in one EEA state – say, Sweden – could establish subsidiaries in another – for example, Germany – without the need for approval of the German authorities. Instead its 'home country' (Swedish) authorities would supervise it. A free market in traffic and transport means an end to the charging of different rates for carrying the same goods over the same transport links on the grounds of the country of origin or destination (EFTA Secretariat, 1992a, 9). Bilateral arrangements separate from the EEA were made between the EC and Austria and Switzerland on the transport of EC goods across those countries, thus making aspects of the EEA transport provisions non-applicable to those countries. This was to allow the two Alpine states to regulate the heavy flow of EC-based traffic across their countryside.

Free movement of capital aimed at creating a non-discriminatory basis for loans, investments and capital transfers across EEA frontiers. Some exceptions were made for foreign ownership in the EFTA countries: Norway and Sweden were to be allowed two years to bring in new laws; Austria, Finland and Iceland three years; and Switzerland and Liechtenstein five years. Norway and Iceland would be allowed to keep national laws on investment in the fishing industry.

The second major element of the EEA agreement was that involving 'flanking and horizontal policies' that would extend EC–EFTA cooperation beyond that associated with the four freedoms. Current cooperation in the fields of education, research and development, statistics, and the environment would be strengthened and formalized, while new cooperation would be started in social policy, tourism and company law (EFTA Secretariat, 1992a, 11). Also associated with the agreement was a promise by the EFTA states to create a 'cohesion fund' of soft loans and grants which would be used to support environmental and educational projects and those involving small and medium-sized firms. The money will be distributed to Portugal, Spain, Greece and Eire, mainly through the European Investment Bank, with the EFTA fund subsidizing the interest rate by 3 per cent. The total cost of the scheme has been reckoned at ECU495 million for the grants

(EFTA Secretariat, 1992a, 12) with another ECU1.5 billion being made available in soft loans (DTI, 1991, 1).

The third aspect of the agreement involved institutions. The EEA Joint Committee, consisting of EC and EFTA high officials meeting at least once a month, would exchange information and views and make and take decisions. The EC Commission, when drawing up legislation affection a field covered by the EEA agreement would also seek advice from EFTA experts on the same basis as it would from EC experts. The Joint Committee would be responsible for the daily working of the EEA and could establish other committees to assist in its work. The EEA Council is the highest political body of the EEA and would consist of the ministers who are members of the EC Council, members of the EC Commission and ministers from each of the seven EFTA states. The EEA Council – which is planned to meet at least twice a year – should make its decisions by consensus between the Community on one side and EFTA speaking with one voice on the other side. In the end one or more country can decide to hold up – or opt out of – an agreement on an EEA matter, though its government would have to decide on whether the possible costs of doing so were worth the benefits. Other EEA institutions include a Joint Parliamentary Committee as a forum to discuss common EEA matters, and the EEA Consultative Committee representing the social partners (such as trade unions, employers, consumers) in the Area.

EFTA would also be obliged to establish new institutions. Within the EC, the Commission would monitor the appliance of the EEA agreement. EFTA will have to establish an EFTA Surveillance Authority (ESA), similar in nature to the Commission, to undertake this task in the EFTA part of the EEA. The ESA would consist of one member from each EFTA state who would, however, act independently of governmental or other instructions in making sure that the rules of the EEA agreement were adhered to in the EFTA countries. The ESA would cooperate closely wiht the Commission. The EFTA Court, consisting of one judge from each EFTA state, would exercise judical control over the proper functioning of the agreement. It would handle disputes between EFTA states, or between the ESA and EFTA states and would consider appeals regarding ESA decisions. Finally, the EFTA Standing Committee would have one representative from each EFTA state and would provide a forum within which the EFTA countries would consult before the EEA Joint Committee meetings. It would be serviced by the EFTA Secretariat.

To make the EEA work, the EFTA countries would be obliged to adopt all the backlog of EC legislation and court decisions – the *acquis communautaire* – thus providing a common legal basis for the Area.

After the rejection of the EEA by the Swiss electorate, the whole idea has been thrown into confusion. The 18 participants took the option of going ahead without Switzerland, hoping that it might join later. A new protocol was signed between the remaining EEA states, adjusting the contributions to the Cohesion Fund to take account of Switzerland's absence. The rest of the EFTA states would contribute between 60 and 70 per cent of the 27 per cent of the Cohesion Fund made up by the Swiss contribution. It was then agreed to implement farm concessions (benefiting the EC Mediterranean states) by 15 April 1993 before the EEA came into force in July 1993. However, the Spanish government indicated that it might hold up the ratification of the EEA in response to the slow process of ratification of the Maastricht Treaty by the United Kingdom during the first half of 1993 (*Financial Times*, 9 March 1993, 18).

What has EFTA achieved? Clearly it brought about industrial free trade between the original seven members and did so rapidly. According to Victoria Curzon (1974, 84) part of this success 'must be attributed to the fact that agriculture was not included in the free trade arrangement, that revenue duties were permitted to remain, that certain limited *decalage* arrangements were made, and that Portugal . . . was allowed to retain the greater part of her tariff during the ten-year period . . .' Even in the post-1972 EFTA there has been difficulty in ending non-tariff barriers to trade, and agricultural trade is still not covered.

It is more difficult to assess EFTA's role in creating one trading bloc in all of Western Europe. While this came about by a series of individual trade agreements with the EC, the fact that a free trade area had been established within EFTA was a major factor that allowed its members 'to participate from the same date in an integrated European market'.

On the other hand, the establishment of EFTA has been seen as counter-productive. Miriam Camps (1964, 217–18) has portrayed the original British strategy of creating EFTA as adding another obstacle to later British efforts to join the EC. However once the step to create EFTA had been taken, it made sense for all the countries to be included in a settlement with the EC, although the individual agreements insisted on by the Communities has been typified as 'falling short of a joint EC–EFTA agreement' (Curzon, 1974, 231). The difficulties experienced in obtaining such a bilateral settlement in the EEA demonstrate the wisdom of originally settling for such limited agreements.

Contribution

What contribution has EFTA made to the organizing of Western Europe? The Association has never claimed political aims and it would be unfair to compare it with the European Communities, but it has made a contribution in three ways.

First, it has helped to break down economic barriers between a number of European countries. It is to be noted that the Nordic countries, similar in background as they are, were unable to end trade restrictions between themselves before joining EFTA. Despite its liberal scheme of rule-application and adjudication, EFTA can thus claim some role in the creation of a West European market.

Secondly, EFTA acted as a training ground for British cooperation with other West European states. Clearly Britain was not ready to join the EEC between 1957 and 1961 and was not allowed to join from 1963 to 1970. EFTA required Britain to cooperate closely on trade and economic matters with six other European states in a detailed, regular, multilateral fashion from 1960 to the end of 1972. Though they did not always use the opportunities offered, there is some evidence that British governments learned from their experiences within EFTA: for example, the introduction in 1968 of an import deposit scheme took into account the lessons of the 15 per cent surcharge of 1964. Thus EFTA undertook an important socialization task with the United Kingdom.

Finally, EFTA has offered most of the West European non-EC states a forum for discussion of broad economic questions, including relations with the EC. Because of its diverse membership, EFTA at first had some difficulty in articulating and aggregating its members' interests – especially in relation to the EC – as can be seen in the 1961 London Declaration. However, since 1989 it has responded to the challenge to negotiate as a body with the EC and has shown a willingness to develop new institutions arising from the EEA agreement. Regardless of the fate of this agreement, the EEA demonstrates that the EFTA states have found that they have developed a considerable overlap of economic interests not only among themselves but with their EC neighbours.

References

Archer, C. 1976: Britain and Scandinavia: their relations within EFTA, 1960–1968. *Cooperation and Conflict* XI, 1–23.
Camps, M. 1964: *Britain and the European Community 1955–1963.* London: Oxford University Press.
Corbet, H. and Robertson, D. (eds.) 1970: *Europe's Free Trade Experiment.* Oxford: Oxford University Press.
Court of Justice 1991: Press Summary of 16 December 1991. Luxembourg: Information Office of the Court of Justice of the European Communities.
Curzon, V. 1974: *Essentials of Economic Integration. Lessons of the EFTA Experience.* London: Macmillan.
Curzon Price, V. 1985: EFTA and the European Communities: what future for 'Greater Europe'? *European Yearbook* 33, 109–36.
DTI 1991: Department of Trade and Industry, *Single Market News,* 13.
EFTA Bulletin, August/September 1961, 2/84, 4/85, 1/89, 2/89 3–4/91.
EFTA Secretariat 1967: *Convention Establishing the European Free Trade Association.* Geneva: EFTA.
—— 1992: *EFTA's New Partners.* Geneva: EFTA.
—— 1992a: *The EEA Agreement.* Geneva: EFTA.
Griffiths, R.T. 1992: The importance of fish for the creation of EFTA. *EFTA Bulletin* 1.92, 34–40.
Pedersen, T. 1991: EC–EFTA relations: an historical outline. In H. Wallace (ed.), *The Wider Western Europe* (London: Pinter), 13–27.
Reisch, G. 1989: 1992 a tremendous challenge for EFTA. *EFTA Bulletin* 1.89, 6–9.
Truninger, C. 1976: *Swiss Relations with the United Kingdom in the Formation and Development of EFTA until 1967.* Aberdeen: PhD thesis, Department of Politics.

8

The Nordic Council

Establishment

After the Second World War, many Nordic politicians considered that the time had come to formalize and advance Nordic cooperation. With the independence of Iceland in 1944, the political fragmentation of the two old Nordic kingdoms – those of Denmark and Sweden – seemed to have come to an end. Norway had gained independence from Sweden in 1905, Finland had been taken from Sweden and given to Russia in 1809 but had become fully independent in 1917, whilst Iceland had gained dominion status from Denmark in 1918.

This centrifugal process created the possibility of cooperation between the new states. In 1907 a Nordic Inter-parliamentary Union was established to allow Danish, Norwegian and Swedish parliamentarians to meet together. During the First World War the three Scandinavian states – Denmark, Norway and Sweden – had made a joint declaration of neutrality at Malmö on 18 December 1914. In 1919 the Norden Association, an organization of private citizens, was formed in order to promote Nordic cultural ties. Intergovernmental cooperation after 1918 was desultory especially with the ending of Scandinavian monetary union in 1924, but it picked up again in the 1930s with a number of ministerial meetings. The three Scandinavian states and Finland made a joint declaration of neutrality in 1939 but changed conditions meant that by the end of 1941 Sweden was the only Nordic area not occupied or at war.

Events after the Second World War – Marshall Aid and the 'Easter Crisis' of 1948 (see p. 20) – persuaded the Nordic countries to start discussions about a Nordic Customs Union in 1947 and about a Nordic Defence Union from 1948 to early 1949. Both sets of negotiations failed but talks on uniform citizen laws in 1950 and on improving communications in 1951 were more successful and formed the basis of a passport union.

The former Danish Prime Minister, Hans Hedtoft, urged the 1951 session of the Nordic Inter-parliamentary Union to take up the suggestion of the Norden Association for a Nordic Council. This idea had previously been put forward by the Danish Foreign Minister, Peter Munch, in 1938 and by the Swedish Prime Minister during the war. The formation of the Council of Europe in 1949 provided a model for action. A report was soon transformed into an agreement which by the end of 1952 had been passed by the Danish, Icelandic, Norwegian and Swedish parliaments. Due to Soviet hostility Finland was not a founder member of the Nordic Council despite participation in the original discussions. A change in Soviet attitudes after Stalin's death allowed Finland to join in 1955 with the understanding that Finns would not take part in debates on security and defence issues.

With their strong democratic tradition and the experience of the Norden Association, the Nordic Inter-parliamentary Union and the Council of Europe, all the Nordic countries wanted the Nordic Council to include a consultative parliamentary, as well as a governmental element. After the failure of the defence and customs union negotiations, it was felt wise for the Council to concentrate on questions of less 'high political' moment but which had a more immediate effect for the citizen. The Nordic states, mindful of their national sovereignty, did not want an intricate organization. Each of the Nordic parliaments adopted an identical statute of 15 articles with Article 1 defining the Council as a body for consultation between the parliaments and between Nordic governments 'in matters involving joint action by any or all of these countries'. Cooperation existing at the time of the Council's creation – on a passport union, communications, social security and harmonization of domestic legislation – was to be continued but no programme for further action was laid down. Furthermore it was never considered that all Nordic cooperation would be undertaken through the Nordic Council.

Institutions

Much of the original Statute of the Nordic Council deals with its institutions. Article 2 states that the Council consists of elected members and government representatives, though under Article 3 the latter do not have the right to vote. Denmark, Finland, Norway and Sweden have 20 parliamentary representatives each (16 up to 1971 and 18 from 1971 to 1984) and Iceland has seven (formerly five) giving a total of 87. Each delegation consists of members chosen by their home parliament to reflect the political opinions there and as many ministerial representatives as the government wishes. Since 1970 the Faeroe Islands and Aaland, which both have home rule, have been accorded representation within, respectively, the Danish and Finnish delegations. After Greenland attained home rule in 1979, a similar arrangement was made for it within the Danish delegation but the suggestion that these three autonomous island communities should be granted separate representation in the Council was rejected by a commission in 1982. However, Iceland, Greenland and the Faeroe Islands have formed their own regional West Norden Committee with regular meetings of ministers, parliamentarians and non-governmental organizations and with funding from the Nordic Council.

The Council has six standing committees: Budget, Cultural, Economic, Legal, Social and Environmental. These prepare the work for the biannual Council sessions, the venue for which rotates among the Nordic countries. According to its statute, the task of the Council is to discuss questions of common interest, to make recommendations to governments and to receive information from these governments about action taken on previous resolutions.

At each session a Presidium is formed with one President and four Vice-Presidents elected by the Council to service it until the next session. In practice it is the leader of each national delegation who joins the Presidium with the member from the host nation becoming President. The Presidium meets several times a year, sometimes together with the Nordic Prime Ministers, and carries out political and administrative tasks. It can organize studies, receive reports on the governmental implementation of Council recommendations, encourage activity and act as a central point for pressure groups. It also allocates the Council's expenses among the five states, appoints secretaries, fills vacancies in the Council in consultation with the delegations and generally supervises the Council's activities.

On its establishment, the Council relied on each delegation to provide its own Secretariat with a Secretary-General. The Secretary-General of the host delegation became the Secretary and Chief Clerk of the Council meetings. The Secretariats tended to specialize in particular areas – the Danes on information services, the Swedes on legal questions, for example.

The original pattern of Nordic business followed that of the members' home parliaments. Subsequent changes have streamlined it. Proposals are initiated by either the parliamentary members, by the governmental representatives, by the Presidium or by mixed government-interest-group bodies. After a short first reading, proposals are sent for detailed discussion in committee where ministerial representatives can have their say (though not vote). The proposition, often suitably amended, is then returned to the plenary Council for a second reading. At all stages voting is by a simple majority but if only particular Nordic states are affected by a resolution 'only the delegates from those countries may vote' (Article 70 of the Statute of the Nordic Council). Recommendations are signed by the session President and Secretary and communicated to the member governments (Nordic Council, 1989, 6).

Since its establishment the Nordic Council has developed its institutions and has been joined by the Nordic Council of Ministers. During its early years much of the groundwork for Council resolutions was done by outside bodies such as the Nordic Cultural Commission, the Nordic Economic Cooperation Committee, the Nordic Social Welfare Committee and Nordic Traffic Commission, all of which were intergovernmental. The Council itself only had *ad hoc* committees, established if and when they were needed: it was only in 1964 that five (later six) standing committees were established.

Nordic cooperation through the Council became more institutionalized by the signing of the Helsinki Treaty in March 1962. Previously the Council statutes had been agreed by each Nordic parliament but not by treaty. The 1962 Treaty itemized the major areas of cooperation – something not previously done – and laid down, but did not change, the means of cooperation as being ministerial meetings, special organs of cooperation, meetings between the authorities in each country, and the Nordic Council and its agencies (Article 35, Helsinki Treaty of Cooporation).

The 1962 Treaty was drawn up to provide an international basis for the Nordic Council and Nordic cooperation generally so that it could be safeguarded during Norway and Denmark's negotiations for EEC membership. A major revision of the Treaty was made in 1971, when Norway and Denmark were again in the midst of membership negotiations with the European Community. Another reason for the 1971 changes was the failure of the attempt to build a Nordic Economic Union (Nordek). This idea had once again been taken up in 1968 after which the Nordic countries (excluding Iceland) drafted a treaty for such a Union together with a framework of common institutions more advanced than any previously accepted (Nordisk udredningsserie, 1968, 44–6). The Nordic states disagreed over the relationship of Nordek with the European Communities, which two of them intended to join, and the plans were finally shelved in March 1970. However, some of the institutional innovations were not scrapped.

In 1971, as well as increasing the number of delegates to the Council from 69 to 78, the Nordic countries agreed that the Council's Presidium should appoint a Secretary-General who, together with the five national Secretaries-General, would form the Secretariat of the Nordic Council. This Secretariat was established in Stockholm in 1972 with the former leader of the Norwegian Liberals, Helge Seip, as the first Secretary-General.

Another addition in the 1971 revised Helsinki Treaty was that of the Nordic Council of Ministers. Ministers had attended and spoken at Council sessions, though without voting rights, but the proposed Nordek Treaty had included a ministerial council. The next step was to establish the Nordic Council of Ministers which could, by unanimity and subject to parliamentary approval, make binding decisions in the general area of Nordic cooperation. After some temporary arrangements, a permanent Secretariat of the Council of Ministers was established in Oslo in 1973 with a Secretary-General and a staff working independently of governments (Drzewicki, 1980, 344–53) and in 1986 this Secretariat moved to Copenhagen and merged with the Secretariat for Nordic Cultural Cooperation (see below). By 1974 each Nordic country had agreed to appoint a contact minister responsible for coordinating questions of Nordic cooperation. These ministers (who often have other portfolios) attend the Nordic Council of Ministers, together with ministers more directly responsible at home for the subjects under discussion. This ministerial cooperation is underpinned by a structure of cooperation between officials in the Nordic states. The Council of Ministers has a Committee of Deputies consisting of senior officials charged with aiding cooperation and there are 14 committees consisting of such civil servants. Furthermore, in each Nordic country every government department or agency has a Nordic contact person who deals with his or her opposite member in other Nordic countries (Wendt, 1981a, 660).

During 1971 the Nordic governments signed the Nordic Cultural Treaty which in 1972 established a Secretariat for Nordic Cultural Cooperation, with a Director in charge and situated in Copenhagen. This Secretariat had a similar relationship to the Council of Ministers as the Oslo General Secretariat (Drzewicki, 1980, 345–53). In 1987 the Secretariats for Cultural Cooperation and of the Council of Ministers were merged and placed in Copenhagen.

The Council of Ministers has proved to be an active instrument of Nordic cooperation, overseeing agreements on the Nordic Fund for Technology and Industrial Development, the administration of Joint Nordic assistance projects, the Nordic Investment Bank, part of the Nordic Cultural Fund and a number of communications projects. On all these matters the Council of Ministers has worked in consultation with the Nordic Council and has been aided by cooperation among senior government officials.

In November 1991 the five Nordic Prime Ministers, meeting in Mariehamn, decided on an initiative that could once more give some direction to official Nordic cooperation. They initiated a reassessment of this cooperation, including its organizational form. At a Heads of Government meeting in Bornholm in August 1992, the Prime Ministers discussed a report from their personal representatives and suggested making themselves 'directly responsible for drawing up the political guide-lines for the cooperation between Nordic governments' and introducing a system of a rotating presidency of all meetings of the Nordic governmental representatives (Nordic Council, 1992, 45). A committee examining these proposal will report back to the Prime Ministers.

Achievements

It is difficult to assess the success of the Nordic Council. This is partly because the Council originally had no programme of action which can be used as a checklist of achievement. Even the 1971 revised Helsinki Treaty only suggests five general areas of cooperation – communications and transport, cultural, economic, juridical and social – with protection of the environment being added in 1974. Secondly it is almost impossible to isolate the effect of the Nordic Council's existence from that of the other Nordic institutions such as the Nordic Council of Ministers, Nordic Cultural Secretariat and Nordic Investment Bank, let alone from the work of non-governmental organizations. Indeed, an opinion survey conducted in the region showed that while 83 per cent of respondents had heard of the Nordic Council, a mere 16 per cent spontaneously referred to it as an example of Nordic cooperation while only 20 per cent had a reasonably accurate conception of what kind of organization the Council is (Andersen and Ussing, 1983, 9).

The Council has continued work started before its creation in the area of transport and communications – indeed, the Council took over the work of the Nordic Parliamentary Committee for Freer Communications. The Scandinavian Airline System was created by the merger of the Danish, Norwegian and Swedish airlines in 1951 and the Council has encouraged the integration of the state railway systems and a coordinated road-building programme north of the Arctic Circle. Travel has been eased by the achievement of a full Nordic passport union in 1958 and since then the Council has sought the minimalization of customs formalities between Nordic states. Under the 1972 Treaty of Coordination in the field of Transport and Communication (which included posts and telecommunication), responsibility for collaboration in this area was given to the Nordic Council of Ministers and their Committee of Senior Officials. A 1976 Convention provided a more formal basis for transborder cooperation in tourism, road construction and communications between local authorities. One area where the Nordic ministers have tried to make progress is that of direct satellite broadcasting radio and TV programmes for all the Nordic region (NORDSAT). After eight years of discussion, in November 1985, the governments of Finland, Iceland, Norway and Sweden decided to go ahead with plans for a satellite channel (TELE-X), but these plans were abandoned in 1988 (Nordic Council, 1989, 13). The whole process has been called 'a display of vacillation' (Nordic Council, 1988, 15).

The aim of legal coordination has been to attain 'the highest possible degree of juridical equality between nationals of any Nordic country, resident in a Nordic country other than his own, and the citizens of his country of residence' (Article 2, Helsinki Treaty). The Nordic Council has encouraged equality in commercial, consumer and criminal law, though agreement on family law has proved to be more elusive with the Christian Peoples parties in Denmark and Norway resisting agreement on marriage and abortion legislation.

Cultural cooperation is based on the recognition of the diversity of national cultures in the Nordic region. This has allowed common structures to promote exchanges and to support minority interests. The replacement in 1971 of the Nordic Cultural Commission, established in 1947, by the Nordic Cultural Secretariat was a triumph for the Nordic Council which had also played an important part in the creation of a Nordic Cultural Fund in 1966. The Council provides half the members of a 10-member administrative board for the Fund – the other five are civil servants – though the Fund's secretarial services were provided by the Cultural Secretariat (Wendt, 1981b, 296–7). Almost half of the Fund's money is spent on education and research, two areas in which the Nordic Council has always taken an interest. The Council has encouraged the creation of joint research institutes – such as NORDITA in Denmark which deals with theoretical atomic physics and the Nordic Volcanological Institute in Iceland – has helped the common recognition of education degrees and diplomas and has been particularly active (together with the Cultural Fund) in the area of the Nordic languages. Indeed, in 1978 the Council of Ministers, on a recommendation from the Nordic Council, established a Nordic Language Secretariat in Oslo. However, this and other activities such as the publishing of books on Nordic history, the creation of a Nordic language and information centre in Helsinki, the establishment of the Nordic Council Literary Prize, all pale when compared to the Nordic organizations' failure to deal with the cultural impact of television, typified by the long and unsuccessful attempt to establish NORDSAT.

Economic cooperation has had rather limited success in the Nordic region. Attempts to create a Nordic customs union in the late 1940s and 50s came to an end when the three Scandinavian states joined EFTA in 1960 causing the Swedish Prime Minister, Tage Erlander, to remark that 'the Nordic Market has been gained inside the Outer Seven'. The idea of a Nordic customs union surfaced again in 1968 with the Nordek negotiations but faded after Denmark and Norway commenced membership negotiations with the EEC in 1970. The following year the Nordic Council of Ministers established a Commission for Nordic Economic Cooperation consisting of senior civil servants; in 1973 the Nordic Fund for Technology and Industrial Development came into being; and in 1975 it was agreed to establish a Nordic Investment Bank centred in Helsinki, with the ability to grant loans to projects with a Nordic angle such as the expansion of the area's electricity supply or the improvement of Nordic harbour facilities. Both the Nordic Council and the Nordic Council of Ministers have turned their attention to the dilemma of unemployment, especially among the young, but have been no more successful than other politicians in solving the problem. They have, however, managed to sustain the common Nordic Labour Market, first established in 1954 to allow free movement of labour and expanded in 1966 and 1970. A new agreement signed in 1980 includes Iceland and emphasizes the rights of employees. In preparation for the EC's single European market, the Nordic Council of Ministers started in 1988 to study how the Nordic Region might ensure the best possible conditions for itself in this market, and the Presidium has instigated a further study, but the parliamentarians declined to support a proposal for intensified Nordic cooperation in relation to the EC's internal market (Nordic Council, 1989, 13, 16, 22, 35, 37).

In 1974 the Nordic Council's Committee on Social Affairs was widened to include environmental questions. This topic has taken up an increasing amount of the Council's interest in recent years: one-third of the 1978 recommendations of the Council concerned the environment and a special session on the environmental crisis in Northern Europe was held in November 1988. The action programme resulting from the 1974 Convention on the Protection of the Environment is supervised by the Nordic Senior Officials' Committee for Environmental Questions and is particularly concerned with nature conservation. In the late 1980s Nordic environmental ministers became particularly involved in the problem of the pollution of the seas around the Nordic area (Nordisk Kontakt, 1988, 6) and, more recently, the environmental effects on the Nordic region of emissions from East and Central Europe have concerned both the Nordic Council and the Nordic Council of Ministers (Nordic Council, 1992, 25).

Another more recent area of Nordic cooperation has been that of energy. Electricity distribution has been coordinated through NORDEL since 1963 and a Nordic Liaison Committee for Atomic Energy was set up in 1957 but became most active in the 1970s. Cooperation in oil, gas and coal supplies after the energy crisis of 1973 proved a harsh test. Attempts to get Norwegian and Danish North Sea oil and gas piped ashore to Sweden were passed over in favour of plans to land them in Britain and Germany. A 1978 agreement to allow Norway to buy into Swedish Volvo in exchange for Volvo acquiring North Sea interests collapsed after shareholder opposition within Volvo (Wendt, 1981b, 179). Later cooperation stressed energy and the environment, energy conservation (Nordic Council, 1989, 19) and cooperation with the Baltic Sea states (Nordic Council, 1992, 34).

Perhaps the most enduring cooperation encouraged by the Nordic Council has been in welfare and social policy. The Council had a history of common action on which to build and little encouragement was needed for Nordic ministers to sign the Nordic Social Security Convention of 1955 which gave a Nordic citizen living abroad in the Nordic region equal social welfare rights to the citizen of the country of residence. This codified previous agreements and exceptions were whittled away in 1967 and 1977.

In the area of foreign policy, the Nordic governments have often coordinated their efforts at the UN or in economic institutions such as the OECD, GATT or the World Bank, with one of the five sometimes acting as spokesman for all. Since 1968 the Nordic countries have had an agreement on joint Nordic assistance projects in the Third World, placing these under the direction of the Council of Ministers, with an Executive Council including representatives of the Nordic aid authorities and a project secretary appointed for each project. Joint action only covers a small part of aid given by the Nordic states and does not make it more disinterested (Rudebeck, 1982, 143–76).

An area where there has been minimal cooperation has been that of Nordic security. In deference to Finland's delicate relations with the Soviet Union, the topic was originally excluded from Nordic Council discussions. However, the idea of a Nordic nuclear-weapon-free zone has given the area a security dimension again and this issue was brought up in the Council in 1961 (ironically by Finnish delegates), again in 1981 and at a Nordic Foreign Ministers meeting in that year (Archer, 1984, 37). In the end, it was agreed to establish a committee of Nordic top civil servants to examine the ramifications of the creation of a zone, a task that was overshadowed by the end of the Cold War.

The whole question of the external relations of the Nordic countries was placed firmly on the agenda by the Nordic Prime Ministers meeting regularly after 1991. The pace of integration in the form of the proposed European Union (see pp. 40–1) and the consequences of the Cold War both demanded a Nordic response and allowed it. The Nordic states were no longer strung out along a dangerous dividing line between East and West, and were all – with the exception of Iceland – candidates for European Communities' membership. The Prime Ministers wished to ensure close cooperation 'on issues on the European agenda in the EEA, the EC and other regional fora' (Nordic Council, 1992, 45). It seems that the one area were there may be a common Nordic front is that of the need to maintain regional policies (op.cit., 41). Furthermore the Prime Ministers were willing to contribute to the debates in the Nordic Council by providing information on European and other foreign policy issues, and even wished to extend inter-governmental cooperation on foreign and security policies (op.cit., 45).

The regional initiatives taken by the Nordic states include those in the Baltic and the Barents seas. In the Baltic region, Nordic institutions have been active in sponsoring two parliamentary con-ferences on cooperation in the Baltic Sea area (NORD, 1992), and the ministerial Council of the Baltic Sea States, the first session of which was held in Copenhagen in March 1992. Representatives of the three Baltic states (Estonia, Latvia and Lithuania) have been allowed to observe at Nordic Council meetings, the three states have been encouraged to form their own Baltic Council and Baltic Assembly on the models of the Nordic Council of Ministers and Nordic Council, and have been provided with aid from the Nordic Environment Finance Corporation (a subsidiary of the Nordic Investment Bank) and from the Nordic Council of Ministers. The latter's allocation was of ECU75 million for a three-year period (Tiveus and Emborg, 1992, 53).

The Nordic countries have also institutionalized their coopera-tion with Russia in the Barents Sea region. Norway and Finland have been concerned with the environmental legacy left in nor-thern Russia after the collapse of the Soviet Union (op. cit., 66–71) and perhaps have been anxious to broaden the basis of their cooperation in the region, to make it less one-sided. In January 1993 ministers from the Nordic states, a representative from the EC Commission and the Foreign Minister of Russia signed an agreement in Kirkenes establishing a Barents Euro-Arctic Council (BEAC – see *The World Today*, March 1993, 46–7). Cooperation will take the form of regular meetings of ministers and common action in a number of areas, especially those involving environ-mental matters (Norinform, 1993, 1–2). There will also be a Regional Council of local government representatives from north Norway, Sweden and Finland, from north-west Russia and Sami (Lapp) representatives. Both schemes for cooperation – in the Baltic and the Barents – demonstrate the willingness of the Nor-dic states to build up regional networks in the post-Cold War period that would not have been possible before. They may also represent attempts by the individual Nordic states to present themselves as being central in the Nordic region (Neumann, 1993). Thus the Norwegians (and perhaps the Finns) may hope to take an Arctic dowry with them to the EC, while Denmark and Finland have stressed a Baltic legacy in that context.

Contribution

As it is difficult to assess the contribution of the Nordic Council to the Nordic political system, it is even more hazardous to estimate its value for European cooperation generally. Perhaps it has contributed in two distinct ways.

First, the Nordic Council has served its own part of Europe well. By means of democratic representation, consensus-building and debate, it has guided public activity in the Nordic region to give the citizen even greater rights and wider choices. However, the modest nature of Nordic governmental cooperation should be remembered: one commentator has remarked that 'the Nordic governments are often motivated to cooperate in order to increase their international influence' (Sundelius, 1982, 191). Nordic cooperation also needs resources: perhaps it worked best in the 1950s and 60s when the economies of Northern Europe were still growing and the spirit of social change and welfarism dominated governments in the area. The politics of tax cuts, controlled government spending, market stagnation and the intrusion of world economic forces have not boded well for Nordic cooperation.

Secondly, Nordic cooperation offers an alternative model to that of the European Community. It is comprehensive: cooperation has pervaded non-governmental organizations, civil servants, parliamentarians and government agencies. Yet unlike the EC it does not rely on highly-staffed central institutions, a host of legislation or a power-battle between member states and organizations. Of course, the starting point has been different: the Nordic states can draw upon linguistic, cultural and juridical similarities. The Nordic Council, unlike the EC, has been able to build on the activities of existing non-governmental pressure groups. The Council has no power except that of recommendation – yet it attracts the top politicians of the Nordic area. The Council of Ministers has the power of decision-making yet exercises it sparingly, mindful of parliamentary and public opinion. Nordic civil servants work together through the contact person or on commissions and committees. Indeed Article 38 of the Helsinki Convention encourages such direct contact without going through the foreign ministries, something that civil servants in the EC states are also increasingly attempting. All this activity encourages what Nielsson calls 'parallel national action by the five political systems' of the Nordic region (1978, 295). It has created 'cobweb integration' with a 'fine-meshed net of small interdependencies that is being spun over the Nordic countries' (Andren, 1976, 17) and a system with ' "contacts" which are plentiful, and "commitments" which are few' (Haskel, 1976, 19).

References

Andersen, O. and Ussing, A. 1983: *Working Together?* Uppsala: Nordic Council.

Andren, N. 1967: Nordic integration. *Cooperation and Conflict*, 3–4, 1–25.

Archer, C. 1984: *Deterrence and Reassurance in Northern Europe*. Aberdeen: Centre for Defence Studies, Centrepiece, 6.

Drzewicki, K. 1980: The conception of administrative organs in the Nordic Council of Ministers. *IRAS*, 4, 343–53.

Haskel, B. 1976: *The Scandinavian Option*. Oslo: Universitetsforlaget.

Neumann, I.B. 1993: Regions in International Relations Theory. Oslo: NUPI, Research Report No. 162.

Nielsson, G. 1978: The parallel national action process: Scandinavian experience. In Taylor, P. and Groom, A.J.R. (eds.), *International Organisation: A Conceptual Approach* (London: Frances Pinter), 270–316.

NORD 1992: *Cooperation in the Baltic Sea Area*. Stockholm: The Nordic Council, NORD 1992, 24.

Nordic Council, 1988: *Nordic Council 36th Session in Oslo 7–11 March 1988: Summary and Recommendations*. Stockholm: Secretariat of the Presidium.

—— 1989: *Nordic Council 37th Session in Stockholm 27 February–3 March 1989. Summary and Recommendations*. Stockholm: Secretariat of the Presidium.

—— 1992: *Nordic Council 41st Session, Århus 9–11 November 1992. Summary of Business and Recommendations*. Stockholm: Secretariat of the Presidium.

Nordisk Kontakt 1988. Nordiska initiativ i miljöfragor. Nordisk Kontakt 9–10/88, 8–9.

Nordisk Udredningsserie 1969: *Udvidet nordisk okonomisk samarbejde*. Stockholm: Nordic Council.

Norinform 1993: Oslo: Norwegian Information Service, No. 2, 19 January.

Rudebeck, L. 1982: Nordic policies toward the Third World. In Sundelius, B. (ed.) 1982, 143–76.

Sundelius, B. (ed.) 1982: *Foreign Policy of Northern Europe*. Boulder, Colorado: Westview Press.

Tiveus, Y. and Emborg, K. (eds.) 1992: *Meet Your Nordic Neighbours*. Copenhagen: Nordic Council of Ministers.

Wendt, F. 1981a: Nordic cooperation. In Wisti, F. (ed.), *Nordic Democracy* (Copenhagen: Det Danske Selskab), 653–76.

—— 1981b: *Cooperation in the Nordic Countries*. Stockholm: Almquist & Wicksell.

9

The North Atlantic Treaty Organization

Establishment

The name of this organization is important. Though the North Atlantic Treaty was signed in April 1949, the association organization, especially its military aspects, only started to grow after the outbreak of the Korean War in June 1950. The membership is drawn from both sides of the North Atlantic – Canada and the United States on the North American continent and Belgium, Denmark, the Federal Republic of Germany, France, Greece, Iceland, Italy, Luxembourg, the Netherlands, Norway, Portugal, Spain, Turkey and the United Kingdom in Europe. The main security concerns of the organization are in Europe and it is the major international security institution for Western Europe. However, its special importance lies in the link it has forged between the West European states and the United States.

The signing of the North Atlantic Treaty reflected the need of the West European countries to have American assistance in order to secure themselves against what, in 1948, they considered to be the Soviet threat. The governments of these states thought themselves at risk internally from political and economic collapse and menaced by the presence of the Red Army in Eastern Europe. They did not appear able to defend themselves against this insecurity as they were still suffering from the deprivations of war.

The creation of NATO has been interpreted in a number of different ways. It has been seen as an imposition on the West Europeans of an American view of the world – one which saw the Soviet Union as the natural enemy of capitalism that had to be opposed on all occasions. Another viewpoint saw the signing of the North Atlantic Treaty as the saving of Western Europe from Soviet expansionism by bringing in the USA, with its then monopoly of nuclear weapons, to guarantee the independence of West European members. More current research tends to stress the active role of the West Europeans in inviting the Americans to join them in a collective defence treaty clearly aimed at what had become the dominant resident power in Europe at the end of the Second World War – the Soviet Union. J.L. Gaddis (1985, 71–2) sums up this view: 'If there was ever a time when one nation was invited to extend its influence over another part of the world, then surely the experience of the United States in Europe after World War II came close to it'. A Norwegian government adviser had previously described his country's Atlantic policy as being aimed at trying 'to nail the Anglo-Saxon Great Powers to their responsibilities in Europe' (Riste, 1985, 21). Part of this duty was to act as providers of security for small West Europeans countries that did not have the resources to maintain their own defences at what was considered to be the appropriate level.

The provenance of the North Atlantic Treaty can be found in the Brussels Treaty of 1948 (see Chapter 10) and in its predecessor, the Dunkirk Treaty of 1947. Whilst these were ostensibly directed against the military renaissance of Germany, it became increasingly apparent that Britain, France and the Low Countries regarded the Soviet Union as the main threat to their security. These pacts offered both a model for any Atlantic treaty and also demonstrated West Europeans willingness to combine together for their own security. However, the United States' Administration was not about to become involved uninvited in what George Washington had described as 'entangling alliances'. Events throughout 1947 and early 1948 had edged the Americans towards further involvement in Europe. On 12 March 1947 the Truman Doctrine was proclaimed and the United States promised military assistance to Greece and Turkey after the United Kingdom had declared its inability to devote further resources to those countries' security. On 5 June 1947 Secretary of State Marshall had unveiled his plan for economic aid for the development of Europe. It was the Soviet and East European withdrawal from the subsequent Paris Conference on European Reconstruction 'that reconciled American officials once and for all to the inevitability of a divided Europe' (Gaddis, 1985, 69). Throughout 1947 and early 1948 this division continued, with Communists taking over the running of East European governments and Communist parties being expelled from governments in Western Europe.

Events in early 1948 galvanized the West European governments into action. After Soviet pressure on Finland and the Communist takeover in Czechoslovakia, France, the United Kingdom
and the Benelux states signed the Brussels Treaty (see Chapter
10). This provided an effective response to what Theodore
Achilles has identified as the US stance towards the West Europeans then: 'Show us what you are prepared to do for yourselves
and each other and then we will see what we can do' (1985, 31).
Arthur Vandenberg, the Republican Chairman of the Senate
Foreign Relations Committee, steered a resolution through Congress on 11 June 1948, by which the Senate advised President
Truman, who was a Democrat by party, to develop regional and
other collective arrangements for self-defence in line with the
United Nations' Charter, to associate the United States with such
agreements and to make clear America's determination to exercise its right of individual or collective self-defence 'should any
armed attack occur affecting its national security' (NATO, 1970,
237). This bipartisan approach helped to clear the domestic
political ground in the United States ready for an acceptance of
a collective defence arrangement. However, there were deep differences in the US Administration as to the format and extent of
any such commitment (Petersen, 1982, 100–10). In the month
following the Vandenberg Resolution and in the shadow of the
Berlin Blockade, the Washington Exploratory Talks (WET) on the
nature of any possible treaty began between the United States,
Canada and invited West European countries. From that time until
April 1949, the details of the North Atlantic Treaty were refined
and the West European states divided themselves into the Alliance
sheep that signed the final agreement and the neutral goats that
remained outside. The core signatory countries of the Treaty in
April 1949 were the Brussels Treaty powers – France, the United
Kingdom, Belgium, Netherlands and Luxembourg – and the United
States and Canada in North America. During the WET, membership of certain countries was mooted but in the end only five
others became original signatories of the North Atlantic
Treaty – Denmark, Iceland, Italy, Norway and Portugal. Three of
these provided important island stepping-stones between North
America and Western Europe – Iceland, Denmark (in the form of
Greenland) and Portugal (the Azores) – whilst Norway and Italy
had strategic coastlines bordering, respectively, the North Atlantic and the Mediterranean, as well as having democratic governments insistent on joining the Atlantic Alliance.

The Treaty is perhaps stronger than might have been expected from the rather vague Vandenberg Resolution but not as trenchant as the Brussels Treaty. Its preamble states that the Parties are determined 'to safeguard the freedom, common heritage and civilization of their peoples, founded on the principles of democracy, individual liberty and the rule of law'. The signatories are also 'resolved to unite their efforts for collective defence and for the preservation of peace and security'. Article 1 affirms that the Treaty is consistent with the United Nations Charter and Article 2 promises the development of free institutions and economic cooperation. In Article 3 the Parties determine – 'separately and jointly, by means of continuous and effective self-help and mutual aid' – to 'maintain and develop their individual and collective capacity to resist armed attack'. This represents a compromise between the expectation of US materiel assistance to the Europeans ('mutual aid') and the American hope that the West Europeans would reciprocate by organizing their own defences more efficiently ('effective self-help'). Article 4 allows for consultation between the member governments when 'in the opinion of any of them, the territorial integrity, political independence or security of any' is threatened. This ensures that even the smallest of the members can institute the consultative process.

Article 5 is the touchstone of the North Atlantic Treaty. It is agreed by the Parties that

> an armed attack against one or more of them in Europe or North America shall be considered an attack against them all and . . . if such an armed attack occurs, each of them . . . will assist the Party or Parties so attacked by taking forthwith, individually and in concert with the other Parties, such action as it deems necessary, including the use of armed force, to restore and maintain the security of the North Atlantic area.

This is to be done in the context of Article 51 of the UN Charter which allows individual and collective self-defence. Again, this article is a compromise between the Americans and the Europeans. The West European negotiators would have preferred an exact copy of Article 4 of the Brussels Treaty by which the five Parties guarantee 'all military and other aid' to any country under attack. However, the US Administration, mindful that Congressional consent had to precede a declaration of war, could only stretch to the words cited above. The article does contain the Musketeers' Oath principle – 'All for one and one for all' – on which successful collective defence depends; it does introduce a note of urgency by requiring action 'forthwith'; and it specifically mentions armed force as a response option. As such, it represents about the best deal that the West Europeans could have wrung from the Americans in 1949.

Article 6 limits the scope of the 'armed attack' mentioned in Article 5 – to which Treaty members should respond – to such an attack 'on the territory of any of the Parties in Europe or North America' and also on the occupation forces of any Party in Europe, on their islands in the North Atlantic north of the Tropic of Cancer or 'on the vessels or aircraft in this area of any of the Parties'. This section was modified in 1951 when Greece and Turkey signed the Treaty, to include the territory of Turkey (much of which is outside Europe) and to include the Parties' forces, vessels or aircraft on or over the Mediterranean. Originally Article 6 also referred to the Algerian Departments of France but in July 1962 this became inoperative after Algerian independence. A distinguished commentator has pointed out that Article 6 merely defines the area of a *casus belli* for the NATO countries and that it was not the intention of its drafters that this should prevent 'collective planning, manoeuvres or operations' south of the Tropic of Cancer in the Atlantic or in other areas of importance to NATO members (Achilles, 1985, 37).

Article 10 opens up the possibility of Treaty signature by any other European state that can further the principles of the Treaty and can contribute to the security of the North Atlantic area. Greece and Turkey have been members since 1952, the Federal Republic of Germany joined in 1955 and Spain acceded in 1982.

Article 12 allows for the review of the Treaty after 10 years, should this be requested by any of the Parties, and Article 13 secures the right – after a period of 20 years – of any state that gives one year's notice, to withdraw from the Treaty.

Institutions

It was mentioned at the start of this chapter that the organizational side of the North Atlantic Treaty took some time to develop. Nowadays, this organization – NATO – is fully fledged both on the civilian and military side. Article 9 of the North Atlantic Treaty established a Council of representatives of all the member states which was to consider 'matters concerning the implementation of this Treaty'. The Council was charged with immediately establishing a defence committee to recommend measures for the implementation of Articles 3 and 4, and was allowed to set up 'such subsidiary bodies as may be necessary'.

The Council, meeting for the first time and at Foreign Ministers level in September 1949, decided to meet annually and also established a Defence Committee which would draw up coordinated defence plans for the North Atlantic region; a Military Committee consisting of the Chiefs of Staff of member states, which was to advise the Council on military matters; a Standing Group responsible for strategic guidance and consisting of the French, United Kingdom and United States representatives; and five Regional Planning Groups to develop defence plans for their own areas. By May 1950 the Council had decided to establish meetings of Deputies to the Foreign Ministers in order to discuss business on a more regular basis.

In the period between the outbreak of the Korean War in June 1950 and the accession of West Germany to the North Atlantic Treaty in 1955, the Organization underwent a number of important changes. The military structure was reorganized with the aim of creating 'an integrated European force under centralized command' (NATO, 1984, 28). In December 1950 General Eisenhower was appointed as Supreme Allied Commander for Europe (SACEUR) with the Supreme Headquarters Allied Powers Europe (SHAPE) being established near Paris in April 1951; and in 1952 two new commands were established: Atlantic Command at Norfolk, Virginia, headed by a United States admiral as Supreme Allied Commander Atlantic (SACLANT), and Channel Command under a British admiral as Allied Commander-in-Chief Channel (CINCHAN). The civilian institutions were also rationalized and new ones created. The Defence Committee and the Defence and Economic Committee were abolished leaving the North Atlantic Council as the one ministerial body. The Council Deputies took on further tasks and at the Lisbon Ministerial Meeting of 1952, it was decided to create a permanent body – the North Atlantic Council – able to make binding decisions by common consent and meeting at various levels – most often that of Permanent Representatives (taking over from the Council Deputies), sometimes that of Foreign and Defence Ministers and, rarely, that of Heads of Government or State. The Council had its headquarters in Paris with the Permanent Representatives being supported by national delegations of advisers and experts. It was serviced by an International Staff headed by the Secretary-General of NATO, an international civil servant appointed by the member governments by consensus. On 12 March 1952, Lord Ismay of the United Kingdom was created Secretary-General.

From 1956 to 1966 there were few institutional innovations within NATO. Member governments were required after the December 1956 Ministerial Council Meeting 'to develop effective political consultation and cooperation' and the Secretary-General was empowered to initiate peaceful settlement procedures in disputes involving member governments (NATO, n.d., 101–4). Other important developments were the creation in December 1957 of a Science Committee of the Council, consisting of outstanding scientists, the appointment of a Science Adviser to the Secretary-General and the establishment in 1963 of a Defence Planning Committee with the task of coordinating and making decisions on matters concerning NATO's integrated military structure.

The North Atlantic Treaty Organization underwent a major upheaval in 1966 when President de Gaulle of France decided to withdraw from the NATO integrated military command structure and requested the transfer from France of most Allied units and installations, including NATO Headquarters and SHAPE. These were relocated in Belgium and the NATO Defense College was placed in Rome. However, the refusal of France to participate in Alliance discussions about military policy offered a challenge to NATO's institutions: the French decided to maintain only a liaison mission with the Military Committee and with the major NATO Commands. France did not participate in the discussions of the Defence Planning Committee of the Council. The Standing Group was abolished and in 1966 the Defence Planning Committee decided to establish two permanent bodies for nuclear planning – the Nuclear Defence Affairs Committee, a policy body open to all NATO members, and a subordinate body, originally of seven members, to handle detailed work, the Nuclear Planning Group. France has not participated in either of these institutions. Furthermore, when, in 1968, the European members of NATO decided to coordinate their defence effort in the Alliance by the creation of the informal group called the Eurogroup, the French again absented themselves.

An institution often associated with, though not part of, NATO is the North Atlantic Assembly, founded in 1955 and originally known as the NATO Parliamentarians Conference. The Assembly consists of 184 parliamentarians, and as many alternates, appointed by the parliaments of the 16 NATO countries, using nationally determined procedures. To this have been added associate delegates from the East and Central European states (Lunn, 1992, 13). The delegations tend to be multi-party, reflecting the political complexion of national legislatures, but serving government members or ministers cannot be delegates to the Assembly (Charman and Williams, 1981, 195). The Assembly is served by a modest Secretariat based in Brussels and it has five committees – Economics, Cultural Affairs and Information, Military, Political, Scientific and Technical – which meet twice a year, analyse specific subjects through sub-committees and report to the plenary sessions of the Assembly held once or twice a year. The role of the Assembly has been described by one of its mentors, Sir Geoffrey de Freitas, as 'that of a critical observer of NATO policies and activities and as a forum for trans-atlantic exchanges at parliamentary level' (Charman and Williams, 1981, Foreword).

The existing structure of NATO is headed by the North Atlantic Council composed of the Foreign Ministers of the 16 member countries or their Permanent Representatives. The Foreign Ministers normally meet biannually. At the latter level it meets at least weekly, more often if circumstances demand. It can meet at two hours notice. The Permanent Representatives raise and discuss political matters of interest to the Alliance, without the restrictions of official records or public debate. Other Council work includes discussion of reports from Council committees. The Council does not take votes; decisions are arrived at by consensus, though members may reserve their position on issues where their national policy differs from that agreed by the other NATO members. Throughout the 1980s, Denmark, Greece and Spain did this on a number of occasions. The Defence Planning Committee consists of those members participating in the NATO integrated defence structure and it meets biannually in sessions attended by the Defence Minister and the rest of the time at Permanent Representative level. The Council has a number of major committees, the most noticeable being the Political Committee, the Economics Committee, the Defence Review Committee, the Conference of National Armaments Directors, the Science Committee, the NATO Air Defence Committee and the Committee on the Challenges of Modern Society. The Council has also created a number of special committees and agencies, such as the Committee for European Airspace Coordination and the various production and logistics organizations.

The Secretary-General chairs the North Atlantic Council and some of its most important committees such as the Defence Planning Committee. He also heads an international staff with divisions covering the main areas of NATO interest – for example, force planning, political affairs, logistics, science programme development. The tradition of appointing a distinguished political figure as Secretary-General has, over the years, increased the status of that post.

The Military Committee is the highest military authority in NATO and consists of the Chiefs-of-Staff or their permanent Military Representatives. France and Spain, not being part of the integrated military structure, are represented only by a military mission. In 1967 an International Military Staff was created at NATO Headquarters to be the executive agent of the Military Committee. It is headed by a Director of three-star rank and has a staff of some 400 people. The Military Committee's main task is to recommend measures for the common defence of the NATO area, and subordinate to it were three Commanders – the Supreme Allied Commander Europe, the Supreme Allied Commander Atlantic, the Commander-in-Chief Channel – as well as the Canada–United States Regional Planning Group. The peacetime missions of these Commanders was to establish unified Allied defence plans, to make recommendations to the Military Committee, and to organize, train and equip forces assigned or earmarked to their command. In wartime, they would have controlled military operations in their area of authority. The Commanders had a number of subordinate commands directly responsible to them; for example, SACEUR had ones in Northern Europe, Central Europe and Southern Europe, as well as those for United Kingdom Air Forces and for the Allied Command Europe Mobile Force, under him.

After the Rome North Atlantic Council of December 1991, NATO's institutional structure was changed to take account of what was regarded as the end of the Cold War. This led to the adoption of the Alliance's New Strategic Concept (see, p. 233), which in itself necessitated changes in the NATO command structure. The 'linear defensive posture in the central region' was no longer required and the overall size of Allied forces was to be reduced (*NATO Review*, December 1991, 30). As a result of NATO's reorientation, the three major commands mentioned above were to be cut to two, with the Commander-in-Chief Channel disappearing. At the next layer down, Allied Command Europe would be divided into Major Subordinate Commands, with one in Southern Europe, Allied Forces Central Europe extending north to include Denmark, and Allied Forces North-West Europe taking in Great Britain, Norway, and the North and Baltic seas.

An institutional innovation that arose from the Rome North Atlantic Council was the creation of the North Atlantic Cooperation Council with its membership drawn from NATO states and the former members of the Warsaw Treaty Organization, including the successor republics of the Soviet Union. This was formed on the eve of the collapse of the USSR, partly as a response to that event and partly as a reply to requests by East and Central European states – such as the CSFR and Hungary – to join NATO. There was a reluctance to extend NATO membership and its collective defence arrangements beyond its existing members, but the need was seen to bring the ex-WTO countries into a close strategic relationship with NATO (see p. 222 below). A High Level Working Group was established by the NACC states to deal with questions of CFE ratification and implementation.

In summary, the North Atlantic Treaty Organization has a fairly stable structure developed over a period of more than four decades and of massive political change. The system has had to be flexible enough to accommodate the sensitivities of 16 nations in what is after all the core area of a state's activity – defence; but NATO is also a useful arena for common action and the institutions reflect the wide scale of defence cooperation undertaken by most of the Alliance members. Some parts of the organization, such as the Secretary-General and his staff, are international actors in their own right, though there are strong restraints of prudence on their freedom of action.

Achievements

NATO can be evaluated in many ways. Most simply, it can be judged as a means by which its member states can promote their collective defence and preserve their peace and security more easily. That it has outlived the WTO and the Soviet system can be seen as a triumph for NATO, but in truth it is more an indication of the failure of Communism in the USSR and Eastern Europe. Whilst the North Atlantic area has been a comparatively peaceful zone since the formation of NATO and certainly avoided the sort of incursion by Soviet troops feared by some in 1948, there is no way of estimating to what extent this has been because of the existence of the organization. However, an examination of the political consultation and military activity undertaken through NATO may elucidate its utility for its members.

Political consultation within NATO has covered four broad interrelated areas: transatlantic relations, East–West relations, problems between individual NATO states and out-of-area questions.

The *transatlantic relationship* has been at the very core of NATO's existence. Together with the OEEC and OECD (see Chapter 3), NATO has provided one of the major institutional mainstays for governmental cooperation between the two North American countries and most of the Western European states. Without this organization, there may still have been a United States military presence in Europe, residually as an occupying power in Germany and possibly through bilateral agreements with the United Kingdom and countries with islands in the North Atlantic – Iceland, Denmark, Norway and Portugal. However, North American–West European relations would not have been carried out on such a regular, familiar and continuous basis without the existence of what one former US Ambassador to NATO has called the 'transatlantic bargain' between the United States and the Europeans in the form of NATO (Cleveland, 1970, 5).

The American–West European relationship spans a wide range of topics and, whilst NATO has primarily concerned itself with defence questions, economic problems – especially the question of the resources that the United States is willing to commit to the defence of Europe – have been a constant source of discussion, if not dispute.

From the beginning, it was the intention of American politicians that the West Europeans would eventually be able to provide for their own defence. Successive Administrations in Washington, DC have encouraged schemes for European unity to this end. In particular, Secretary of State John Dulles threatened an 'agonizing reappraisal of basic American policy' towards Europe should the West Europeans fail to establish the European Defence Community (EDC) in 1954 (Fursdon, 1980, 231). While this did not have the desired effect of persuading the French National Assembly to accept the EDC, subsequent British proposals for a Western European Union were eventually welcomed by the US Administration as a demonstration of European resolve. This British commitment followed, after all, a period during which the perception of a military threat to Western Europe from the Soviet bloc had been heightened by the Korean War and in which the USA had committed more money and troops to the defence of Europe. Following 'the Great Debate' on this subject in early 1951, the US Senate had decided to back President Truman on the issue, albeit with the expectation in many quarters that direct participation in West European defence at that time would eventually lead to a greater effort by the European Allies and a gradual diminution of American effort (Williams, 1984, 13–14).

During the early 1950s the United States was also moving nuclear weapons into Europe, ostensibly as a means to bolster the defence of the West against what was seen as an overwhelming Soviet conventional superiority. This move was to complement the 'shield' of conventional forces, which the Americans hoped the West Europeans would supply, with the 'sword' of the United States Strategic Air Command's nuclear strike force (Osgood, 1962, 67–72). It was also true that 'the turn to nuclear weapons averted serious allied quarrels over burden-sharing and over the reconstruction of conventional capability for defense of Europe' (Etzold, 1985, 311). However, it created a political problem that has continued to affect the Alliance – that of the influence that the West Europeans have on American nuclear policy in Europe. This question is inextricably tied to that of burden-sharing within NATO, insofar as the greater the European contribution of conventional forces, the weaker would be the demand for nuclear weapons, and the more the West Europeans gave to the Alliance, the more their voice would be heeded on nuclear matters. By the end of 1953, the US Administration, still hoping for the formation of the EDC, decided to share with its allies information about nuclear weapons, thereby making NATO planning of nuclear strategy a possibility. However, circumstances in the mid-1950s worked against a logical and planned deployment of nuclear weapons, on a NATO-wide basis and ideas for using them had not been fully thought through (Etzold, 1985, 298).

US–West European relations in the late 1950s and early 60s underwent a number of trials. The Suez Crisis of 1956 produced a transatlantic rift when the Eisenhower Administration in the United States not only refused to back the British and French expedition against the Egypt of Colonel Nasser, but hastened British withdrawal from occupation of the Suez zone by placing economic pressure on Britain. While this disagreement reminded the Europeans that they could not rely on American support in all their escapades, it did not affect the general United States commitment to the defence of Europe. What caused concern was the growing arsenal of American nuclear weapons stored in Europe under exclusive American control. From about 1958 to 1964 the problem of 'nuclear sharing' was one that both sides tried to solve but without much success. On one side, the United States administrations wanted to keep control of nuclear weapons – wherever they might be – as they had paid for them and because they feared that secret elements, if shared with certain allies, might leak to the Soviets. They were also aware of the hostile reaction of the Soviet Union to any idea that the Federal Republic of Germany might gain control of any nuclear weapons (a notion that other West European states themselves rejected in the Paris Agreements of October 1954 – see Chapter 10). On the other side, the West Europeans were concerned by the implications of total American control of nuclear systems on their soil. The doctrine of Massive Retaliation demanded that any attack on the West by the Soviet Union would be met by a full-scale atomic riposte from the United States. Some Europeans asked whether the Americans would make such a self-destructive reply to, say, a Russian incursion on an uninhabited Norwegian island and, thus, whether the doctrine would not be more credible if Europeans themselves had an input into any nuclear decision. Others wanted a European finger not so much on the nuclear trigger as on the atomic safety-catch: their fear was that the Americans might be too willing to incinerate the European battlefield and thought that West European governments should have a say on such vital matters.

There were two main responses to this quandary. The British and French governments sought a way out by developing their own nuclear weapons which, in the last resort, might be used separately from US systems. Also, American administrations tried to invent forms of 'nuclear sharing' acceptable to their European partners. One idea was that of the Multilateral Force (MLF) which surfaced in 1964. The original intention was to have a mixed-man crew of American and Allied military personnel for one of the strategic nuclear systems such as the Polaris submarines that the Americans were building for their own – and the British – seaborne deterrent, but with the warheads still being controlled by the United States. After the Polaris idea was dropped, a proposal was advanced for a fleet of mixed-manned surface ships carrying nuclear weapons. By September 1965 the idea was scrapped. Apart from the practical details of running a ship manned by sailors from six or seven navies, the MLF proposal was rightly seen as a political palliative to soothe European concerns about not being consulted on nuclear matters. Even if the plan had been adopted, there would still have been only a minimal European voice on the use of America's other strategic and tactical weapons in and around Europe (Cleveland, 1970, 48–53).

A more successful method of bridging the transatlantic gap on 'nuclear sharing' was found in the creation of the Nuclear Planning Group (NPG) in 1966. Originally a select band of the United States, Britain, the Federal Republic, Italy and one other state, its creation got over the hurdle of discussion nuclear topics within NATO but without France, and also allowed the United States to take other NATO countries into its confidence about nuclear targeting and nuclear affairs generally. It was by using the NPG that NATO countries introduced the new Alliance doctrine of 'flexible response' in 1969.

This is not to say that the institutional innovation of the NPG solved transatlantic disagreements. The problem of burden-sharing was taken up from 1966 to 1970 by Mike Mansfield in the US Senate where he requested that the Europeans made 'military contributions commensurate with their new-found economic strength' and that the United States should substantially cut its forces in Europe (Williams, 1984, 14). This pressure, together with the 'Nixon Doctrine' (whereby the United States would ask its allies throughout the world to take on a greater share of their own defence) worried the European members of NATO. During the early 1970s, the United States continued its agony over the war in Vietnam, an episode which ended with the withdrawal of US support from its former ally in South Vietnam; the dollar declined as a world currency and Western economies seemed transfixed by the spectre of the wealth and power of the Middle Eastern oil producers; the USA and the USSR were pursuing detente with an almost indecent haste and the White House in Washington was immersed in the Watergate scandal. It was ironic that in 1973, declared by the Nixon Administration to be the Year of Europe, the Europeans denied landing rights to US military flights to the Middle East during the Yom Kippur War between Israel and its Arab neighbours. Especially after the United Kingdom joined the European Community in 1973, the European allies in NATO started to develop their own foreign policy initiatives (see Chapter 6), some of which had international security implications and some of which were not always in tune with mainstream American thinking, the Middle East providing an example in both cases.

Since the mid-1970s, the West Europeans and the Americans have continued their ambiguous relationship. On the whole the Europeans have recoiled from the intensity of America's relationship with the Soviet bloc, whether this was the close Superpower to Superpower relations of the Nixon–Ford presidencies or President Carter's moral condemnation of the Soviet human rights record or the doctrinaire approach of President Reagan. A change at the end of the 1980s led West Germany to be more reactive to Soviet proposals, while the United States, under the presidency of George Bush, became more reflective.

A good example of the problems that can arise within the Alliance because of different perspectives on the Soviet Union was that of the Urengoy Pipeline dispute in 1982. Aware of their over-dependence on Middle Eastern oil and gas, seven European countries contracted with the Soviet Union to buy some of their gas which would come to the West through extensions of the Soviets' Urengoy Pipeline project made possible by the export of Western pipeline technology. After the imposition of martial law in Poland in December 1981, the Reagan Administration decided to ban all US-made parts of the pipeline and, six months later, this prohibition was extended to include American subsidiaries and licensees abroad, which meant many of the European firms involved. This action sparked a heated transatlantic debate in which the Europeans complained about American incursions on their right to trade, accused the Reagan Administration of endangering what was left of detente in Europe and pointed to American grain trade with the Soviets as a measure of double standards. The United States riposte was to question the wisdom of the European allies depending too much on Soviet gas, to emphasize that the pipeline technology could also be used for military purposes and to accuse the Europeans, in making payments to the Russians, of providing the Soviets with resources to spend on their armed forces. In the end, the dispute between the United States and its allies was settled by diplomacy and compromise but not after more damage had been done to the Alliance than to the Soviets (Woods, 1983, 1–3; Treverton, 1985a, 65). The dispute reflected badly on NATO as the Organization had not been used to consult on a matter over which the United States clearly felt very strongly; it demonstrated conflicting views of security

issues by the US and the West European members; and it demon-
strated a wide difference between the Reagan Administration and
West European governments about relations with the Soviet
Union.

While the Urengoy Pipeline issue showed maladroit American
handling of their allies, two other subjects have shown some of the
difficulties the United States must face when dealing with the
West Europeans. In 1977 President Carter announced his intention to place US Enhanced Radiation Weapons (ERWs or 'neutron
bombs') in Western Europe, should West European political
leaders request such a move. The European politicians found
themselves faced with an intense domestic campaign against
ERWs – which looked far too usable to many of their citizens – and
they refused to grant the request. Learning from this failure in
consultation and loss of nerve, the Alliance members took a new
approach to their next major decision – that of introducing US
land-based cruise and Pershing missiles into five NATO-Europe
countries. A long process of consultation was undergone in which
the United States was seen to be responding to a European need
to feel that the American nuclear umbrella over their countries
still existed. The decision taken at a special meeting of NATO
foreign and defence ministers in December 1979 was unanimous.
However, the following five years saw difficulties in deploying the
missiles, with parties that had supported the 1979 package in
government condemning it when in opposition and some governments distancing themselves from the decision completely. The
United States was thus given the impression that its allies were
fractious, ungrateful and untrustworthy. This spurred Senators
Nunn and Cohen to call on the Europeans to do more for their own
defence, otherwise cuts could be expected in the US contribution
to Europe (Eberle *et al.*, 1984, 549). European members of NATO
responded by publicizing their existing effort rather than substantially increasing it (Eurogroup, 1985; Van Eekelen, 1988, 7–11).

This is not to say that all transatlantic relations within NATO
have descended into an abyss of misunderstanding. In 1979 NATO
created a group of foreign office experts to examine arms control
opportunities which, after the December 1979 'Dual Track' decision, became the Special Consultative Group through which the
United States kept its European allies appraised of its Geneva
negotiations with the Soviet Union on the question of Intermediate-
range Nuclear Forces in Europe. However, this did not prevent
President Reagan from going over the heads of the network of

NATO diplomats and politicians in offering his own deal on INF (and on strategic weapons) to Mr Gorbachev in their Reykjavik Summit in October 1986. Despite later US efforts, there was still an air of ambiguity to US–European relations, summed up by Professor Ernst van der Beugel (1986, 18) thus: 'Europeans have asked for strong American leadership until they get it at which point they complain that they are being pushed around'.

As the Cold War began to fade toward the end of the 1980s, the sheer pace opened up some divisions between the United States and some of its European allies, for example over whether a new generation of short-range nuclear weapons should be placed in Europe. However, once it was clear – by early 1989 – that relations with the Soviet bloc were undergoing a qualitative change, the USA and the NATO European states worked closedly together in such arms control forums as the Conventional Forces in Europe (CFE) and the 35-nation Confidence– and Security-Building Measures (CSBM) talks. They cooperated in responding to the fall of Communist governments in Eastern Europe and, in the summer of 1990, at NATO's London Summit, were able to put together the London Declaration that, in effect, ended the Cold War and presaged a change in NATO's doctrine. This document looked forward to a continued American presence in Europe which was seen as a means of assuring a continuing US commitment to European security and defence. The intention of reducing short-range nuclear forces and abolishing nuclear artillery shells in Europe was expressed (*Survival*, 1990, 469–72), thereby reducing and removing two sources of conflict between allies.

In June 1991, the Copenhagen meeting of the North Atlantic Council set out NATO's four core functions after the end of the Cold War: to provide a foundation for European stability; to act as a forum for transatlantic consultations; to deter and defend against attacks on member states; and to preserve the strategic balance in Europe (*NATO Review*, June 1991, 30). Even at that stage it seemed clear that a United States presence in Europe could facilitate all these aims. However, with the collapse of the Soviet Union at the end of 1991, strategic considerations changed even further. Basic questions about the need for NATO had to be asked, and – even if the continuation of NATO was considered desirable – the old problems recurred about what overall effort was needed and how much the USA and European members should contribute. By early 1992, the United States had announced large defence cuts as a response to the changing world situation and, not least, to domestic political and budgetary pressures. US troop strength in Europe had already declined from 314,000 in September 1990 to 227,000 in February 1992, with the figure dropping to some 200,000 by the end of 1992. At that stage the plan was to decrease the number to 150,000 by 1995 (United States Information Service, 1992, 4). By the time the Clinton Administration had come into office in January 1993, it was clear that this figure would be 100,000.

Despite this decline in US presence, the US still wishes to maintain its interest in European security. It has viewed the attempts of the EC countries to develop a security dimension to their cooperation with some trepidation. In February 1991 the Bush Administration sent the EC members of NATO a memorandum in which it warned of the dangers of creating a European defence caucus (Mortimer, 1992, 58). A draft Pentagon document, made public in March 1992, sought to prevent the emergence of 'Europe-only security arrangements which would undermine NATO' (cited in Menon et al., 1992, 116–17). This seems to give some credence to Treverton's view (1992, 124) that

> Reshaping NATO to make it fit Europe's present security problems would not restore the old state of affairs for which Americans can easily be nostalgic: Americans liked NATO because they ran it. They will not run it the same way in the future; little by little . . . Europe's security order will be Europeanized.

As can be seen, it has often been in the area of *East–West relations* that Alliance solidarity has been tested. It has not just been Western governments that have disagreed in their perception and handling of the Soviet bloc; quite often there has not been a consensus on these issues within administrations (Petersen, 1982, 93–114). At the time of the formation of NATO, there was general agreement within Western governments as to the existence of a Soviet menace, though there may have been some discussion about the best way to confront it. The presence of the Red Army in Eastern Europe and Soviet actions in Czechoslovakia and Berlin seemed to present the West with a military as well as an ideological challenge. Any inclination by politicians in, say, the United Kingdom or Norway to give their former wartime ally, the Soviet Union, the benefit of the doubt was soon swept away by the ineptitude of Moscow. As Michael Howard commented, 'One of the most remarkable aspects of this whole period is the astonishing stupidity of Soviet policy'. Other Western leaders could not fail to agree with Attlee's sentiment that the Russians were 'behaving in a perfectly bloody fashion all over Europe' (Howard, 1985, 14–15).

The explosion of the first Soviet nuclear device in September 1949 and the outbreak of the Korean War in June 1950 confirmed NATO governments in their belief in 'the Soviet threat' and there was little effort made to treat with Stalin. After his death in March 1953, it seemed that the new leadership in Moscow was more prepared to coexist with the West. An armistice was signed in Korea and, in 1955, both Soviet and Western governments agreed to end their occupation of Austria, leaving it a neutral, democratic state. Even after the entry of West Germany into NATO and the formation of the Warsaw Treaty Organization in May 1955, the Soviet Union and the three major Western powers agreed to meet at a Four-Power Conference in Geneva. While little came out of this meeting, it offered NATO the opportunity to discuss East-West relations and for the 'Big Three' - the United States, Britain and France - to consult with the other members. The breakdown of the Geneva talks, the Soviet's suppression of the Hungarian Uprising in November 1956 and the constant pressure placed on West Berlin - set in the Communist sea of East Berlin and East Germany - by the Soviet Union, confirmed NATO governments in their old suspicions about Moscow, and this was reflected in the communiques of NATO Ministerial meetings well into the early 1960s.

After the trauma of the Cuban Missile Crisis in November 1962 when it became clear that both Superpowers could threaten the world with nuclear destruction, NATO countries felt that relations with the Soviet Union should be placed on a more stable basis. At the North Atlantic Council of December 1963, it was decided to seek 'agreement on limited measures which would help to reduce tension' and would achieve 'a genuine and fundamental improvement in East-West relations' (NATO, n.d., 153-4). In 1966 the Council commissioned a study of East-West relations from their Permanent Representatives and at their December meeting that year, the Alliance Ministers agreed 'to undertake a broad analysis of international developments since the signing of the North Atlantic Treaty in 1949' (NATO, n.d., 179). This became known as the 'Harmel Exercise' after the Belgian Foreign Minister who had proposed the study. In the Report to the December 1967 Council meeting entitled 'The Future Tasks of the Alliance' it was stated that the Alliance had two main functions, the first of which - to maintain its military strength and political solidarity to deter aggression - had been successfully fulfilled. The second function was to search for a more stable relationship with the

Soviets so that underlying political issues could be solved. In the view of the Report, 'Military security and a policy of detente are not contradictory but complementary' and collective defence was seen as a necessary condition for policies aimed at relaxing international tension. It was recognized that a number of NATO countries had started to improve relations with the Soviet bloc on a bilateral basis and NATO offered itself as 'an effective forum and clearing house' for information and views on these efforts. The German question, arms control and possible balanced force reductions in Europe were seen as areas of negotiation with the Soviet bloc, in which a concentrated Allied effort might be made with NATO as a 'clearing house' (NATO, n.d., 199–200).

Meeting in Reykjavik in June 1968, NATO Ministers decided to continued their search for detente and in particular to invite the USSR and other East European countries to discussions on Mutual and Balanced Force Reductions in Europe, an offer that was eventually taken up. This 'Reykjavik Signal' to the East was somewhat clouded in August 1968 by the invasion of Czechoslovakia by Soviet and Warsaw Treaty Organization troops in order to replace the reformist Communist government by one more amenable to Moscow. This move had the side-effect of uniting the NATO countries after a period of uncertainty and, paradoxically, spurring their governments towards the achievement of an internationally accepted settlement of outstanding political issues in Europe. Indeed, the process of detente continued apace when the Warsaw Treaty Organization, meeting in Bucharest in March 1969, called for a Conference on European Security and the May 1970 Rome North Atlantic Council responded positively. This was also the time when Western Germany was conducting its *Ostpolitik* of normalizing relations with its East European neighbours and the Soviet Union and when Washington and Moscow were conducting the Strategic Arms Limitation Treaty (SALT) talks which led to the SALT agreements of May 1972. All these positive developments in East–West relations tested NATO's intention of acting as a forum within which its members could develop a coherent strategy of detente. In this it relied upon the process of consultation which was particularly close and successful over the Helsinki Conference on Security and Cooperation in Europe, 1973–5, for which a Coordinating Committee was established, and over the Vienna Mutual and Balanced Force Reduction negotiations which started in October 1973.

From the mid-1970s the process of detente first faltered and then stalled with East-West relations descending into what is sometimes called the New Cold War (Chomsky *et al.*, 1982). Detente came to mean different things to East and West and the momentum of improving relations could not be sustained in the face of other negative events (Frei and Ruloff, 1983, 276-83). When the Soviet Union invaded Afghanistan in December 1979 and martial law was declared in Poland in December 1981, it was clear that the Western response would not be positive. The more combative approach displayed by the Reagan Administration towards the Soviet Union from 1981 until 1986 led to disagreements within the Alliance about how to handle the Soviet Union. Council meetings about responses to Soviet actions often become more concerned with US-West European relations than with East-West dealings. A classic example could be seen as late as May 1989 when the NATO Heads of Government and of State Summit in Brussels looked like becoming more a diplomatic wrangle between the West Germans, supported by most of the other European NATO members, and the United States, supported by the British. There was opposition to US plans to update their tactical nuclear weapons in Europe, after a Soviet offer to abolish this class of missile completely. The situation was saved by intense NATO diplomacy and by President Bush's own initiative on arms control.

Since 1989 NATO's involvement in East-West relations has changed dramatically. The collapse of communism in East Europe led to the final reconsideration by NATO of its former largely adversarial relationship with the fragmenting Soviet bloc. The London Declaration of the July 1990 North Atlantic Council, took a major step to ending that relationship and looked forward to successful arms control negotiations to limit both the conventional and nuclear forces in Europe (*Survival*, 1990, 469-72). Since then, NATO's concern with Eastern Europe and the former Soviet Union has been over arms control and the management of the collapse of the Soviet empire.

The negotiation of a CFE agreement between the NATO and WTO states throughout 1990 kept NATO engaged in the arms control and disarmament process which was also taking place in other forums, such as the superpower Strategic Arms Reduction Treaty (START) talks. The final CFE agreement represented not only an agreement to reduce troop and armament levels in Europe quite substantially but also, together with the CSBM agreement, put in place an intrusive system of verification from the Atlantic to the Urals.

The final details of the CFE Treaty were agreed in June 1991 and START was agreed the following month. However, with the break-up of the Soviet Union in December 1991 – not to mention the disintegration of the WTO earlier that year – there was the danger that these agreements would fall apart. In case of the CFE this was because many of the carefully planned zonal limits were based on the Soviet military districts which do not necessarily correspond to the borders of the Soviet Union's successor republics. In the case of START, some 30 per cent of the USSR's strategic forces are now deployed outside Russia (the successor state of the USSR in the Security Council of the UN) in Belarus, Kazakhstan and Ukraine (IISS, 1992, 196).

The response of NATO to this dilemma was to create NACC (see p. 210) in which was represented the NATO countries, and the ex-WTO states including the successor states of the Soviet Union. Attached to NACC has been a High Level Working Group that has been dealing with the implementation of CFE and its successor CFE-1A which set national limits on manpower levels. An Open Skies Agreement that should help with the verification of CFE was signed in March 1992. The question of strategic weapons has been dealt with on a much more bilateral level with the states involved, by the United States (Miller, 1992, 15–21).

NACC has also been used to try to socialize the ex-WTO states in a number of international security matters by bringing them into a dialogue with NATO states. A Work Plan has been organized which includes cooperation on such matters as the structure of defence-oriented armies, approaches to arms control, military doctrines and defence conversion (*NATO Review*, April 1992, 34–5). A Group on Defence matters has been established to deal with such questions as defence strategies, defence management, military contributions to humanitarian aid and similar matters (Worner, 1992, 7).

Within a short period of time, the NATO bureaucracy has dealt remarkably well with the translation of its former opponents into states that wish cooperation with it on security matters – indeed, the governments of a number of ex-WTO states have expressed the wish to join NATO. If NATO's concern is to be the security and stability of Europe from the Atlantic to the Urals, then it would certainly make strategic sense to have countries such as Poland, Hungary and the Czech and Slovak Republics as members, though the possibility of such an extension in 1993 is low.

The process of consultation within the Alliance has also been used to deal with *differences between two or more NATO members*, apart from those clearly in the category of North American–West European differences.

It has been particularly difficult for the North Atlantic Council to act as moderator in some of the more important rifts between Alliance members, such as the differences between France under General de Gaulle from 1958 to 1969 and the 'Anglo-Saxon' countries of the United States and the United Kingdom. The task was made more arduous as de Gaulle regarded international organizations that had powers such as those exercised by NATO and the European Communities as being a threat to French sovereignty. He preferred to solve any outstanding differences with Allied countries – such as West Germany – on a bilateral basis (Willis, 1968). NATO's institutions have had more success in helping to prevent other disagreements between member states from reaching the point of no return.

One example can be seen in the so-called 'Cod Wars' between Iceland and the United Kingdom. These involved the extension of Iceland's exclusive fishing limits out to four (1952), 12 (1958), 50 (1972) and then 200 miles (1975) from its coast, thereby effectively excluding the distant-water British fishing fleet from some of its most lucrative traditional grounds. Britain protested against these unilateral actions and sent the Royal Navy to guard British trawlers against the small Icelandic fishery protection fleet (Iceland has no armed forces). By all reckoning, the United Kingdom should have been able to use its superior force to bring the Icelanders to heel. However, the fisheries question was seen by the Icelanders to be one of the utmost national interest for their maritime country and they were not prepared to give in to what they regarded as bullying. They also had an important bargaining card in the form of the United States' base at Keflavik which was of importance both for transporting US troops to Europe in an emergency and as a surveillance and communications centre for the North Atlantic.

The base had been created as a result of an agreement in 1951, by which the United States also established an all-American force in Iceland called the Iceland Defence Force. During the latter two fisheries disputes, Icelandic governments pointed out that the security of their population depended upon exclusive access to the fish off their coast, the main threat to their island was from the Royal Navy and that they might request the Iceland Defence Force to defend their coastguard against the superior strength of the British. There was also the hint, from left-wing politicians in particular, that, if the disputes escalated, the presence of the US base would be challenged. This placed pressure not only on the Americans but also on the Norwegians, Danes and British whose territories were the prime alternatives for the Keflavik base but who, for political reasons, did not want to host such a base. Between the last two disputes, the Icelandic government renegotiated the base agreement, reminding NATO Allies of its strategic importance.

The dispute was discussed at the Oslo North Atlantic Council in May 1976 and, after both the Norwegians and NATO's Secretary-General intervened, the British capitulated. A former Icelandic Prime Minister wrote of the 1958 dispute that 'There is no doubt that NATO had a great deal to do with the final settlement' (Grondal, 1971, 65). An American writer commented that 'Since the mid-70s, there has been a growing understanding among politically aware Icelanders of the leverage Iceland exerts in international negotiations as a result of the NATO connection' (Fairlamb, 1981, 141). This case demonstrates the utility of membership of an alliance by a small, strategically important country such as Iceland and the ability of NATO's institutions to facilitate a settlement in a dispute threatening the defence capability of the Alliance.

A more dangerous clash of interests within the Alliance has been that between Turkey and Greece. There has been a traditional enmity between the two states and their borders were only drawn after a war in 1920 which still left disputed areas. New problems arose after the independence in 1960 of Cyprus which, though closer to the Turkish mainland than to Greece, had a Greek majority and Turkish minority. In the early 1960s other NATO countries played down the rivalry between the two by encouraging the economic development of both states, to which other members contributed. When civil war broke out in Cyprus in 1963 it seemed at one stage that NATO forces might intervene. Although Cyprus had its status guaranteed by three NATO countries (Britain, Greece and Turkey), it was not a NATO member and a United Nations peacekeeping force was sent in. NATO countries and the NATO Secretary-General managed to prevent both Greece and Turkey from intervening directly. From 1964 to 1974 the Secretary-General reported back to the North Atlantic Council on the 'watching brief' on Cyprus that the Council had given him. Events deteriorated after the military took over power in Greece and in 1974 removed the Cypriot President and encouraged the Greek community there to seek union with Greece. Turkey invaded Cyprus in July 1974 and its troops remained in occupation of the north-east part of the island. The collapse of military rule in Athens prevented any armed response by Greece: once again direct conflict between two NATO countries had been avoided, but – this time – not by NATO action.

However, Greece and Turkey remained adversaries, with the Cyprus dispute as well as air and maritime border disagreements between the two countries leading to the cancellation of some NATO exercises in the area and Greek withdrawal from the integrated military structure of the Alliance from 1974 to 1980. Having the two states as NATO members certainly meant that the southern border of the Alliance was unstable, with both countries directing much of their military effort at each other rather than at the Soviet bloc. However, there is no guarantee that the situation would be any better with Greece and Turkey out of NATO and there is reasonable evidence that action by the NATO Council and Secretary-General (as well as by individual members) has prevented fighting between the two states.

With the advent of NACC (see above, p. 210). the prospect exists of NATO involvement in preventing conflict between what could be seen as 'associate members'. There is some indication that NATO's good offices have been used to ease friction between Russia and the Baltic republics over military matters and that the Organization has made a positive contribution in assisting the CSCE obesrver mission to Nagorno-Karabakh, a region disputed between Armenia and Azerbaijan (Worner, 1992, 4).

The last area of political consultation within NATO is that in the Third World, covered by the term '*out-of-area*', the area being that specified in Article 6 (see p. 205). On the whole, NATO members have been cautious about discussing their out-of-area policy in a NATO context. This has mainly been because the Alliance is seen to refer primarily to the Atlantic area but also because NATO members have widely differing views about security questions in the Third World. Up to the 1960s much of this area was either in the direct American sphere of influence (Latin America) or was under colonial rule by NATO European members. In the remaining parts of the world such as the Middle East, Alliance members often pursued different policies, as was the case in the Suez Crisis (1956) when the United States opposed French and British use of force against Egypt. After this, it was agreed that NATO countries would consult each other on broad foreign policy questions affecting the Alliance.

Whilst there have been Council discussions about wider global problems and more specific examinations of how out-of-area operations might affect NATO's preparedness (as in the case of the Falklands War between Britain and Argentina in 1982), the North Atlantic Council discussions have continued to be centred on Europe. Indeed, a number of West European governments became critical of United States out-of-area activities from the 1960s onwards. France and some of the smaller states voiced their opposition to American policy on Vietnam from 1965 to 1975; NATO European states would not grant landing rights to US aircraft on their way to the Middle East in the Yom Kippur War between Israel and its Arab neighbours in 1973; and a number of NATO countries would not allow overflight facilities to US F-111 aircraft on their way from bases in Britain to bomb Tripoli in April 1986. These divisions of opinion have prevented deep discussion of such issues in the North Atlantic Council. Even when the West European states – or some of them – have given support to US out-of-area actions, as in the case of their mine-sweeping operations in the Gulf from 1987 to 1988, this was studiously coordinated through the Western European Union (which excludes the United States) rather than through NATO.

Two out-of-area problems have recurred for NATO since 1990. The first was the Iraqi invasion of Kuwait in August of that year and the subsequent events, and the second has been the disintegration of Yugoslavia.

In the case of Iraq and Kuwait, the North Atlantic Council met and condemned the Iraqi invasion, but the action taken was that by individual NATO nations together with other states. In doing this, these countries utilized both the operational experience gained through NATO and weapons and troops already deployed in the NATO area. Coordination of the European naval contribution was, however, undertaken through WEU. NATO did send the ACE mobile force (its 'fire brigade' force) to Turkey – a NATO member – to deter any Iraqi attack on that country. This seemed to demonstrate that, even in the changed circumstances of early 1991, NATO members were not prepared to use that institution and the North Atlantic Treaty in areas outside those mentioned in Article 6 (see p. 205).

The Yugoslav problem has offered a more serious challenge to NATO. The break-up of Yugoslavia in 1991 and the subsequent conflict between Serbia (and, originally, the Yugoslav National Army, the YNA) and, in turn, Slovenia, Croatia and (together with Croatia) Bosnia, have sorely threatened the peace of the Balkans and of Europe. Of course, the EC and ECP have been involved (see above p. 113) as has the WEU (see below), the CSCE (see below p. 247) and the United Nations Security Council. So NATO could be excused action – as an institution – in an area seemingly not covered by its Treaty and which is also being treated by other security institutions. However, though not in the Article 6 area, former-Yugoslavia is a neighbour of two NATO states, Italy and Greece, and a serious conflict there could bring in Turkey and Russia. Anyhow Article 6 does not restrain NATO – or, of course, its members – from taking joint action in conflicts outside the Article 6 domain (Achilles, 1985, 37).

Indeed, the North Atlantic Council has shown an interest in the Yugoslav situation from the beginning and this has increased over time. By November 1991, NATO ministers were condemning the YNA for its actions against the Croats, giving support to the work of the UN, the EC, the CSCE, the UN High Commissioner for Refugees and the International Red Cross, but were studiously avoiding any action – except for consulting closely – through NATO (*NATO Review*, October 1991, 23; and February 1992, 27). This was partly because the United States saw the crisis as a European one which should be dealt with by the plethora of European institutions, and the European members of NATO were not then prepared to send forces into the area, which action through NATO may have required. By December 1992, the Alliance was helping in the implementation of the UN Security Council resolutions. 'For the first time in its history, the Alliance is taking part in UN peacekeeping and sanctions enforcement operations' (*NATO Review*, December 1992, 29). Specifically mentioned are supporting (with WEU) the enforcement of UN economic sanctions against Serbia and Montenegro and the arms embargo on the whole Yugoslav area; NATO's NORTHAG command contributing elements for the UNPROFOR (UN protection force in Bosnia) operational headquarters; and NATO airborne early-warning aircraft monitoring the UN-mandated no-fly zone over Bosnia (op.cit.,

29). This seemed to reflect both the failure of other institutions – especially the EC and EPC – to deal with the situation and the increased willingness of the US to become involved – albeit at arm's length – in the conflict.

The Yugoslav conflict points up the need for NATO to consider out-of-area operations, especially those in Europe. The Copenhagen North Atlantic Council in June 1991 gave prominence to providing 'the indispensable foundations for a stable security environment in Europe', not just in the North Atlantic Treaty area, thus backing up the idea of 'security for a Europe whole and free' (*NATO Review*, June 1991, 30). The Rome Council went further in the Alliance's New Strategic Concept. It recognized that the 'security challenges and risks' that faced NATO were different from those of the past, and that the risks that remained were 'multi-faceted and multi-directional', making them hard to assess. Sources of such risks were identified as being instabilities arising from economic, social and political difficulties in East and Central Europe, outside the 'NATO area'. These could give rise to armed conflict which them might then directly affect the security of the Alliance. Furthermore, Alliance security had to be seen in the global context and the Alliance could consult on these wider matters, though there was little propensity to use Alliance forces, as such, in out-of-area roles (*NATO Review*, December 1991, 25–32). By the time of the Oslo Council in June 1992, NATO ministers had agreed 'to support, on a case-by-case basis ... peacekeeping activities under the responsibility of the CSCE, including making available Alliance resources and expertise' (*NATO Review*, June 1992, 31). In December 1992 the North Atlantic Council reported that ministers wished to 'further strengthen Alliance coordination in peacekeeping' and that the Alliance was willing to support 'on a case-by-case basis' peacekeeping operations of the United Nations Security Council (*NATO Review*, December 1992, 29). Thus the ground has been laid for the Alliance (as distinct from just its members) to participate in either a UN or CSCE peacekeeping operation in an out-of-area conflict. Indeed, this is precisely what NATO ministers claimed they had done, by December 1992, in Yugoslavia (see above).

NATO is a *military* as well as a political alliance, and its achievements in this area are considerable. As seen, the Alliance started out in 1949 with an American guarantee and only the bare outlines of defence cooperation. The advent of the Korean War saw the adoption, in September 1950, by the United States Administration of its National Security Council's report, known as NSC 68, which recommended a 'major conventional and nuclear build-up of military strength' (Wells, 1985, 183). This move transformed the military strength of NATO, especially after the members adopted the Medium Term Defence Plan and appointed General Eisenhower as SACEUR in December 1950. In 1952 the North Atlantic Council held in Lisbon adopted goals for the enlargement of its conventional forces, but these proved to be too ambitious (Etzold, 1985, 291). The core of NATO's deterrent strategy was that of the threat of 'massive retaliation'. This meant that the United States would hit back with the full panoply of its nuclear arsenal against any aggressor that had struck against one or more of the NATO members. The problem was that this strategy offered few incentives to the West European NATO members to reach their conventional force goals as long as they felt that the American 'nuclear umbrella' would protect them. It was also a ploy that would only work as long as the United States had an undoubted nuclear superiority. Once the Soviet Union started to build up its nuclear stocks, the United States' calculation changed. It had to consider the possibility that the Soviets might strike back against America when under attack from US massive retaliation. In these conditions, the United States might lose part of its homeland because it had come to the rescue of West European countries being attacked by the Red Army. Such costly supportive action might no longer have seemed credible to ally and adversary alike.

The United States' response to this dilemma was to place short-range nuclear weapons in Western Europe from the mid-1950s onwards. This bolstered the credibility of the US nuclear deterrent's extension to Western Europe and helped to postpone Alliance disagreements about the sharing of the conventional rearmament burden but also created the problem of how much the United States could share the control of nuclear weapons with its European Allies (see p. 213).

By the early 1960s the credibility of massive retaliation was stretched to breaking. Within the Alliance, the French had made it clear that they no longer believed that the United States would start a nuclear war in response to a loss of Alliance territory in Europe when such a move could lead to the destruction of America. France had decided to build its own deterrent force rather than gamble that an American President might be prepared to place New York at risk to save Paris from the Russians. From 1962 to its formal adoption by NATO in 1967, the concept of 'flexible response' was developed in the United States by the Pentagon. It based Western strategy on 'a flexible and balanced range of appropriate responses, conventional and nuclear, to all levels of aggression or threats of aggression' (North Atlantic Council communique, 14 December 1967). Massive retaliation implied the existence of a 'trip-wire' which, if crossed by Soviet troops, would bring a full-scale American nuclear riposte; flexible response suggested a range of possible replies by NATO to any aggression, from the conventional, through the use of tactical nuclear weapons up to a strategic nuclear exchange. An attack would be met at the equivalent level but the option of escalation to a higher level of conflict would be maintained in the case that the opponent's aggression proved successful. The concept thus involves a more credible reply to any low-level attack by not threatening an immediate nuclear holocaust but at the same time requires NATO to show competence at all levels of defence. Critics also pointed to the possibility that the concept of flexible response might allow the two Superpowers to fight a limited war in Europe and remain relatively unscathed themselves (*New Statesman and Society*, 1989, 13). This was one of the reasons why the French did not subscribe to the new concept.

The adoption of flexible response did little to alleviate NATO's military problems: if anything, it made them more apparent (Schwartz, 1983, 190). As it implied that NATO countries would at first respond to a conventional attack with non-nuclear weapons, the concept placed a greater responsibility on the Allies to provide such forces that could credibly deter an attack and could, if need be, keep an attack at the conventional level rather than be forced to choose the nuclear response. However, this was at a time – in the early 1970s in particular – when there was United States pressure to cut its troop levels in Europe and negotiations had started with some Warsaw Treaty countries to lower the general level of forces in Europe (see p. 214). Furthermore, most of the European NATO members were suffering from economic problems and were either reluctant or unable to devote more resources to conventional weapons at a time of detente. Indeed it was May 1978 before NATO ministers adopted the wide-ranging Long-Term Defence Programme and a number of members promised to increase their annual defence expenditure by 3 per cent in real terms. The early to mid-1980s saw a fresh debate over the role of conventional forces in NATO's deterrent and defence strategy (ESECS, 1983; Clarke, 1985; Miller, 1986; Pierre, 1986).

In 1984 NATO's Allied Command Europe started developing the concept of Follow-on Forces Attack (FOFA) aimed at making the conventional defence of Europe more credible and General Rogers (then SACEUR) called for more resources to reach this goal (Rogers, 1984, 1–9). Questions about what each member should contribute brought the Alliance back to familiar problems over burden-sharing (Golden, 1983).

NATO required a triad of forces to implement its strategy: strategic nuclear, theatre nuclear and conventional. Apart from the French and British deterrents, strategic nuclear weapons are held by the United States outside mainland Europe. Theatre nuclear weapons always were the most apparent manifestation of the nuclear deterrent for the Europeans, as they were based on their territory for the most part. At the end of the 1970s, some West European leaders – especially Chancellor Schmidt of West Germany – were anxious lest Superpower talks about Strategic Arms Limitation led to a stalemate in this area whilst the Soviet Union established a superiority of conventional forces in Europe. This turned attention to the second leg of the triad – theatre nuclear weapons – especially as the Soviets were deploying new SS-20 intermediate-range ballistic missiles. For a number of political and military reasons, NATO ministers decided in December 1979 to replace some of their existing ageing theatre nuclear missiles with new intermediate nuclear missiles (INF) – 108 Pershing II and 464 cruise missiles – and at the same time called on the Soviet Union to join arms control negotiations on these systems (Boutwell, 1985, 67–74). This 'Dual Track' decision exposed some of the problems of dealing with nuclear strategy in an alliance. The process of consultation that led to it was 'more painstaking than any in the history of NATO, a model blend of European involvement and American leadership' (Treverton, 1985b, 107). Despite this, the Dual Track decision led to troubled times for the Alliance, especially when the new Reagan Administration decided to hold back on the arms control strand. When talks did start, they were stalemated as long as the Soviet Union thought that the missiles would not be deployed, and were then broken off by the Soviet leadership when the first Pershing IIs were placed in West Germany. In 1985, the United States and the Soviet Union resumed arms control negotiations, including those on INF. As one commentator has remarked:

Because the December 1979 decision is viewed as a response to concerns about the US nuclear guarantee in an era of strategic parity, as a test of US leadership of the alliance, and as a test of alliance cohesiveness and resolve,

it has taken on an importance totally out of proportion to the size and scope of
the military role the new weapons systems are likely to play in the event of war
(Schwartz, 1983, 250).

It may have been realization of this position that allowed the
American leadership to respond positively when President Gorbachev took up the original US offer of a 'zero option' on INF,
aimed at their complete banishment. In US eyes, the Alliance had
triumphed – it had obtained concessions from the Soviet Union by
deploying the INF. Some Europeans saw it differently: INF had
been a means of tying the United States more closely to the
defence of Europe and of providing an intermediary nuclear 'rung'
in the 'ladder' of deterrence. The disappearance of these forces
brought doubts about the US commitment to the defence of Europe
and increased pressure for another 'zero option' – that of removing all short-range nuclear missiles from Europe (Binnendijk,
1989, 137). This issue almost managed to spoil NATO's fortieth
birthday celebration and the diplomatic papering over the cracks
did not hide the reality that NATO's military posture had been
severely challenged by Mr Gorbachev's peace initiatives.

With the beginning of the Vienna negotiations on Conventional
Forces in Europe (CFE) in March 1989, NATO had to adjust its conventional force plans, not only to meet individual national capabilities, but also to suit what could be a moving target of bloc-to
bloc (NATO and Warsaw Treaty Organization) agreements on the
future size and structure of conventional forces in Europe. The
1988 NATO Summit laid down the ground rules for this task – they
aimed at a secure and stable balance of such forces at lower
levels, the elimination of disparities prejudicial to security and
stability and the elimination of the capability to launch a surprise
attack and for initiating large-scale offensive actions (NATO,
1988, 4–5).

The CFE negotiations resulted in an agreement about sizeable
reductions in both NATO and WTO troops and conventional
weapons in Europe (IISS, 1991, 247–51). However, both the end of
the Cold War and the budgetary-driven cuts in the armed forces
of most European and North American countries, has led to a
changed strategic position for NATO. This was recognized at the
Rome NATO Summit in November 1991 in the Alliance's New
Strategic Concept.

This Concept reflected the realization that the major threat to
NATO – a full-scale attack on all fronts – had effectively disappeared and that the security challenges and risks were going to be

multi-faceted and multi-dimensional, and thus hard to predict and assess. In response NATO had to take a broad approach to security, using dialogue, cooperation and a collective defence capability. The first two elements would be used to reduce the risks of conflict, but the Alliance would still have to maintain the ability to act collectively.

A new force posture was agreed in pursuit of the Rome strategy. The size of the forces was to be reduced but they were to be more flexible and mobile. Also there was to be less reliance on nuclear weapons, especially the sub-strategic forces which, after the October 1991 Taormina decision by NATO's Nuclear Planning Group, will be reduced by about 80 per cent of the stockpile at that time (*NATO Review*, December 1991, 25–32; Schulte, February 1993, 17–19). The new force structure meant that there would be three types of forces. There would be the main defence forces, still the bulk of NATO's armoury, that would ensure the Alliance's territorial integrity. There would be an augmentation force for reinforcing particular forces in one of the NATO regions. Both these types would comprise active and mobilizable elements. Rapid reaction forces would be suited for rapid and selective employment, 'to assist in crisis management or to respond to aggression' (*NATO Review*, June 1992, 35).

Since the Rome Summit the NATO countries have been attempting to put together the military jigsaw puzzle by deciding which member's troops undertake what task. They have had some success in maritime defence, but then the Standing Naval Forces were already in place in the old system. Also Allied Command Europe had, by the end of 1992, activated the Rapid Reaction Corps under a British commander and with a multinational headquarters. However, the Defence Planning Committee, meeting in December 1992, noted that 'a number of planned national force reductions will have an effect on the future size and capabilities of main defence forces' and a review of the consequence of these effects was initiated (*NATO Review*, December 1992, 33). This was an admission that the various cuts made by the members in their armed forces had undermined the new planned force structure. Without an obvious threat at their door, the electorates of Western Europe and their governments were not prepared to devote resources to a defence effort that may have been logical to NATO planners. This is perhaps indicative of the uncertainly within NATO about its future military role.

Contribution

Schwarz's epitaph for the Dual Track decision is in many ways fitting for much of NATO's current collective military effort. What is done by whom, with whom, how and where is more determined by political considerations than by questions of potential military effectiveness. This is not to say that the Alliance has had a weak defence posture – far from it. But it remains primarily a political alliance, utilizing American strength for the defence of Western Europe. In doing so, it helped to perpetuate the division of Europe between the Soviet bloc and the Western bloc, with just a few neutrals in between, and demonstrated that the Continent is an object of international relations, with its governments reacting to Superpower stimulus and trying to adapt to new conditions. At the same time, NATO provided its European members with a very real instrument of influence on the North American Superpower and fashioned a collective defence system for West European countries that contributed considerably to their feeling of security during the Cold War.

It is a hard task for NATO to aggregate its members' defence interests as these go to the very core existence of the sovereign state. However, the member countries realize that a collective approach to defence can bring dividends and, in its various communiqués and policy statements, NATO has articulated that common interest. The existence of the organization has contributed to the stability of Western Europe by recruitment to the system – in the case of the Federal Republic of Germany – and in upholding certain norms of behaviour between members, which has encouraged the settling of disputes by non-warlike means. It can be argued that NATO, with its emphasis on the Soviet threat, has socialized the leadership of its member states into an adversarial and military approach to international relations. This perhaps overestimates the ability of such an organization to insist on loyalty to a line in the face of opposition or even apathy, and it underestimates attempts made through NATO to pursue detente with Eastern Europe.

NATO's rule-making and rule-application powers are limited. It has never tried to take on a judicial or semi-judicial role and defence policy is not an easy area for judicial settlement. On some occasions – for example in the disputes between Iceland and the United Kingdom over fishing rights – NATO institutions have adopted a quasi-adjudication role, ruling in favour of one party and against another, though it should be said that the settlement tended to be political rather than legal by nature.

NATO does have strong information and operational functions. Its output of information is prodigious and self-serving and the functions performed by its various institutions range from the crucial defence role of SACEUR to the mundane – though nevertheless important – activities of those in the Brussels headquarters who scrutinize the fine details of members' armaments programmes. NATO also has associated with it a number of civilian and military agencies, performing specialist tasks such as the NATO Integrated Communications System Organization (NICSO), the Advisory Group for Aeroplane Research and Development (AGARD) and the NATO Defense College.

Whatever contribution it made to the political development of Europe during its first 40 years of existence, its most testing time has come since the end of the confrontation between the two hostile military blocs in Europe. Since the end of the Soviet system and the collapse fo the Warsaw Treaty Organization, NATO has been without an adversary and thus without its most obvious role, that of protecting its member states through a form of collective defence. However, the end of the Cold War was not followed by a period of peace and stability in Europe – far from it.

NATO ministers have identified a series of threats to the security of their members (see above p. 209), but the question remains whether NATO is the best medium through which to tackle these. Attempts to reshuffle the NATO pack to create new command structures and a new strategy have foundered on the rocks of public indifference and budgetary savings, that exist on both sides of the Atlantic. However, NATO does have some advantage over other institutions: it is experienced in dealing with security issues and it seems to be sharing this experience with new states in NACC. It does have an integrated military structure that can perhaps be adapted to meet the new political needs of its European members to create a 'defence identity' (see above p. 218), though here it may have to vie with the WEU. Finally, it still acts as a bridge between North America and Europe. If US military power is to be put to good use to help solve – or limit – conflict, then NATO can provide an operational context for such action – taken together with European allies – in the European theatre or on its borders. Twice during the twentieth century American troops have been called into Europe to end wars. Perhaps it is the fate of NATO to make sure that such forces stay on the European continent to prevent another such war from starting.

References

Achilles, T. 1985: The Omaha milkman. In De Staercke, A. 1985, 30–41.
Binnendijk, H. 1989: NATO's nuclear modernization dilemma. *Survival* 31:2, 137–55.
Boutwell, J.D., 1985: NATO theatre nuclear forces: the third phase, 1977–85. In Boutwell, J.D., Doty, P. and Treverton, G.F. 1985, 67–86.
——, Doty, P. and Treverton, G.G. 1985: *The Nuclear Confrontation in Europe.* London: Croom Helm.
Charman, S. and Williams, K. 1981: *The Parliamentarians' Role in the Alliance.* Brussels: North Atlantic Assembly.
Chomsky, N., Steele, J. and Gittings, J. 1982: *Superpowers in Collision. The New Cold War.* London: Penguin.
Clarke, M. 1985: The alternative defence debate: non-nuclear defence policies for Europe. Sussex: ADIU, ADIU Occasional Paper 3.
Cleveland, H. 1970: *NATO: The Transatlantic Bargain.* New York: Harper & Row.
De Staercke, A. 1985: *NATO's Anxious Birth.* London: C. Hurst.
Eberle, J., Roper, J., Wallace, W. and Williams, P. 1984: European security cooperation and British interests. *International Affairs* 60:4, 545–60.
ESECS (Report of the European Security Study) 1983: *Strengthening Conventional Deterrence in Europe.* London: Macmillan.
Etzold, T.H. 1985: The end of the beginning, NATO's adoption of nuclear strategy. In Riste, O. (ed.) 1985, 285–314.
Eurogroup, 1985: *Western Defense: The European Role in NATO.* Brussels: Eurogroup Secretariat.
Fairlamb, J.R. 1981: *The Evolution of Icelandic Defense Decision Making 1944–1981.* Ann Arbor: University Microfilms International.
Frei, D. and Ruloff, D. 1983; *East–West Relations, Volume 1: A Systematic Survey.* Cambridge MA: Oelgeschlager, Gunn & Hain.
Fursdon, E. 1980: *The European Defence Community: A History.* London: Macmillan.
Gaddis, J.L. 1985: The United States and the question of a sphere of influence in Europe, 1945–1949. In Riste, O. (ed.) 1985, 60–91.
Golden, J.R. 1983: *NATO Burden-Sharing, Risks and Opportunities.* New York: Praeger, The Washington Papers 96.
Grondal, B. 1971: *Iceland. From Neutrality to NATO Membership.* Oslo: Universitetsforlaget.
Howard, M. 1985: Introduction. In Riste, O. (ed.) 1985, 11–22.
International Institute for Strategic Studies (IISS) 1991: *Strategic Survey 1990–1991.* London: Brassey's.
International Institute for Strategic Studies (IISS) 1992: *Strategic Survey 1991–1992.* London: Brassey's.
Lunn, S., 1992: The hand of friendship. *NATO Review* 40:1, 12–18.
Menon, A., Forster, A. and Wallace, W. 1992: A common European defence? *Survival* Autumn 1992, 98–118.
Miller, S.E. (ed.) 1986: *Conventional Forces and Americans Defence Policy.* Princeton: Princeton University Press.

—— 1992: Western diplomacy and the Soviety nuclear legacy. *Survival* Autumn 1992, 3–27.

Mortimer, E. 1992: *European Security after the Cold War*. London: Brassey's for IISS, Adelphi Paper 271.

NATO, 1970: *The North Atlantic Treaty Organization: Facts and Figures*, 6th edn. Brussels: NATO Information Service.

——.1984: *The North Atlantic Treaty Organization: Facts and Figures*. Brussels: NATO Information Service.

—— 1988: *Conventional Arms Control: The Way Ahead. Statement issued under the authority of the Heads of State and Government participating in the meeting of the North Atlantic Council in Brussels*. Brussels: NATO Press Service.

—— n.d.: *NATO Final Communiques 1949–1974*, Brussels: NATO Information Service.

NATO Review June 1991, October 1991, December 1991, February 1992, April 1992, June 1992, December 1992.

New Statesman & Society 1989: An end to Europe? *New Statesman and Society* May 1989, 13.

Osgood, R. 1962: *NATO: The Entangling Alliance*. Chicago: Chicago University Press.

Petersen, N. 1982: Who pulled whom and how much? Britain, the United States and the making of the North Atlantic Treaty. *Journal of International Studies* 11:2, 93–114.

Pierre, A.J. (ed.) 1986: *The Conventional Defense of Europe: New Technologies and New Strategies*. New York: Council on Foreign Relations.

Riste, O. (ed.) 1985: *Western Security: The Formative Years*. Oslo: Universitetsforlaget.

Rogers, B.W. 1984: Follow-on forces attack (FOFA): myths and realities. *NATO Review* 32:6, 1–9.

Schulte, G.L. 1993: NATO's nuclear forces in a changing world. *NATO Review*. 41:1, 17–27.

Schwartz, D.N. 1983: *NATO's Nuclear Dilemmas*. Washington, DC: The Brookings Institution.

Survival 1990: September/October, XXXII:5.

Treverton, G. 1985a: *Making the Alliance Work*. London: Macmillan.

—— 1985b: Theatre nuclear forces: military logic and political purpose. In Boutwell, J.D., Doty, P. and Treverton, G.F. (eds.) 1985, 87–112.

—— 1992: America's stakes and choices in Europe. *Survival* Autumn 1992, 119–35.

United States Information Service 1992: US is Reshaping Military and Reducing its Size. *Official Text* Feb. 28, 1–4.

Van der Beugel, E. 1986: The Atlantic family – managing its problems. *NATO Review* 34:1, 13–18.

Van Eekelen, W.F. 1988: the Eurogroup and the US-European dialogue. *NATO Review* 36:4, 7–11.

Wells, S.F. Jr. 1985: The first Cold War buildup: Europe in United States strategy and policy, 1950–1953. In Riste, O. (ed.) 1985, 181–97.

Williams, P. 1984; *US Troops in Europe*. London: Routledge & Kegan Paul, Chatham House Papers 25.

Willis, F. Roy 1968: *France, Germany and the New Europe 1945-1967*, revised edn. London: Oxford UP.

Woods, S. 1983: *Pipeline Politics*. Aberdeen: Centre for Defence Studies, Centrepiece 5.

Worner, M. 1992: A vigorous Alliance - a motor for peaceful change in Europe. *NATO Review* 40:6, 3-9.

10

Western European Union

Establishment

Although the Western European Union was formally constituted in May 1955, its background can be found in the Brussels Treaty of 1948 and the immediate reason for its establishment lies in the failure of the European Defence Community negotiations.

The signing of the Brussels Treaty between the United Kingdom, France, Belgium, the Netherlands and Luxembourg came at a time when the West Europeans feared what they saw as an emerging Soviet threat. The French government, in particular, felt under attack from the Communist Party at home and the smaller countries were worried by rumours that they were to be the objects of a Soviet demarche. The United Kingdom saw an agreement with the other four countries as a logical follow-up to the Treaty of Dunkirk with France but was spurred on less by concern with the revival of Germany than by the negative attitude of the Soviet Union at the Council of Foreign Ministers meetings, Communist advances in Greece and Czechoslovakia and the need to show that West Europe was worthy of American help. Indeed, on signing the Brussels Treaty the foreign ministers of the five countries sent a telegram pleading for American support for their endeavours (Dilks, 1985, 53).

The Brussels Treaty, signed on 17 March 1948, reflected the dual fear of the five signatory governments – that their countries were open to economic and social collapse and that they might not be able to defend themselves from outside military intrusion. It was therefore designated a 'treaty of economic, social and cultural collaboration and collective self-defence', by which the parties were pledged to preserve 'the principles of democracy, personal freedom and political liberty, the constitutional traditions and the rule of law, which are their common heritage'

(Preamble). While the first three articles of the Treaty dealt with economic, social and cultural affairs, it was Article 4 which became the centrepiece of the agreement. In this the countries undertook that, if any one of them became the object of an armed attack in Europe, they would – in accordance with Article 51 of the UN Charter (which allows for collective self-defence) – 'afford the Party so attacked all the military and other aid and assistance in their power'. The Treaty was valid for 50 years. The five countries thus gave each other a direct and far-reaching commitment of help in the case of aggression. Though the Brussels Treaty was a preparation for the North Atlantic Treaty, it was by no means made redundant by the latter. It is true that the economic aspirations were taken over by the Organization for European Economic Cooperation and that it was NATO which became the collective self-defence organization of importance for Britain, France and the Benelux states. Despite this, a feeling remained that the West European countries should develop a closer relationship within the context of NATO. From 1950 to August 1954 the members of the European Coal and Steel Community, with the uneven support of the United Kingdom, attempted to develop a European Defence Community (see Chapter 6, p. 87) but the effort was stopped by a combination of a lack of British commitment to a Community-centred defence arrangement and the absence of French political support for the final agreement.

After the French parliament's rejection of the EDC, Sir Anthony Eden, the British Foreign Secretary, took an initiative to call a conference in London from September to October 1954 for the six Community states, the United States, Canada and the United Kingdom. Eden announced that Britain would maintain four army divisions and the Tactical Air Force in Europe, if needed by the Brussels Treaty powers. It was within the context of the Brussels Treaty that a new arrangement emerged for European security. West Germany and Italy were to join the Treaty, the British, United States and French occupation of the Federal Republic would end and German sovereignty would be restored, and certain controls would be exercised over German rearmament.

The understanding hammered out in London was formalized in the Paris Agreements of 23 October 1954. These included a document signed by France and the Federal Republic of Germany aimed at ending their dispute about the future of the Saarland; documents signed after a Four-Power Conference of the USA, the United Kingdom, France and West Germany which dealt with German sovereignty; documents signed by the five Brussels Treaty powers, inviting Italy and West Germany to accede to the Treaty; documents signed by the five Brussels Treaty powers plus Italy and West Germany, forming the basis of the new Western European Union; and documents signed by the 14 North Atlantic Treaty countries which admitted the Federal Republic to NATO.

This package dealt with a number of related political problems. First, it created the sovereign state of the Federal Republic of Germany, bringing that country into the comity of Western nations. To do so, the one main outstanding contentious issue between Germany and France – the Saar – was placed to one side with the promise of a European solution. Secondly it brought this new state (and Italy) into the network of Western defence by inviting it to join NATO and the Brussels Treaty. This provided a phoenix – the WEU – to rise from the ashes of the EDC and gave the promise of West German manpower to strengthen NATO armed forces. Thirdly, it also kept some restraints on West Germany, most noticeably the ban on Germany manufacturing atomic, biological or chemical weapons, as well as on long-range guided missiles, warships and strategic bombers. Finally, it saw the commitment by the United Kingdom to place under the command of NATO's Supreme Allied Commander Europe, in peacetime and on the mainland of Europe, four divisions of troops and the Second Tactical Air Force.

The central part of the Paris Agreements is the protocol modifying and completing the Brussels Treaty. In particular, it replaced the Preamble's former aims – 'to take such steps as may be held necessary in the event of renewal by Germany of a policy of aggression' – with the new 'to promote the unity and to encourage the progressive integration of Europe'. A new Article 4 expressed the intention of the parties to work in close cooperation with NATO and promised to rely on the Military Authorities of NATO for information and advice on military matters. The new organization was called the Western European Union (WEU) and Italy and West Germany joined the Brussels Treaty states as full members.

The second protocol covered the forces of WEU. This included the existing strength and number of formations to be placed under the Supreme Allied Commander Europe after the EDC negotiations, together with the new British commitment and one regimental combat team from Luxembourg. The British, in Article 4, promised not to remove any of their forces from mainland Europe against the wishes of the majority of the members, except in the case of an acute overseas emergency. However, if maintaining these forces strained the external finances of the United Kingdom, the North Atlantic Council would review the financial conditions.

Protocols number three and four dealt with the control of armaments, as outlined above. An agency for this purpose was established with a Director (and staff) responsible to the WEU's Council. The task of the Agency is to see whether the arms control measures are being observed by scrutinizing budgetary and statistical information and by running test checks and inspections. It is to report to the Council. In a resolution, the WEU states agreed to convene a Working Group to look at the rational production of armaments and the standardization of weapons and their components.

Institutions

The Brussels Treaty had a simple institutional structure. Article 7 created a Consultative Council organized to exercise its functions continually and to meet when deemed fit. It could be immediately convened to consult about any possible threat to the peace or about any danger to economic stability. In fact, the Council rarely met at foreign minister level but instead a Permanent Commission consisting of a British Foreign Office official and the Ambassadors in London of the other member countries met monthly. A small international Secretariat was formed and committees established to examine cooperation in social and cultural matters.

This structure was strengthened and expanded with the creation of the Western European Union. The Consultative Council became the Council of Western European Union and a consultative Assembly composed of WEU representatives to the Council of Europe was established. As mentioned, an Agency for the Control of Armaments (ACA) was set up under Protocol number four. The Council was also empowered to establish subsidiary bodies as necessary. The small Secretariat in London continued in existence and in May 1955 the Council decided to establish a Standing Armaments Committee to examine how the members' armed forces might best be equipped.

As a result of the revival of the WEU in the mid-1980s, the Agencies were reorganized and the Council meetings revitalized with foreign and defence ministers gathering twice a year. The ACA was reorganized and its staff drastically cut (Assembly of Western European Union, 1992, 28).

Further institutional changes were introduced after the end of the Cold War and with the prospect of the well becoming more closely connected with the emerging European Union. The Secretariat and Council were moved from London in early 1993 to Brussels. The idea was that the WEU's institutions should be close to those both of the EC (and the European Union) and of NATO. Furthermore, a Planning Cell was established by the WEU in Brussels to map out the military aspects of WEU operations. Chiefs of the members' defence staffs, who had already met together on an *ad hoc* basis during the 1990-1 Gulf War, met again in May 1992 and it was decided that they should meet twice yearly prior to the meetings of the Council of Ministers (Assembly of the Western European Union, 1992, 29). An Institute for Security Studies was also established in Paris by the Council, starting work in July 1990.

A joint session of the North Atlantic Council of NATO and the Council of the Western European Union was held on 8 June 1993, promising closer cooperation between the two organizations. This session dealt mainly with the operations the two organizations had been operating since July 1992 in the Adriatic, and it also arranged a single command and control arrangement for these combined operations. Further such joint NATO-WEU sessions are promised should additional political guidance be needed.

Achievements

The first major task faced by the WEU was that of the Saarland settlement. The Franco-German agreement made at the same time as the Paris Agreements had accepted that the territory should have a 'European Statute within the framework of Western European Union'. The Saar would have a home-rule government but with a Commissioner, appointed by and responsible to the WEU, to represent it in defence and foreign affairs. This task was withdrawn from the WEU's ambit after the Saarlanders rejected the settlement in a referendum on 23 October 1955.

WEU activity in the two areas mentioned in protocols two to four – arms control and armament standardization – has been fairly marginal. Its work in the latter has been overshadowed by NATO and by undertakings such as the meetings of the Conference of National Armaments Directors and the Independent European Programme Group (IEPG) (Taylor, 1982, 24–33; Taylor, 1984, 24 and 60–1). The Agency for the Control of Armaments was more active than the Standing Armaments Committee, producing a number of reports on force levels, arms stocks and manufacture. However, the non-ratification of the instrument that would have allowed inspection without prior consent, refusal by WEU's Council to finance the recruitment of trained inspectors and French disregard for provisions about the production and stockpiling of nuclear weapons undermined the Agency's work (Gordon, 1973, 250). Also the restrictions on West German conventional armed strength have been loosened over the years and were abolished altogether as from 1986.

The Assembly of the WEU has had a fairly undistinguished career. Having no real powers in an organization whose workload seemed to be taken over by other institutions, it attracted members (who were parliamentarians nominated by governments but not only from the governing party) with a high sense of duty but mostly of little standing. It often sparred with the Council and in June 1967 referred back the Council report as being insufficiently informative. Indeed the main use of both the Assembly and the Council of the WEU up until the early 1970s was as meeting points for British and European Community politicians in a forum where they could discuss political developments in Europe (Gordon, 1973, 253; Westhof, 1977, 94–123).

In 1968 Pierre Harmel, the Belgian Foreign Minister, proposed that the WEU Council should discuss questions not covered by the Treaty of Rome, such as foreign and defence issues. This was a clear attempt to keep Britain in close political contact with the Europeans Communities' governments after President de Gaulle of France had issued his second veto on British entry the previous year. When the Middle East situation was placed on the agenda of the Permanent Representatives of WEU the following year, the French government boycotted the meeting and that of subsequent Councils for more than a year. In the end, the EC enlargement negotiations began and it was mutually agreed that the WEU should not dabble in European Communities' matters.

Once Britain joined the Communities, the WEU lost its bridging role. It allowed a core of European Communities' members to discuss ideas of common defence in a European context, something not covered by the Treaties of Rome. In this, it was – and is – only one of a number of forums. The Communities did eventually entertain questions of international security and both IEPG and NATO's Eurogroup take on defence-related topics, though the former is concerned mainly with procurement programmes and the latter lacks French participation. However, the WEU has not faded away. In September 1983 President Mitterrand of France proposed that WEU should form the basis of a 'European identity' in defence matters. This can be seen as an attempt to broaden the close defence cooperation that France had been developing with West Germany in the early 1980s (John, 1985, 2), though without diluting the effort by too many participants. French and West German proposals for a resurrection of WEU were met with British scepticism at first but in June 1984 ministerial meetings were revived after a lapse of many years and all seven member governments felt able to subscribe to the Declaration of Rome made at the foreign ministers' meeting of 26–27 October 1984 (Hoppe, 1991, 274–7). WEU ministers would meet biannually, the ACA and Standing Armaments Committee were reorganized (as outlined above), the political directors of the ministries of foreign affairs and of defence were to meet regularly and the question of a revivified Assembly was discussed. The Permanent Representatives then in London were meeting more often – nearly every two weeks – and a new and active Secretary-General, Alfred Cahen, was in office from 1985 to 1989.

The Rome meeting was followed by gatherings of the WEU's foreign and defence ministers in Bonn (April 1985), Rome (November 1985), Venice (April 1986), and Luxembourg (November 1986 and again in April 1987), leading to the October 1987 meeting in the Hague at which the 'Platform on European Security Interests' was adopted. This 'Platform' became the creed of the revivified WEU. It referred positively to the need to construct an integrated Europe in security and defence, to NATO solidarity and the validity of the Harmel Report, to the strategy of deterrence and defence relying on conventional and nuclear elements, to the irreplaceable nature of US forces in Europe, to the European contribution to the defence of the Alliance – including that of the independent nuclear forces of France and the United Kingdom – to overall deterrence and security, and to arms control and disarmament being an integral part of Western security policy. It was stated that the WEU states intended to assume fully their responsibilities in the field of Western defence, in the fields of arms control and disarmament and in the area of East–West dialogue and cooperation (Western European Union, 1987, 1–9).

The reason for this reactivation of WEU lay not only in the search for a European identity within NATO. There was also a concern, especially by France, to limit changes in West German security policy, and a mistrust of United States security policies

(Mahant, 1988, 22). In the latter case, the American approach to the Reykjavik Summit in 1986, when their negotiating position went way beyond anything agreed in NATO, and the subsequent US–Soviet INF agreement, together with long-standing European reservation about SDI, led some Europeans politicians to call for greater West European defence cooperation. This was aimed both at encouraging a continued US commitment to the defence of Europe – by showing that the Europeans were pulling their weight – and at exploring alternatives should the United States start to cut back on its military presence in Europe.

The Hague 'Platform' seemed long on words and short on action. There have, however, been two major developments in the WEU from its rebirth in 1984 until 1990.

The first was the extension of membership to include Spain and Portugal, which signed accession protocols in November 1988. The significance here was in Spain's acceptance of the 'Platform' and its inclusion of the nuclear policies of the member states as an essential part of the defence of the West. This came at a time when the Socialist government of Spain had been negotiating the removal of certain US bases from its territory because of its aversion to their nuclear nature. Furthermore, Spain was not part of NATO's Integrated Military Command structure and WEU membership provides it – like France – with a multilateral forum for military cooperation with its neighbours.

Secondly, the WEU states coordinated their naval presence in the Gulf during the latter stages of the Gulf War (1980–8) between Iran and Iraq. From August 1987 there was political consultation within WEU on this matter. Technical coordination on the spot and at the admiralty level by the five members with naval vessels in the area took place under WEU's aegis (Cahen, 1987, 11). The two states not directly involved – West Germany and Luxembourg – showed their solidarity in other ways. The Federal Republic replaced units in the NATO area where its partners had left gaps by taking resources to the Gulf, and Luxembourg made a financial contribution.

A further activation of WEU came after the Iraqi invasion of Kuwait on 2 August 1990. Western countries felt their interests threatened by this aggression and WEU foreign and defence ministers met in Paris on 21 August 1990 to discuss their reaction. Also present were observers from Denmark, Greece and Turkey. The ministers called upon Iraq to respect UN resolutions and to withdraw from Kuwait, and agreed to make effective the embargo of Iraq under UN Security Council Resolution 661. They decided to ensure coordination of their response both at a political level and in the region by agreeing on areas of operation and on sharing tasks, logistical support and intelligence. Their defence chiefs of staff then met to translate this agreement into practical measures and to fit the WEU activities into wider cooperation. Zone commanders of WEU naval forces met before similar meetings of all naval representatives of forces in the region. WEU nations decided on a division of the Gulf area into five patrol sectors with vessels from six WEU states (the Federal Republic of Germany, Portugal and Luxembourg did not send ships) patrolling these in turn. By September 1990 WEU ministers had agreed on the further coordination of ground and air forces, especially their transport to the Gulf, and had extended the escort of shipping to the Mediterranean and Red seas (van Eekelen, 1990, 525–9). This helped the integration of these forces, led by the United States, that defeated Iraq early in 1991.

The experience from the Gulf was used at a later stage: by the end of 1992 the WEU was again coordinating the naval vessels of its members in their contribution to the UN blockade of Serbia/Montenegro. After much discussion within the institutions of the WEU, it was finally decided that ground and air forces from the WEU would not become involved in the disputes in former-Yugoslavia until there was a lasting truce. The Council, meeting in Helsinki in July 1992, did however agree on a naval and air surveillance of the UN Security Council embargo on Serbia and Montenegro. Six members contributed vessels and airplanes to the WEU's first European operation, 'Sharp Vigilace', in the Strait of Otranto and the Adriatic Sea (Assembly of Western European Union, 1992, 20–1).

December 1991 saw another development in the role of the WEU in West European defence policy. The Intergovernment Conference of the 12 EC governments agreed on the Maastricht Treaty on European Union, signed in February 1992 (see pp. 158–9). One of the objectives of the Union was to 'assert its identity on the international scene, in particular through the implementation of a common foreign and security policy which shall include the eventual framing of a common defence policy' (Treaty in European Union, 1992, Title I, Common Provisions, Article B). In the body of the Treaty, it is stated that the Union 'requests the Western European Union, which is an integral part of the development of the European Union, to elaborate and implement decisions and actions of the Union which have defence implications'. The necessary practicalities are to be decided by the Council of the European Union and the institutions of the WEU (op.cit., Article J.4.2). Furthermore, the provisions of this 'defence' article of the Maastricht Treaty can be revised on the basis of a report in 1996 by the European Council (the meeting of that Union's heads of state or government), bearing in mind that the 1948 Brussels Treaty – the basis for WEU – comes to the end of its life-span in 1998.

Thus the Maastricht Treaty took the first steps to formalize the position of the WEU as the basis for the defence component of the European Union. At the same time – December 1991 – the member states of the WEU, which were also nine of the founder members of the European Union, declared that 'a genuine European security and defence identity and a greater European responsibility on defence matters' would be a gradual process. They agreed to strengthen the WEU in the context of a common defence policy within the European Union 'which might in time lead to a common defence, compatible with that of the Atlantic Alliance'. Drawing together the two strands of the WEU, they saw it being developed as 'the defence component of the European Union' and as a means 'to strengthen the European pillar of the Atlantic Alliance' (op.cit., Annex II.29).

Two practical problems arose from these declarations. The first was that of the memberships of the European Union and the WEU. In 1991 there were three signatories of the European Union Treaty that were not members of the WEU – Denmark, Greece and Ireland. Also if the WEU was planning to be 'the European pillar of the Atlantic Alliance', then there were three European members of NATO that were members of neither the WEU nor the proposed European Union – Iceland, Norway and Turkey. This problem was dealt with in a Declaration by the member states of the WEU, appended to the Maastricht Treaty, that offered full membership of (or observer status in) the WEU to all members of the European Union, and associate membership of the WEU to other, non-European Union, European members of NATO. These relationships were fleshed out in the Petersberg Declaration of the Western European Union Council on Ministers of 19 June 1992. Obervers could attend WEU Council meetings that were not otherwise restricted and could be invited to working groups. They would have the same rights and responsibilities as full members for functions transferred to the WEU from other institutions of which they were members (for example the CSCE or the European Union). Associate members could, under most circumstances, participate fully in WEU Council meetings and subsidiary bodies. They could not, however, block a decision agreed on by the full members. As a result, from 1 January 1993 Greece became the tenth member of the WEU and Norway and Turkey became associate members. Denmark has become a 'permanent observer' and Eire has accepted observer status, though has not activated it.

The second practical aspect of the Maastricht Treaty was that of turning promises into action. In order to develop a close relationship between the WEU and the European Union, the headquarters of the WEU's Secretariat and the Council has been moved to Brussels, and the meetings of the two organizations will eventually be synchronized. The move to Brussels also helps closer cooperation with NATO.

WEU's operational role will be strengthened by a meeting of the Defence Chiefs of Staff to be held prior to the ministerial Council, by military delegations supplementing the WEU institutions in Brussels, and by the creation as from April 1993 of a Planning Cell within the WEU. This was to prepare military contingency plans, recommend command, control and communications arrangements and list units that could be used for WEU operations. Members were prepared to make available conventional armed forces for tasks under the WEU's authority, and in May 1992 Chancellor Kohl of Germany and President Mitterrand of France decided to create a Franco-German army corps 'with a European vocation' that could take up collective self-defence missions – as in the North Atlantic Treaty and the Brussels Treaty, peacekeeping and humanitarian operations. It is to consist of a French division, a German division and a Franco-German brigade and should be operational by October 1995. In January 1993, SACEUR (see above p. 206) and the Chiefs of Staff of France and Germany agreed on the formation of a 'Eurocorps' – with the Franco-German contribution as its basis – for employment within the Atlantic Alliance (Van Beveren, 1993, 22 – 7).

The plan seems to be to create a European army that can be tasked by WEU and other organizations. Apart from common defence, these military units could also be used for humanitarian and rescue tasks, peacekeeping activities, and contributions to crisis management (Western European Union, 1992, p. 8). Experts are also to examine the possibility – with IEPG (see above p. 243) – of creating a European Armaments Agency, and there are plans for the Eurogroup (see above p. 244) to transfer some or all of its functions to the WEU. An experimental WEU Satellite Centre has been established in Spain (Sheehan, 1992). WEU has made a contribution to NATO on the issue of arms control verification and has started its own dialogue with East and Central European countries. The groundwork has been laid for an active role by the WEU until either its demise in 1998 or its full inclusion into the European Union after 1996.

Contribution

The role of the WEU in the integration of Europe has changed over time. Some of the original powers it had in its constitution – to solve the Saarland question and to check on German rearmament – went by default, and for a time the organization was overshadowed by the divide between the United Kingdom and France over the future of the European Communities. However, since the mid-1980s the WEU has taken on two complementary tasks: those of representing the European pillar of the Atlantic Alliance and of forming the defence component of Western European integration as more recently displayed in the European Union. 'The role of the WEU in relation to the Atlantic Alliance seems to be more a "ginger group" than a "caucus"' (Jorgensen, 1990, 150). The WEU's 1992 Petersberg Declaration put some flesh on these intentions but the members of the organization showed a marked reluctance, in September and October 1991, to send an armed WEU force into the fragmenting Yugoslavia, even to protect and support EC monitoring efforts (Salmon, 1992, pp. 250–1). A further weakening of the defence element in West European cooperation could come with the extension of the European Union to include neutral countries such as Austria, Finland and Sweden. There are some indications that these countries after the end of the Cold War will be more willing to participate in defence cooperation, perhaps as observers at first. However, there have been some demands from those that wish a stronger European defence posture that the neutral candidate members should commit themselves in advance to supporting the development of the Union's defence role in 1996.

While the WEU is busy creating the mechanisms for the implementation of an eventual European Union defence policy, there remains some doubt as to whether the member states will allow out of their hands the control of such vital policy. If they do, then some of the dreams that inspired the European Defence Community proposal will at last be realized.

References

Assembly of Western European Union, 1992: *Thirty-eighth Ordinary Session Report Submitted on Behalf of the Committee for Parliamentary and Public Relations* (Document 1334, draft). Paris: Assembly of WEU.

Cahen, A. 1987: *La contribution de l'Union Occidentale au processus de construction européenne.* London: WEU.

Dilks, D. 1985: The British view of security: Europe and a wider world, 1945–1948. In Riste, O. (ed.), *Western Security: The Formative Years* (Oslo: Universitetsforlaget), 25–59.

Gordon, C. 1973: The WEU and European Defence Cooperation. *Orbis* XVII, 1, 247–57.

Hoppe, U. 1991: The Western European Union. In Jopp, M., Rummel, R. and Schmidt, P., *Integration and Security in Western Europe.* Boulder: Westview Press, 270–82.

Mahant, E. 1988: *Western European Union – or the Reactivation of the Platitude.* St Louis: International Studies Association (mimeo).

John, I. 1985: West European Union. An organisation in search of a role. *The Council for Arms Control Bulletin* 18, 1, 2 & 5.

Jorgensen, K.E. 1990 The Western European Union and the Imbroglio of European Security. *Cooperation and Conflict* XXV:3, 135–52.

Salmon, T. 1992: Testing times for European political cooperation: the Gulf and Yugoslavia 1990–1992. *International Affairs* 68, 2, 233–53.

Sheehan, M. 1992: *Western European Military Space Cooperation.* BISA Conference Paper, December 1992 (mimeo).

Taylor, T. 1982: *Defence, Technology and International Integration.* London: Frances Pinter.

—— 1984: *European Defence Cooperation.* Chatham House Papers 24. London: Routledge & Kegan Paul.

Treaty of European Union 1992: Luxembourg: Office for Official Publications of the European Communities.

Van Beveren, R. 1993: Military cooperation: what structure for the future? *Chaillot Papers* 6. Paris: Institute for Security Studies.

Van Eekelen, W. 1990: WEU and the Gulf Crisis. *Survival* XXX:11, 6, 519–32.

Western European Union 1987: *Platform on European Security Interests The Hague, 27 October 1987.* London: WEU (mimeo).

—— 1992: *Petersberg Declaration, Bonn, 19 June 1992.* London: WEU (mimeo).

Westhof, J. 1977: L'Union de l'europe Occidentale avant et après l'élargissement des Communautés européennes. *Annuaire européen* 23, 94–123.

11

Comecon and the Warsaw Treaty Organization

Establishment

An effective international organization linking the states of the Soviet bloc was not needed by the Soviet leadership before 1954. Until his death in March 1953, Stalin held a tight grip on power not only in the Soviet Union but also in the states of Eastern Europe. The communist parties were entrenched in government in Bulgaria, Czechoslovakia, the German Democratic Republic (as Soviet-occupied East Germany became), Hungary, Poland and Rumania, and any dissident voices were purged from the Party so that only leaders faithful to Stalin were left. The Communist Information Bureau (Cominform) was established in September 1947 to impose Moscow's party line on communist parties world-wide, including those in Eastern Europe. However, once communist power was established in the East European states, the Cominform seems to have had less importance with the Communist Party of the Soviet Union and its leader – Stalin – communicating their wishes directly to East European leaders. Furthermore, a series of bilateral defence treaties were signed between the Soviet Union and the East European states and after 1948 their armies were remoulded along Soviet lines, often with Soviet officers (of the appropriate nationality) in charge. By 1953 the conscript armies of Eastern Europe made up 15 divisions and could be used either to defend the Soviet Union or as part of an offensive operation (Johnson, 1976, 40). On the economic side, Stalin made sure that no regional cooperation was allowed in Eastern Europe, and economic activity was determined by the needs of the Soviet Union.

However, the Council on Mutual Economic Assistance – often known as Comecon – was created in the Cold War period immediately following the Second World War. As a result of the

Marshall Plan, Western countries had established the OEEC in 1948 (see Chapter 3) but the Soviet Union had made sure that the East European states had been excluded from what Stalin regarded as an American effort to impose its economic and political system on the whole of Europe. One communist-run government that had started to fall out with Stalin was that of Yugoslavia. Its President Tito had come to power as a resistance leader and, unlike the communist leaders in other East European states, did not feel that he owed his position to the Soviet army. In an effort to bring Tito to heel, Stalin withdrew economic support from Yugoslavia in 1948, but Tito went instead to the United States for assistance. To bring the rest of the East European states publicly into line and also to respond to the creation of the OEEC, Stalin established the Council on Mutual Economic Assistance in January 1949 with the Soviet Union, Bulgaria, Czechoslovakia, Hungary, Poland and Romania as its original members. In fact the Council was a propaganda ploy – it scarcely existed except on paper. Its only activity at that time was to make sure that the East Europeans followed the Soviet trade embargo of Yugoslavia.

Comecon later widened its membership to include the German Democratic Republic and Albania in the 1950s, Mongolia in 1964, Cuba in 1972 and Vietnam in 1978. Angola, Laos, North Korea and China (until 1966) were observers in Comecon and Yugoslavia became a semi-associate. Joint committees were established with Finland, Iraq, India and Mexico after 1975. In 1964 Albania ceased to attend meetings of Comecon when its leadership fell out with Moscow. The German Democratic Republic ceased to be a member when it became part of the Federal Republic of Germany in October 1990, and the remaining nine states – the Soviet Union, Bulgaria, Cuba, Czechoslovakia, Hungary, Mongolia, Poland, Romania and Vietnam – dissolved the organization at a ministerial meeting held in Budapest on 26 June 1991.

The Warsaw Treaty Organization (WTO) was set up in May 1955 but its background was that of the Cold War in the late 1940s. At that time, the Soviet Union had installed Communist governments in East and Central Europe that were in reality puppets of the Kremlin in Moscow. After Stalin died in 1953, the new leadership in the Soviet Union started an internal debate on defence. Kruschev – who eventually became the new leader – wanted to cut down the number of troops built up by Stalin, a move that would have military consequences for the East European states. Furthermore, the death of Stalin had ended his personalized control of Eastern Europe (as well as the Soviet Union), which suggested that the Soviet domination of its satellite states might have to be more institutionalized above and beyond the existing bilateral treaties the Soviets had with most of those states.

The need for a multilateral defence agreement between the Soviet Union and its East European satellites became more immediate in May 1955. On 14 May 1955 the Soviet Union, Albania, Bulgaria, Czechoslovakia, the German Democratic Republic (East Germany), Hungary, Poland and Rumania signed the Warsaw Treaty. Some of the ministers arriving in Warsaw did not even know why they were being brought there. The immediate reasons for the establishment of the resulting Warsaw Treaty Organization lay in events in Western Europe. On 5 May 1955 the Federal Republic of Germany (West Germany) had joined NATO and the WEU and its remilitarization began. The Soviet Union had made every diplomatic attempt to forestall this move, even applying for NATO membership for itself in May 1954. The NATO countries rebuffed these Soviet moves. The leadership in Moscow then considered that the creation of a defence alliance in Eastern Europe, superficially similar to NATO, might give them a base from which to negotiate the abandonment of both institutions and the creation of an all-European organization within which the Soviets could have some influence. The signing of the Warsaw Treaty thus represented a diplomatic riposte to the NATO states and its preamble specifically mentions the integration of West Germany into NATO as a menace 'to the national security of the peaceloving states' (Vaughan, 1976, 134).

In 1954 the new government in the Soviet Union, as part of its attempt to improve relations with the West after the Stalin period, had negotiated a treaty that gave Austria a neutral status. Like Germany, Austria had been occupied in 1945 by the USA, the Soviet Union, the United Kingdom and France. By giving Austria its independence back, by taking out the occupation troops and by creating a neutral country, the new Soviet leadership had not only shown that they were prepared to make deals with the West but also created a model for a German settlement. However, any hope of a neutral unoccupied Germany had disappeared by early 1955 and the withdrawal of Soviet occupying troops from Austria as a result of the Austrian State Treaty to be signed on 15 May 1955 caused a problem for the Soviet Union. The need for military access to Austria had been given as the reason for the presence of their troops in Hungary and Rumania: if Soviet troops were to leave Austria, then their legal basis in those two states was undermined. The Warsaw Treaty provided a new excuse for Soviet troop presence in those two countries.

Finally, there was an internal Soviet reason for the creation of the WTO. The new leadership in the Soviet Union – especially Kruschev – was anxious to dismantle the remnants of personal rule created by Stalin. One example of this was the use of Soviet officers in command positions in the armies of East European countries such as Poland. With the creation of WTO, the relations between the Soviet and East European armed forces could be placed on a more internationally acceptable basis and the Soviet officers replaced by national officers, albeit those trained and closely controlled by the USSR.

Albania ceased to attend WTO meetings during the 1960s and left the organization after the intervention in Czechoslovakia by the troops of Warsaw Treaty countries in August 1968. The military structure of the WTO was dismantled in March 1991 and the Organization was disbanded at a meeting of the Political Consultative Committee (see below) in Prague on 1 July 1991.

Institutions

Comecon was more or less a paper organization after its establishment in 1949. It held the first meetiag of a Council – in which all states were represented – in August 1949 and set up a Bureau, being its permanent executive organ in which each state was represented by a delegate (John, 1980, 113). In 1954 a permanent Secretariat, based in Moscow, took over the administrative functions of the organization from the Bureau. It was only in December 1959 that a statute appeared in which the organization of Comecon appeared and this came into effect, after ratification, in April 1960. The main body of Comecon was the Council which could make recommendations and take decisions, though the latter only applied to organizational and procedural matters (Vaughan, 1976, 142). Neither recommendations nor decisions could be applied to states that had not agreed to them. The session of the Council was to meet at least annually and was to decide Comecon's major policies and could establish subordinate organs. The Executive Committee consisted of a representative from each member at the Deputy Head of Government level and it could adopt recommendations, make decisions and submit proposals to the Council. Standing Commissions dealing with particular issues could be established by the Council. The Secretary of the Council was to be appointed by the Council and his deputies by the Executive Committee (op. cit., 143). In 1971 an Interstate Commission for Accounting Techniques was set up. The Executive Committee established two important committees, the Committee for Cooperation in Material and Technical Supply and the Committee for Scientific and Technical Cooperation. It also set up a Military–Industrial Commission, under which were 21 permanent branch industrial commissions and which was closely tied in to the WTO (Chechinski, 1987, 18–25).

When the WTO was created in 1955 its highest political authority was the Political Consultative Committee (PCC), comprising of the ministers of defence and of foreign affairs of the member governments and of the secretaries of the ruling Communist parties. In 1956 a Secretariat and a Permanent Commission were established to help give foreign policy guidance to members. A WTO staff was established in Moscow as part of the Soviet Ministry of Defence, and the Commander-in-Chief of the WTO forces was invariably a high-ranking Soviet officer (John, 1980, 116).

During the period from 1955 to 1965 the PCC met only six times and always in Moscow. It did not seem to discuss important issues – such as the Cuban Missile Crisis in 1962 – but was more an instrument used by the Soviet Union to enunciate its policy. In March 1969, in the wake of the invasion of Czechoslovakia, the institutions of the WTO were reformed at the Budapest PCC. The military Combined Command structure was reconstituted and a permanent staff was created in Moscow, and a Military Council was established as a 'consultative and advisory organ of the WTO's military officers' (op. cit., 123). Also a Committee of Defence Ministers (CDM), a Technical Committee and a Military Scientific–Technical Council were set up. National deputy defence ministers were to become Deputy Commanders-in-Chief of the WTO joint command. A Staff of Joint Armed Forces was set up consisting of the Chief of Staff and his deputies and Deputy Chiefs of Staff from the other WTO members. These changes seemed to reflect a willingness of the leadership to tighten up the multilateral mechanism of military control in the region after the debacle of Czechoslovakia in 1968. This also meant a greater institutionalization of relations, with the PCC meeting regularly and by rota in national capitals. It seems that the PCC coordinated foreign policy among members and received reports from the CDM and from the Commander-in-Chief on military questions. The CDM was primarily a means of communications with national defence ministries (Caldwell, 1975, 6–7).

Further institutional developments came after the Bucharest PCC in November 1976 when a Foreign Ministers Committee was set up and a Joint Secretariat of the PCC established to improve the mechanism of political collaboration. This reflected the need for a more united foreign policy stand in a period of detente.

During the late 1970s and early 80s the organization became atrophied, reflecting the ageing – and often dying – Soviet leadership, but once Mr Gorbachev came to power, a renovation took place. At the Berlin PCC in May 1987 it was agreed to institute a new mechanism, namely that of multilateral groups of member states providing information for each other. Furthermore, a special commission on disarmament questions was established.

Achievements

The achievements of both the Warsaw Pact and Comecon must be seen more in terms of the motivations for their creation and continued existence. Also it should be noted that it is often difficult to disentangle the activities of the organizations, and of the members acting within their institutions, from what has been undertaken as a result of bilateral relations between the Soviet Union and one, or more, of the individual members of Comecon or the WTO. Furthermore, the importance of the intimate links before 1989 between the various Communist parties in the member states should be remembered.

Any appreciation of Comecon must bear in mind the aims of the organization which were, as set down in its 1959 Charter, uniting and coordinating the efforts of the members, the planned development of the national economy, acceleration of economic and technical progress in the member states, industrialization of the less developed countries, growth in productivity and an advance in people's welfare. Though many, if not all, of these aims may have been reached, the official statistics of the past may have painted an optimistic picture compared with the real achievements, and little account was made – until recently – of the environmental, economic and social costs of these policies. Furthermore many of the aims were reached by national effort rather than by coordination through Comecon.

At its first meeting in August 1949 Comecon seemingly passed a resolution concerning economic–technical documentation (John, 1980, 113). However, this seems to have been the limit of its activity until 1954, after the death of Stalin. In 1958 the principles of fixing prices between the member states was accepted and a formal Charter for the organization adopted in 1959. This was part of the second stage of the coordination plan for Comecon members (the first having supposedly taken place between 1949 and 1954), whereby an effort was made to 'harmonize the needs and possibilities of the countries in physical terms' (Simai, 1990, 50).

During the 1960s Comecon was given greater scope for activity through the desire of the Soviet leadership to legitimate – especially in the eyes of the emerging Third World – their relations with Eastern Europe. Furthermore, the success of the EEC which strengthened Western Europe both economically and politically seemed to evince from Moscow a determination to copy the example of integration. The third stage of the Comecon coordination plan (1962 to 1975) was meant to establish, joint planning for the region as a whole in the form of a modified version of central national planning (op. cit.,). The idea was that this 'international socialist division of labour' would make for the 'maximum utilization of the advantages of the world socialist system' (Vaughan, 1976, 145). However, this plan was staunchly opposed by Romania which feared it would become merely an agricultural economy designated to feed its neighbours, and it thus opposed the transmitting of the levers of social and economic life 'to the competence of superstate or extrastate bodies' which 'would turn sovereignty into a meaningless notion' (op. cit., 150). In the end, the Basic Principles in Internationalist Division of Labour adopted by Comecon in 1961–2 emphasized the need to coordinate economic plans, and the effort of the Soviet leader, Kruschev, to give Comecon greater power was defeated.

However, some progress was made. In 1963 the International Bank for Economic Cooperation was established and the transferable rouble introduced for trading purposes. An International Bank for Investment was also set up, but neither of these institutions fulfilled their promise because of the difference between Comecon members over the role of central planning. Nevertheless other specialized agencies were established, such as Intermetall in 1964 aimed at coordinating iron and steel production and the Common Wagon Pool for railway rolling-stock.

The onset of detente in the late 1960s and early 70s opened up greater possibilities for trade and contact with the West. Western European integration was continuing apace and the EC had started to adopt a common policy in its dealings with third countries. Furthermore the oil crisis of 1973-4 lead to a massive increase in petroleum and gas prices that affected the world economy, including that of the Soviet bloc. The Soviet Union responded to the latter event by repricing the oil it supplied to Comecon members, though it was still sold at below market price. A system of gas pipelines and an electricity grid was built during the 1970s, perhaps doing more to draw the East European economies together than all of the previous attempts at centralized planning.

More generally, Comecon had adopted a long-term Comprehensive Programme in 1971 which set out the progress of integration for the following 15 years. At the Berlin meeting in 1976, these plans for the completion of integrated Comecon planning by 1980 were dropped in favour of a more sectoral approach (Glendenning, 1977, 16). At the 1974 Sofia meeting Comecon was authorized to conduct relations with other states and international organizations, though attempts to create bloc-to-bloc arrangements with the EC failed as the Communities did not feel that Comecon was at all equivalent to itself. It seemed that the recession caused by the oil crisis and the failure to institutionalize links with Western Europe, if anything, forced the East European states back on dependence on the Soviet Union (Kanet, 1976, 81). This reliance was emphasized by the use of subsidized Soviet oil in their industries.

The process of economic integration between the Comecon countries had become very uneven by the 1980s. Some states – such as Hungary – were looking more to the West for their markets and their economic ideas, while others – such as Romania – were falling back into central planning and autarky. Poland had a massive debt with the West, a leftover of its failed attempt to revitalize its economy in the 1970s. Cooperation within Comecon had become increasingly bilateral, though the various committees of the organization were used. In this period neither 'the domestic nor the international conditions developed favourably from the point of view of furthering CMEA [Comecon] integration' (Simai, 1990, 50).

Nevertheless at its 1985 Council, Comecon confirmed the goals of the close coordination of long-term plans; long-term cooperative agreements for Soviet natural gas; joint action on scientific and technical work; emphasis on trade within the bloc, especially the export of consumer goods to the Soviet Union; and limitations on trade with the West. The reality of the situation was that the 'price structure within the trading bloc is in a shambles' (Kusin, 1986, 42) and countries such as Hungary had little to gain from a tightening of Comecon cooperation.

By the end of the 1980s, most of the East European states had become an economic deadweight for the Soviet Union which had to support them with subsidized oil. From the East European perspective, Comecon trade meant not getting a decent price for manufactured goods which could otherwise be sold in the West for hard currency. However, the economic and political basis of the Communist governments – imposed on the area in the immediate post-Second World War period – was beginning to crumble and, once it became clear that Soviet tanks would not rescue the leaderships of these countries, their days were numbered. Comecon, reflecting its member governments, had just not been able to provide the sort of standard of living that the people of Eastern Europe were increasingly expecting. Instead it was part of a political system that had become ever more despised. With the end of Communist governments in Eastern Europe in 1989, Comecon melted away.

An examination of the achievements of the Warsaw Pact shows that its utility reflects the development of East–West relations, relationships between the Soviet Union and individual WTO states, as well as some of the security–political peculiarities of the members.

From 1955 until 1969 the WTO as an organization was at first quiescent though then started to play a role in the important changes in Soviet military thinking. From 1961, the East European allies of the Soviet Union were given a new mission – that of substituting their troops for those of the Soviet army in Eastern Europe – as the Soviet leader, Mr Kruschev, attempted to cut the size of Soviet ground forces. The armies were modernized, joint exercises held and consultation among defence ministers increased. It seemed that the Soviet bloc was developing a concept of 'coalition warfare', making the East European states an extension of Soviet military power. This treatment encouraged the already nationalist-tinged Romanian Communist Government to try to disengage itself more from the Soviet military grip, but it also had a price in the increased say that the East Europeans wanted in the running of the WTO and, possibly, in the 'rena-tionalization' of their officer class (Remington, 1987, 76–7). While the Soviet leaders may have hoped that the WTO would have pro-vided greater cohesion in Eastern Europe (Johnson, 1976, 43), this did not happen and Romania recognized the Federal Republic of Germany in 1967 against the wishes of other members. WTO members failed to issue a statement backing the USSR in its dispute with China in 1969, and it took force of arms to bring the reformist Czechoslovak Communists into line in 1968. The Brezhnev Doctrine of the Soviet leader suggested that the needs of the Soviet bloc were to be placed above the territorial integrity of WTO members. This view was denounced by President Ceausescu of Romania.

During the period of detente from 1969 to 1976, the WTO was increasingly used by the Soviet Union in its military dealings with the East European states. The more direct means of operation – such as army to army or communist party to communist party – were still the most important means of relationship, but the WTO had come to serve a purpose. It had helped to legitimate in Eastern Europe the Soviet armed intervention in Czechoslovakia in August 1968, in which the armies of other WTO members (except Albania, which then left the WTO, and Romania) participated. Furthermore, the WTO members increased their military expen-diture during this period, though by vastly differing amounts (Nelson, 1986, 18–19) and the Soviet military presence in Eastern Europe was strengthened. Particular importance was attached to the three 'Northern Tier' states – Poland, East Germany and Czechoslovakia – because of their geo-strategic position in rela-tion to West Germany.

From 1976 to 1986 the WTO faced a hardening of East–West relations, under an ageing Soviet leadership. As the New Cold War took hold at the end of the 1970s and the confrontation in Europe took on an increasingly military tinge, it might have been expected that the WTO members would have become more loyal to the Soviet cause. This was not always the case. On the military side, the Soviet Union continued its build-up of forces in Eastern Europe, requiring further East European contributions for the command structure of Combined Armed Forces introduced after 1978. It seemed that the Soviet Union was increasingly moulding the WTO armed forces into a unified war machine. On the political side, they were not so successful. Ceausescu resisted calls for increased WTO military expenditure at the end of the

1970s and Honecker of East Germany pushed for closer relations with West Germany in 1984 against Soviet opposition.

It does seem that even before Gorbachev had come to power in the Soviet Union in 1985, the WTO was not the tight military pact that it was sometimes thought to be. It could at best be described as 'a complex mechanism for coordinating the military and foreign policy activities of its members' (Holloway, 1984, 37) and even 'no longer a tidy instrument for Soviet penetration and control of Eastern Europe, although those purposes are still pre-eminent' (Nelson, 1986, 109).

Though the Warsaw Treaty was renewed for another 20 years in 1985, its days were numbered. It had become more 'a reflection of the Soviet's weaknesses much more than its own strengths' (op. cit.). The decision by Gorbachev to pursue the theme of common security with the West, thereby ending the confrontation of the Cold War, and his increasing renunciation of the Brezhnev Doctrine robbed the WTO of its two main reasons for existence: the defence of the Soviet bloc and the guaranteeing of continued communist rule within that bloc. The WTO became an interlocutor for NATO in the CFE negotiations (see p. 232) and gave political support to Gorbachev's various arms control and disarmament initiatives. In the end, the fall of communism in Eastern Europe took away the last vestiges of cement that held the organization together. The founders of the WTO had, in the Treaty, espoused 'a system of collective security in Europe, with the participation of all the European states, irrespective of their social and state systems' (Vaughan, 1976, 133). Its members came closer to this goal with their membership of CSCE and, after the demise of the WTO, of the North Atlantic Cooperation Council.

Contribution

The WTO and Comecon have often been seen as organizations that merely projected Soviet power into Eastern Europe. That description has a good deal of truth behind it, especially when the earlier days of the organizations are considered. However, both the WTO and Comecon gave the non-Soviet members the chance to articulate and aggregate their views of security and economic affairs within the Soviet bloc. Their voices may have been muted and their requests sometimes overridden, but the existence of the two institutions seem to have given them opportunities that otherwise would have not been available to affect Soviet decisions.

The norms that both organizations were meant to establish were clearly those of the 'Socialist Commonwealth' and the communist system. Thus they can be seen as two of the more subtle methods of Soviet control of Eastern Europe – or, at least, of its leadership. Even there some failure should be noted, especially with Ceausescu of Romania. A greater lack of response can be seen among the people of Eastern Europe, most of whom had little belief in the socialist norms of the two organizations.

Comecon was able to recruit other members of the 'Socialist Commonwealth' – such as Cuba and Mongolia – to its ranks, though neither it nor the WTO had little success in bringing in non-Communist states to the system. Furthermore, both organizations lost members – Albania and East Germany.

The rule-making, rule-application and rule-adjudication functions of the two bodies is hard to estimate in isolation from such tasks carried out on a state-to-state or communist party-to-communist party basis. Within both organizations rules were clearly made and applied, but the most important agreements were probably reached outside the strict confines of the organizations' institutions. It is worth noting that Comecon had some trouble in decision-making because of its consensus system: a number of its plans were stopped by Romanian intransigence.

The operational activities of both organizations can be seen in the Comecon projects and the joint military activities (such as manoeuvres) by the WTO, though the latter may also have been conducted as a result of other bilateral agreements.

The way that both Comecon and the WTO disappeared at the end of the Cold War seemed to suggest that they were unwanted by the peoples of Eastern Europe and were certainly seen as reminders of Soviet and communist dominance. The East and Central European countries have sought a number of regional arrangements in their stead and have also looked to wider organizations such as the CSCE and NACC for security. However, these countries have been so far excluded from the EC and from NATO, the two organizations that Comecon and the WTO opposed for so long; but it is the members of those Western organizations that are now keeping them out. It would seem that the alternatives to Comecon and WTO are not yet available to the former members of those organizations. There is the danger that a new barrier, quite different from that of the Iron Curtain between East and West, is being installed in Europe. It is to be hoped that it will not prove as durable.

References

Caldwell, L.T. 1975: The Warsaw Pact: directions of change. *Problems of Communism* XXIV: 5, 7–19.

Chechinski, M. 1987: Warsaw Pact/CEMA military–economic trends. *Problems of Communism* XXXVI: 2. 15–28.

Glendenning, P.H. 1977: Comecon: progress and prospects. Report of the 6th NATO colloquium. *NATO Review* June 1977, 16.

Holloway, J. and Sharp, J. (eds.) 1984: *The Warsaw Pact: Alliance in Transition*. Ithica: Cornell University Press.

John, I.G. 1980: Co-operation in Socialist Europe: CMEA and the Warsaw Pact. In Twitchett, K.J., *European Co-operation Today* (London: Europa), 110–39

Johnson, A.R. 1976: Has Eastern Europe become a liability to the Soviet Union? The military aspect. In Gati, C., *The International Politics of Eastern Europe* (New York: Praeger), 40–55.

Kanet, R. 1976; East–West trade and the limits of Western influence. In Gati, C., *The New International Politics of Eastern Europe* (New York: Praeger), 204–8.

Kusin, V. 1986: Gorbachev and Eastern Europe. *Problems of Communism* XXXV:1, 39–53.

Nelson, D.N. 1986: *Alliance Behavior in the Warsaw Pact*. Boulder and London: Westview Press.

Okolicsanyi, K. 1993: The Visegrad Triangle's free trade zone. *RFE/RL Research Report* 2:3, 19–22.

Remington, R.A. 1987: Western images of the Warsaw Pact. *Problems of Communism* XXXVI: 2, 69–80.

Simai, M. 1990: Co-operation: the CMEA experience. In Groom, A.J.R. and Taylor, P. (eds.), *Frameworks for International Co-operation* (London: Pinter), 44–55.

Vaughan, R. 1976: *Post-War Integration in Europe*. London: Edward Arnold.

12

Conference on Security and Cooperation in Europe

Establishment

The Conference on Security and Cooperation (CSCE) in Europe has gone through two major changes during its lifetime. In the early 1970s it was indeed just a conference with the aim of ameliorating East-West divisions in Europe and producing a semi-formal peace treaty for the Second World War. The signing of the Helsinki Final Act (which was not an international treaty) in August 1975 by 35 states opened a new chapter for the CSCE by providing it with a 'constitution', while since late 1989 it has become increasingly institutionalized and more concerned with the problems arising from the end of the Cold War.

The genesis of the CSCE lay in the period of detente experienced by Europe in the late 1960s and early 70s (see above pp. 30-2). During that time the two military alliances – NATO and the Warsaw Treaty Organization (WTO) – had prepared international initiatives to further detente, but on their own very different terms.

At the Bucharest meeting of the Warsaw Treaty Organization in July 1966, the Soviet bloc states reiterated an old Soviet idea, that of the creation of a European Conference on Security bringing together all the countries of Europe. Clearly at that stage the Soviet Union thought that such a conference would be to their advantage, especially as it could lead to the uncoupling of the United States from Western Europe. The NATO states, adopting the Harmel Report in 1967 (see above p. 219), suggested that there might be discussions between both the blocs in Europe about a reduction in conventional weapons there, a move that was seen to the to the advantage of the numerically inferior NATO forces in

Europe. By the early 1970s, after a good deal of diplomatic sparring, the two sides – encouraged by the neutral and non-aligned (NNA) states – agreed a compromise formula that entailed the establishment of negotiations between the NATO and WTO countries with forces in Central Europe – the Mutual and Balanced Force Reductions (MBFR) talks in Vienna, and a broader Conference on Security and Cooperation in Europe (CSCE) taking place in Helsinki.

The discussions in the Conference on Security and Cooperation in Europe were long and difficult, but, during a period of detente, the two sides wished to come to an agreement and had sufficient common interests to do so. The Soviets wished to obtain Western recognition of the immutability of the post-war European frontiers – especially the division of Germany – and to gain access to Western technology and credits. The Western states were prepared to accept that frontiers should not be changed, except by peaceful agreement, but that these frontiers should become more porous, with the peoples of the Soviet bloc having access to the other peoples of Europe and their ideas and culture. This seemed to be their price for what the Soviets wanted. Despite these two different views of what CSCE was about, NATO and WTO states – and the NNA countries – were persuaded to subscribe to the Helsinki Final Act on 1 August 1975. A diplomat wrote that 'The Helsinki Summit was the high-water mark of the detente era of the 1970s; it was the very symbol of detente, and its most ambitious manifestation' (Maresca, 1987, xi).

The Helsinki Final Act was agreed by 35 states, all 33 European countries except the isolationist Communist-ruled Albania, and the two North American states that had troops in Europe, the United States and Canada. Although not an internationally binding treaty, the Final Act was a demonstration of political intent. The Act was divided into a preamble, a declaration of principles and three main sections or 'baskets': security and arms control (Basket I), economic cooperation (Basket II); and human rights and humanitarian issues (Basket III). Basically the agreement sets out standards by which states should act towards each other and towards their own people. The latter aspect was a victory for the Western countries which were determined to make human rights a valid factor in the relations between states.

The preamble recognized the 'indivisibility of security in Europe', as well as the common interest of the parties in the development of cooperation throughout Europe (*Survival*, 1975,

295–6). The principles for guiding relations between the participating states included sovereign equality and the respect for the rights inherent in sovereignty such as the rights of states to choose and develop their own political, social, economic and cultural systems. States were to refrain from the use or threat of force against the territorial integrity or political independence of any state, and frontiers were to be inviolable. Other state's territory should not be seized or usurped or made the object of military occupation. However, frontiers could be changed 'in accordance with international law, peaceful means and agreement' (op. cit., 296). States should refrain from intervening in the internal and external affairs falling within the domestic jurisdiction of other member states and thus from armed intervention, coercion or assistance to terrorism.

The states were to respect human rights and fundamental freedoms 'including the freedom of thought, conscience, religion or belief' and were to promote 'civil, political, economic, social, cultural and other rights and freedoms' (op. cit., 297). National minorities were to be accorded equality before the law. It was recognized that the respect of human rights and fundamental freedoms was an essential factor to develop friendly relations and cooperation among states.

States were to respect 'the equal rights of peoples and their right to self-determination . . . all peoples always have the right in full freedom, to determine, when and as they wish, their internal and external political status without external interference, and to pursue as they wish their political, economic, social and cultural development' (op. cit., 297–8). This article had a disruptive potential, given the patchwork quilt of national groups and of 'peoples' (however defined) in Europe.

Cooperation was to be developed between the participating states, in order to bring 'the well-being of peoples' and to contribute to the fulfilment of aspirations through increased mutual knowledge and from progress and achievement in the 'economic social, scientific, technological, social, cultural and humanitarian fields'. Governments, institutions, organizations and peoples have 'a relevant and positive role' to play in achieving the aims of cooperation (op. cit., 298). States were to fulfil their obligations under international law and to settle disputes by peaceful means.

These principles were seen as being unexceptional at the time, but they contained the seeds of change. Apart from the article on self-determination, the link between the respect for human rights and friendly relations between states made that subject an issue of inter-state relationships. In other words, one European state could express disquiet about human rights in another European state not just because of humanitarian concern, but also because of a fear that inter-state relations could be adversely affected.

The part of the Final Act that dealt with confidence-building measures and aspects of security and disarmament ('Basket I') aimed at 'reducing the dangers of armed conflict and of misunderstanding or miscalculation of military activities which could give rise to apprehension' (op. cit., 299). The methods chosen to achieve these aims were prior notification of major manoeuvres; exchange of observers; and an interest in disarmament (op. cit., 300–1). Under the notification scheme, manoeuvres of over 25,000 troops on the territory in Europe of any participating state would be notified through diplomatic channels 21 days in advance. States could also notify other parties of smaller-scale manoeuvres. Participating states would also invite others 'voluntarily and on a bilateral basis' to send observers to the military manoeuvres (op. cit., 300). The signatories also agreed to lessen military confrontation and promote disarmament. In general, the states recognized the complementary nature of the political and military aspects of security, and between the security of each state and Europe as a whole (op. cit., 301).

This section on security was important because in a very modest way it attempted to draw back from the 'balance of terror' – the existence of two opposing stockpiles of weapons and sets of armed forces – as a means of preventing war in Europe. It suggested that the two adversarial blocs had a common interest in not misunderstanding each other's intentions and in informing the other side of at least some military dispositions. It represented the first signs of common security.

'Basket II' contained sections on cooperation in the field of economics, science and technology, and the environment. This was to intensify cooperation between the parties irrespective of their systems. This would involve commercial exchanges, industrial cooperation, trade and industrial cooperation, science and technology, environmental protection and improvement, and cooperation in other areas such as transport, tourism and migration.

'Basket III' covered cooperation in humanitarian and other fields. Here the aim was to strengthen peace and understanding among peoples and the spiritual enrichment of the human personality. It was intended to encourage contacts on the basis of family ties, to help with the reunification of families, to facilitate travel by citizens, and to improve the conditions for tourism. Freer and wider information of all kinds would be encouraged, including access to newspapers from other states. Cultural and educational links were also to be facilitated.

The original membership of the CSCE remained at 35 until German unification in 1990, when it dropped to 34. With the break-up of the Soviet Union, all the successor states were allowed CSCE membership, although a number – such as Uzbekistan and Kazakhstan – are Asian republics. This is somewhat ironic as the CSCE only included the European part of the Soviet Union in its remit and the Russian Federation has chosen to continue with this limitation. The disintegration of Yugoslavia and of the CSFR has expanded membership further – despite the suspension of 'Yugoslavia' as a member – so that by early 1993 it stood at 52. From 1992 Japan has been able to attend CSCE meetings and some links have been made for Israel and the Arab Mediterranean states.

Institutions

At the beginning, the institutions of the CSCE were very basic. The Helsinki Conference that led to the Final Act was a gathering of diplomats with the host country – Finland – providing the secretarial services and often acting as broker between the NATO states and the WTO countries. The only original institutionalization of the CSCE process was the agreement to have a Follow-Up Meeting in Belgrade in October 1977. However, this gathering achieved little, except to establish a number of experts' meetings and to agree on a Second Follow-Up Meeting this time in Madrid in November 1980.

The Madrid Conference (which lasted until September 1983), unlike its predecessor and despite the onset of the New Cold War, did attempt to take stock of the implementation of the Final Act and to develop it. Furthermore, it established another swathe of experts' meetings and seminars, such as the CSCE Experts' Meeting on the Peaceful Settlement of Disputes, held in Athens in 1984, and the CSCE Seminar on Economics, Scientific and Cultural Cooperation in the Mediterranean, which met in Venice in October 1984. Most important of these offshoots was the Conference on Confidence- and Security-Building Measures and

Disarmament (CDE) which opened in Stockholm in January 1984 and which continued negotiations between East and West on arms control and disarmament issues when other forums were deadlocked. In September 1986 it came up with a binding agreement (see p. 272), thereby giving political impetus to the September 1986 Vienna Third Follow-Up Meeting. It should be noted that, at this time, all CSCE decisions were taken by consensus, so that any agreement had the assent of all the membership, however tacitly given.

This Vienna meeting – which was concluded in January 1989 – was the most successful until then. Its success, in a period when a new detente was budding between the two superpowers, led to a further institutionalization of the CSCE process. It agreed to the continuous monitoring of the human rights situation throughout Europe, including an annual meeting of a Conference on the Human Dimension (CDH); it established negotiations on conventional forces in Europe (CFE) between the 23 NATO and WTO states to replace the stalled MBFR talks; and it set up a 35-power CSCE Conference on Confidence- and Security-Building Measures (CSBMs) to follow on from the work of the Stockholm CDE. Finally a raft of other subsidiary meetings were agreed, including a meeting on the Protection of the Human Environment in Sofia, Bulgaria, in September and October 1989, a meeting on the Mediterranean, Palma de Mallorca, Spain, in September 1990, and a Cultural Heritage Symposium in Cracow, Poland, in May–June 1991. These were all in preparation for the Fourth Follow-Up Meeting, held in Helsinki from March to July 1992.

Because of the events of late 1989 that had led to the fall of Communist governments in Eastern Europe and to the unification of Germany, a special Heads of State or Government meeting of the CSCE was held in Paris in November 1990, at which the Cold War was consigned to the dustbin of history and the Charter of Paris for a New Europe was adopted. Furthermore, the Vienna Document 1990 (dealing with CSBMs for all CSCE states) and the CFE Treaty (between NATO and WTO states) were agreed, with the Vienna Document subsequently being updated in 1992. As a result of the Paris summit, the CSCE process – the dialogue between East and West – was changed into a more institutionalized pan-European structure with a Council of Foreign Ministers, a Committee of Senior Officials, an Assembly of Parliamentarians, a Conflict Prevention Centre and an Office of Free Elections being established. A first meeting of the Council of Ministers was held in Berlin in June 1991; the Committee of

Senior Officials met regularly in Prague where a new Secretariat was also set up.

The Fourth Follow-up Meeting held in Helsinki in 1992, and a preparatory meeting of ministers in Prague in January 1992, decided on a number of important changes in the CSCE's format and institutions. These Prague and Helsinki Documents reformulated the CSCE's structure.

At the top of the new structure are summits which are to orientate the process at the highest political level. Review conferences should aim at looking at the range of CSCE activities and propose measures to strengthen the process. There will also be other more specialized evaluation meetings to examine activities under each of the three 'baskets'.

The Council of Foreign Ministers remains the highest regular decision-making body, being assisted by the Committee of Senior Officials (CSO). The CSO is to be responsible for the management and coordination of all CSCE activities. The CSO and/or its chairman-in-office may decide on the use of the variety of CSCE's mechanisms (see below), finding support from *ad hoc* steering groups, special representatives or the chairman-in-office together with his immediate predecessor and successor (the 'troika'). The Office of Free Elections became the Office of Democratic Institutions and Human Rights (ODIHR), which has been given new responsibilities in the Helsinki Document. The office of High Commissioner for National Minorities (HCNM) has been created to both warn and mediate when actions involving national minorities may threaten international peace and security in the CSCE area. The Conflict Prevention Centre's Consultative Committee was allowed to send fact-finding missions and to assist the CSO in peacekeeping. A new Forum for Security Cooperation is to take over the CFE and CSBM activities in disarmament and in confidence- and security-building. As well as negotiating agreements in these areas it will have a consultative role in wider security matters (Ghebali, 1992, 3–8). The idea of 'consensus minus one' has been accepted whereby measures taken under the human dimension of CSCE (Basket III) can be agreed without the consent of the state concerned (Anstis, 1992, 23).

Achievements

The CSCE process is one that has reflected the flow of pan-European politics since the mid-1970s. Its success in the period until 1989 can be seen in its contribution to the amelioration of the

Cold War, and since 1989 it must be judged by its efforts to overcome more deep-seated security, economic, ethnic and political
divisions within Europe. In both cases it is hard to disentangle any
particular input from the CSCE from the activities of the member
states and of the Cold War alliances and other international
organizations. Nevertheless, it is worth examining what has been
attempted through the institutions of the CSCE, in particular in
terms of the three CSCE 'baskets'.

Basket I dealt with security questions and has had a number of
successes. Most notable were the CDE Stockholm agreement and
the CFE agreements. The Stockholm agreement was one of the
first East–West arms control arrangement to be hammered out
after the years of the New Cold War of the early 1980s. It
reviewed the progress of the Helsinki notification of manoeuvres
system and found it to be wanting. Between 1975 and 1984 about
a hundred notifications of military activities involving over million
troops had taken place. As the Helsinki Final Act was not an international treaty, the agreement was not legally binding and,
anyhow, the wording of the 'Basket I' agreement included exception clauses and much of the process was voluntary. It was not
surprising that major Soviet exercises such as ZAPAD 81 were not
notified and that the WTO invited observers to less than half of
the 20 manoeuvres it notified, with none being invited from 1979
to 1983. The CDE agreement tried to improve on this record.
Notifications were to be given of manoeuvres of at least 13,000
troops (or of 300 battle tanks); all the European part of the Soviet
Union was to be covered, not just the limited area mentioned in the
1975 Final Act; manoeuvres of over 17,000 troops were open to
observation by other CSCE states; challenge inspections were to
be allowed, at the rate of up to three a year for each CSCE state,
whereby a team of observers would be allowed in within 36 hours
of the challenge being made and would have 48 hours to carry out
an inspection; and annual calendars of military activities would
be created.

The aims of the CFE talks were to establish a secure and stable
balance of conventional forces at lower levels than then existing;
to eliminate disparities prejudicial to stability and security in
Europe; and as a high priority, to end the capability for launching
surprise attack and for initiating large-scale offensive action. This
spoke to the concern that the two sides in the Cold War had built
up such forces in Europe that their very presence was creating
fear and instability.

The Paris summit in November saw the signing of the CFE agreement between NATO and the WTO. It was seen as a major step to conventional armament parity between the two military blocs in Europe from the Atlantic to the Urals. It limited the size of forces with neither side having more than 20,000 tanks, 20,000 artillery pieces, 30,000 armoured combat vehicles, 6800 combat aircraft and 2000 attack helicopters. There was also a limit on the equipment allowed with active forces: the rest was to be placed in storage units. The armaments held by any one country were limited and regional arrangement created to prevent destabilizing force concentrations of ground equipment. To meet the various ceilings, equipment would be destroyed. An unprecedented system of detailed information exchanges, on-site inspection, challenge inspections and on-site monitoring of destruction was created by the treaty (*Survival*, 1991, 79–82).

The CFE Treaty was meant to deal with the excesses of the alliance system in Europe, but no sooner was it signed than one of those alliances – the WTO – dissolved. This in itself brought certain problems with the ratification and implementation of the treaty. Diplomacy through NATO and the newly-formed North Atlantic Cooperation Council (see above, p. 210) persuaded the successor states of the Soviet Union to adhere to the treaty (de Franchis, 1992, 12–16).

CFE drew a line under the security system of pre-1989 Europe – that of two hostile blocs. Since then, the CSCE has been coming to grips with the security problems of the new Europe which are, in NATO's language, 'multi-faceted in nature and multidirectional'. The system established in the 1982 Prague and Helsinki Documents (see above) is aimed at attempting to deal with these challenges. This new approach has two tracks. First, there are the 'Basket I' institutions. These attempt to prevent threats to the peace from arising by using a number of diplomatic instruments such as the CSO, the chairman-in-office troika, special representatives, and the Crisis Prevention Centre's Consultative Committee. The creation of a Forum for Security Cooperation – the Vienna Forum – brought together these conflict prevention and peacemaking aspects with a new role in European disarmament talks (such as the CSBM and CFE processes) and an encouragement for dialogue on wider security issues such as non-proliferation.

Secondly, there is a development of the link between human rights and international peace and security, as noted in the

Helsinki Final Act. The HCNM's good offices are to be used to attempt to prevent conflict involving national minorities from threatening peace and security (Ghebali, 1992, 5).

The CSCE has also involved itself in a modest way in peacekeeping by suggesting in the 1992 Helsinki Document that it could conduct such operations in the case of inter-state conflict. In doing so, it could call upon the expertise and resources of NATO (which has promised such assistance), the EC, the WEU and perhaps the Commonwealth of Independent States (op. cit., 6).

Finally, the CSCE has declared itself a regional arrangement under Chapter VIII of the United Nations Charter.

'Basket II' has been described as 'the Cinderella of the CSCE' (Ghebali, 1992, 7). The Helsinki Document established an Economic Forum as a specialized session of the CSO, with the job of reviewing annually the achievement of 'Basket II' commitments. The low level of activity in this area reflects the existence of stronger institutions in Europe that encourage more successfully economic and environmental cooperation. The list would include the EC, EFTA, the OECD, the UN Economic Commission for Europe, and the EBRD.

The advent of both elected governments in East and Central Europe and new soverign states arising from the break-up of the USSR, Yugoslavia and the CSFR, has given an added impetus to the CSCE's activities concerning the human dimensions. As mentioned above, an important link has been made between human rights and security with the HCNM playing a crucial role here. The establishment of ODIHR as 'the main institution of the Human Dimension' has allowed the CSCE to monitor members' implementation of this aspect at biennial reviews and more regular specialist seminars. Six CSCE states can now initiate the sending of a mission into a member state to examine human rights questions (Anstis, 1992, 23). The CSCE has also expressed more immediate concern over seeming human rights violations in former-Yugoslavia, in Georgia and in Nagorno-Karabakh. In carrying on its work, the ODIHR has cooperated with other international organizations, both governmental (such as the EBRD) and non-governmental (the International Red Cross).

The International Helsinki Federation for Human Rights (IHF) is an example of an international non-governmental organization that sprouted from the Helsinki Final Act. It had as its stated aim the promotion of compliance with the human rights provisions of the Final Act and by 1993 it was a federation of 23 national

'Helsinki' committees organized across Europe and in North America. It has small executive headquarters in Vienna, led by an Executive Director, and has sought to play an active role in the human rights domain internationally and within the CSCE process.

Contribution

The CSCE has responded to the political changes in Europe by changing its own nature. It has had three main stages in its existence: first as a diplomatic conference before the signing of the 1975 Helsinki Final Act, then as a series of follow-up meetings and negotiations in the period of growing Cold War, and finally as a pan-European-plus organization in a period when bloc confrontation had disappeared in Europe. Established as a way to ameliorate the consequences of the Cold War division of Europe, it became an instrument to manage change peacefully in post-Cold War Europe.

In its first two stages the CSCE saw its member states' interests being articulated and aggregated through the bloc system. Even the neutral and non-aligned states formed their own effective caucus. In the third stage, it has been harder to aggregate interests and divisions have appeared between Western members (for example, between the USA and France in 1992 in relation to the CSCE and NATO). These differences are likely to increase with the return of more nationalist, and perhaps less democratic, governments in Eastern Europe and the CIS states.

The great success of the CSCE has been in establishing norms – standards of behaviour – for states in their relations with each other in Europe and also for their treatment of their own peoples. As yet, these norms may not be respected throughout Europe, but their existence is acknowledged by all the CSCE states.

Attempts at socialization of governments has had some success. The new governments of East and Central Europe have accepted certain modes of behaviour more easily because of the CSCE process.

Likewise the CSCE has recruited new members into the international political system of Europe – even to the extent of accepting Asian republics as members. Whether this proves to be a wise move remains to be seen.

The CSCE has had some success at rule-making in the CSBM and CFE processes and has created a fairly intrusive system of verification to ensure the application of those agreements, although there is no judicial structure attached to the organization.

The CSCE will increasingly carry out other operations such as observing elections or, possibly, peacekeeping. However, it is likely to undertake these in tandem with other organizations such as the Council of Europe, NATO, the EC and the United Nations. The question remains whether the CSCE, with its diverse membership, will be able to compete with the more tightly knit and experienced NATO in the security field or with the EC in the realm of economic affairs.

References

Anstis, C. 1992: CSCE Mark II: Back to Helsinki from Paris via Berlin and Prague. *NATO Review* April, 18–23.

De Franchis, A. 1992: The CFE Treaty – the role of the High Level Working Group. *NATO Review* October, 12–16.

Ghebali, V.Y. 1992: The July CSCE Helsinki decisions – a step in the right direction. *NATO Review* August, 3–8.

Maresca, J.J. 1987: *To Helsinki*. Durham and London: Duke University Press.

Survival: November/December 1975, 295–301; January/February 1991, 79–82.

13

Conclusions

Chapter 1 of this book looked at international organizations, how they might best be defined and classified, and the roles and functions that they might be expected to have in the European political system. Chapter 2 traced the major diplomatic and political events in that system since the Second World War and placed the rise of particular international organizations in an historical context. The remaining chapters have dealt with a number of those organizations, examining their establishment, their institutions, their achievements (and failures) and the contribution, if any, that they made to the international political system in Europe. The aim of this chapter is to bring together the main themes of this book and to examine what role international organizations collectively have played in post-war Europe and what role they may play.

Any understanding of the position of international organizations in Europe depends to a great extent on the image of the how the international political system has functioned there since 1945. This in turn is affected by one's view of international relations more generally. It is not the intention here to examine the various theoretical debates within the study of international relations. Instead two major – and quite contradictory – interpretations of international relations will be used to explain the role of international organizations in Europe. The first of these 'paradigms' can be called 'Pluralist' or 'Liberal Institutionalists', the second 'Realist'.

The *Pluralist* or the Liberal Institutionalist approach to the study of international relations covers a wide range of writings from those of the interdependence school (Robert Keohane) to those who are called 'functionalists' (such as David Mitrany) and 'neo-functionalists' (Ernst Haas and Leon Lindberg). It goes back to the works of Norman Angell and Leonard Woolf in the period just before the outbreak of the First World War (Archer, 1992,

77). Broadly, this group have the following in common:

 i) They reject the exclusive state-centric approach of most of the Realists (see below) and place emphasis on the growth non-state actors such as international non-governmental organizations (INGO's), transnational corporations or of transgovernmental relations (Keohane and Nye, 1974, 39–62).
 ii) They see the international system as being an international society – in other words, it is more than a collection of sovereign states that have between them only those links demanded by state interests. Liberal Institutionalists consider that the ties that bind stretch across frontiers and create interdependencies – as well as rules, norms and institutions – that underpin a form of society in international relations. Their assumption is that of the solidarity, or potential solidarity, of the states comprising international society, with respect to the enforcement of the law, (Bull, 1966, 52).
 iii) Following from this, they consider that the exercise of power by states in the international system is tempered both by the considerations of international society and, in the case of military force, by the varied economic, social and other interests that states pursue which are not best open to achievement by force of arms. They have a nuanced understanding of power in the international system and consider there to be no hierarchy.
 iv) They are particularly interested in international organizations and how their functioning may affect the running of the international system.

The *Realist* approach is one that has deep historical roots in the works of Machiavelli, Clausewitz and in this century Raymond Aron, Hans Morgenthau and Martin Wight. It contrasts with the Liberal Internationalist in a number of ways:

 i) They view the international system as being state-centric and one in which anarchy – lack of government – prevails.
 ii) They thus consider that the existence of an international society is strictly limited. Interests, not feeling of solidarity determine governmental action in the international sphere.
 iii) International politics is the concept of 'interest defined in terms of power' (Morgenthau, 1960) and 'is a struggle for power' (op. cit., 27).
 iv) They regard international organizations as instruments of their member states, nothing more, nothing less.

More recently there has been a revision of this view – by the Neo-Realists such as Stephen Krasner and Richard Gilpin – which has taken into account both changes in international politics and developments in the international relations literature. They have attempted to bring a greater intellectual rigour to their work than some of their predecessors, to deal with the seeming loosening of US hegemony in the 1970s, and to include economic factors in their calculations (Ashley, 1984, 226–86). However, Gilpin does not regard the 'international economy ... as an autonomous sphere', saying that it always works 'in the context of the political struggle' (1984, 295). Likewise, while non-governmental actors in international politics are given their due, the Neo-Realists still regard states as the prime actors on the international scene.

The work of Kenneth Walz is worth mentioning here. While in the Realist tradition as mentioned above, he has shown a particular concern for the *structures* of the international system. He stressed that this system was defined by its anarchic environment and the distribution of capabilities among the states within it (Waltz, 1979, 112). Once the structure of the system changed – for example, from a bipolar to a multipoler set-up – then that distribution of power could change, as could the stability of the system as a whole (op. cit., 192)

The distinctions made above – albeit very crude ones – mean that adopting one of these approaches can subsequently affect one's understanding of the role of international organizations in Europe.

Pluralist or Liberal Institutionalists

The Pluralists would see the last 400 years or so as a transformation of the international political system in Europe from one that was fragmented, where relations were based on power and on the threat and use of force, and where the state was emerging and organizing, to a contemporary system where there is a more integrated system, and in which the state has been penetrated by a series of economic relations and non-state entities acting across frontiers. This has become a system where war is no longer expected to be used or threatened in international intercourse, where instead diplomacy and international organizations are the common mode of interaction.

Thus there has been a reformulation – a reform – of the international system in Europe away from one that was merely the relations of states, based on power, to one that is more akin to international society with generally accepted norms and rules. With this reform has come the rise of international institutions, described by Duverger as 'the collective forms or basic structures of social organisation as established by law or by human tradition' (1972, 68), and in particular international organizations, the formal and material manifestation of those institutions.

The Liberal Institutionalist interpretation of events in Europe since the Second World War is one that stresses the reformulation of the Western European political system to become more than the ungoverned relationship of states, and more an international society.

It is not surprising that a number of authors in this paradigm have placed great emphasis on the creation and development of what can be called Community Europe – the Schuman Plan and the establishment of the European Coal and Steel Community in the 1950 to 1952 period, followed in 1957 by the signing of the Treaties of Rome establishing the European Economic Community and the European Atomic Energy Community (Euratom). After all, Community Europe seemed to link 'authority to a specific activity' and loosen 'the traditional link between authority and a definite territory' (Mitrany, 1966, 125). Secondly, it replaced traditional interstate relations, first with a tight economic and political interdependency and then with a 'security community' in which the members 'will not fight each other physically, but will settle their disputes in some other way' (Deutsch, 1957, 5). Thirdly, it stressed the importance of activities of institutions and organizations working across frontiers, which would lead to a process

> whereby political actors in several distinct national settings are persuaded to shift their loyalties, expectations and political activities towards a new centre, whose institutions possess or demand jurisdiction over the pre-existing national states (Haas, 1958, 16).

The Pluralists have tended to see the European Communities as the power-house of European integration. They considered the process of integration – that of bringing together separate parts into a complex whole – as being progressive. There may have been set-backs, but the march forward to what Jean Monnet called 'building Europe' seemed inevitable: from the ECSC to the EEC; from six members to nine to 10 to 12 and perhaps up to 20 by the end of this century; from the Treaty of Rome to the Single European Act to the Treaty of Maastricht. The nature of the final outcome is disputed, it may be a federation, it may be a 'Union', it may be a Community, or it may be some political formula that is hard to categorize. But it will be an entity within which relationships between the sub-groups are qualitatively different from traditional inter-state relations.

The creation of the European Communities has fulfilled some of the hopes of the Liberal Institutionalists. It has shown that the international system can be reformed and that international relations between states can come to have that element of international *society*. It has demonstrated the utility of international institutions and organizations, and that such organizations can become important actors on the international stage. It has also shown that individuals, political parties, companies, and groups can effectively organize themselves across frontiers, almost as if those borders did not exist. For the federalists among the Pluralist writers, the next step is for the European Communities to aim at the creation of one political entity, the United States of Europe.

In February 1992 the Maastricht Treaty on European Union was signed by the member governments of the European Communities. A Liberal Institutionalist view of Maastricht would be that the Treaty – however imperfect – was another step along the relentless road towards an international society in Western Europe, though whether it would take the form of a federal Europe was still left open. They would place emphasis on the creation of a European citizenship, the move to a common foreign and security policy, the plans for economic and monetary union in the Treaty. On the institutional side they would point to the greater decision-making power for the European Parliament, the move to more majority voting by the Council of Ministers and the establishment of a Committee of the Regions. All these factors weaken the role of the individual nation-state in international relations and strengthen the forces of transnational politics – politics across state frontiers rather than between states.

At the same time that the European Communities were moving towards a European Union, the end of the Cold War – and the subsequent collapse of the Soviet bloc and the Soviet Union – added new challenges to those studying international relations, Liberal Institutionalists could take comfort from these events: the Eastern bloc was an entity that had all the trappings of traditional military power which it was occasionally prepared to use; transnational politics and domestic politics seemed to have been as important in the change of Soviet attitudes towards the West (Risse-Kappen, 1991, 185–8); the economic and social weakness of the Communist states seemed more important than their military strength. Furthermore, since the end of the Cold War, a great emphasis has been placed on international organizations in Europe. The countries of East and Central Europe, not to mention some of the CIS states, have expressed their wishes to join the EC and NATO, and a number have become members of the Council of Europe. The NACC has been formed to accommodate the desire for closer relations with NATO and the EC has signed a series of closer cooperation agreements with these states. The CSCE has become institutionaiized and its membership extended. Much time has been spent by Liberal Institutionalist writers in deciding how this plethora of organizations might interact and divide their labour (for example, Lodgaard, 1992, 57–68; Mortimer, 1992).

Of course, the end of the Cold War has produced problems for Liberal Institutionalist writers. In particular, the descent of Yugoslavia into first civil and then inter-state war has suggested that the use of force in Europe is not off the agenda. A raft of potential disputes between European states await solution: Hungary and Romania over minorities, Hungary and Slovakia about dam projects, the Baltic states and Russia concerning the rights of Russians and Russian troop presence in those states, Greece and Macedonia because of the latter's name, to name but four. Ethnic and racial tensions are growing within states and refugees are again becoming a problem in Europe.

The Liberal Institutionalist would point out that any of these problems – and not just the Yugoslav situation – would have been the cause for war in pre-1945 Europe and in many other parts of the world today. These problems, it would be said, are being dealt with by the institutions in Europe, and if solutions have not yet been found, it is because many of these organizations have only just taken on new powers and are often prevented from taking action by lack of resources or by residual state interference. Eventually international society in Europe will enforce its norms and socialize new states and governments into behaviour more appropriate for a security community, and international organizations will aid this process by performing conversion functions in the European system (Almond and Powell, 1966, 28–9). Eventually, this system will be able to function in a way similar to a domestic polity, deciding on issues of law and order, protecting the security community against outside aggression, and performing wealth-creation and distributive functions within Europe. Such a potential is implicit in the Maastricht Treaty, resting as it does on the three pillars of a common foreign and security policy (external security), home and justice cooperation (law and order), and the European Communities (wealth-creation and distribution).

Two major questions remain for Liberal Institutionalists contemplating this agenda. The first is the format of the eventual political entity: the destination of the European integration 'train' is still unknown. Suggestions range from that of a Union (the Maastricht Treaty on European Union), or a federation (Pinder, 1991), to consociation (Taylor, 1990, 172–84), a confederation (Presidents Mitterrand and Havel), or just 'an experiment in pooling sovereignty' (Keohane and Hoffmann, 1990, 277). Depending on the answer to this question are views about the extent to which the EC – as the presumed core and motor of any future European arrangement – should 'deepen', in other words intensify its policy-making. The more 'state-like' the desired outcome, the more the EC will be expected to 'deepen'.

The second question is related to the first and it concerns the definition of what Europe is. Given that, in the Liberal Institutionalist understanding of events, the EC will continue to be central to any plans to 'build Europe' (whatever form the house may take), which states should be allowed inside the 'house' and which obliged to remain outside? For many, this is just a practical question, the answer to which depends not only on the desire of governments to become part of the EC enterprise, but also on their economic and political ability to do so. Thus, some states can be placed in a sort of 'out-house' where they can prepare for full membership.

However, a deeper consideration of the issue brings out a number of concerns. Is there an eastwards limit of Community Europe? Are there some states – such as Turkey, Russia or the Ukraine – that should not be considered European for this purpose, and, if so, what reason is to be given for any decision? Is there a link between 'deepening' and the widening process? Will the Scandinavian states, with their antipathy to federalism, slow down 'deepening'? If the EC is 'deepened' will this not mean that East and Central European candidates for membership will be kept constantly in the 'out-house' because they are unable to catch up with this process? Can the European Community – in whatever form – continue its present seemingly successful economic policies if it is open to a wide membership? Could this not bring a high economic cost – similar to that experienced by West Germany after German unification – and social discontent among existing EC citizens mixed with unfulfilled expectations of the citizens of new members? Finally, what relations would a widened EC have with the USA? Would the US be willing to continue to contribute to the defence effort of an even greater economic rival than at present? Would it become less an ally, more a rival? The Liberal Institutionalist agenda, with its emphasis on organizations and on cooperation, has so far skirted round many of these issues.

The Realists

How might the Realists and their modern counterparts, the Neo-Realists, interpret the role of international organizations in Europe? (The views here will be called Realist. As many of the original Realist writers are no longer able to comment on events in contemporary Europe, the 'New' Realists can perhaps take on their mantle.)

Unlike the Pluralist approach, the Realists would look back over the past 400 years of European history and they would not see progress within this system. Indeed, they would see two major enduring elements: that of the nation-state and that of the exercise of power. Thus they would not be surprised at the regular occurrence of war when state interest clashes against state interest. They see the main constraint on the descent into war not as being any feeling of international society nor the actions of such international organizations as the UN or the EEC, but a system of balance of power. So, for example, Hans Morgenthau pointed to the balance of power between major powers within the international system as 'an essentially stabilizing factor' (1960, 167). The occasion of war in the period up to the present day could thus be explained mainly in terms of the maintenance or the break-down of a balance of power system.

But what about the post-war period in Europe, the supposed heyday of international society and international organization in Western Europe, according to the Liberal Internationalists? The Realist interpretation is different.

First, the Realists see the process of European integration and the creation of the EC as a result of the power play in the continent, which means the Cold War. The process is explained in terms of both a response to the Soviet threat and as the consequence of US action in Europe, though these two explanations mostly go hand-in-hand. John Mearsheimer claims that cooperation among Western democracies was not caused by interdependence, but that it is 'more likely that the prime cause was the Cold War, and that this was the main reason that intra-EC relations have flourished' (1990, 46). Josef Joffe's opinion is that the United States 'has acted as the indispensable catalyst of integration – as a power greater than each and all that protected the West Europeans not only against others, but also against themselves' (1992, 47). Or put more trenchantly:

With the United States serving as night watchman, relative-gains concerns among the Western European states were mitigated and . . . [they] were willing to allow their economies to become tightly interdependent. . . . In effect, relations among EC states were spared the effects of anarchy . . . because the United States served as the ultimate arbiter within the Alliance (Mearsheimer, 1990, 47).

Taking this view further, the Treaty of Paris which established the ECSC and the Treaty of Rome that set up the EEC can be seen as attempts by the West Europeans to build up their economies – especially the German economy – to counteract the Soviet threat in Europe, and was coalition-building by the USA. The US was faced with the perceived Soviet threat at the start of the 1950s in both Korea in the Far East and in Berlin and Central Europe, and needed strong and united allies. The creation of the ECSC, the plans for a European Defence Community and the signing of the EC Treaty represented solid steps on the way to creating a Western-oriented, capitalistic grouping on the continent of Europe that would be a natural ally of the USA in its attempt to deter the spread of Soviet influence. Finally, the process locked West Germany into a system of alliance and community that guaranteed that its recovery would not be at the expense of the security of its neighbours, especially France.

Indeed, the role of the United Kingdom can be seen by the Realists as proof of their interpretation. When the Community idea was first mooted in the early 1950s, Britain's presence was not needed. It was already tied closely in defence terms to the US, and the United Kingdom had a world role that in many ways supplemented that of the USA. The main aim – in European balance of power terms – was to get West Germany and France cooperating as closely as possible together, and to build up a German army that would be under wider West European control. There was however a subsidiary aim of getting the British more heavily committed to the defence of continental Europe, and this was planned through the creation of the EDC, with which Britain was meant to be associated. Indeed, in that case the US *did* place pressure on the British to sign up, but when the whole enterprise failed and the British produced their own non-Community organization – the WEU – and at the same time committed their troops and air force to the defence of Europe, then the US Administration did not complain. By 1961, the French under President de Gaulle, had become very anti-American. If the EC was going to fail then, reasoned some in the US Administration, it would be better to have the British present to pick up the bits, as they had done with the EDC. If it was to succeed, then the British should be a member to guide the new enterprise along the Atlantic path.

The last great upsurge of integration activity in the EC – that from 1985 to 1990, from the creation of the single European market to the negotiations for the Maastricht Treaty – can be explained by the Realists in similar terms. It was a period when the West European doubts about the US presence in Europe reached new heights. There were those who felt that the US might become more isolationist and no longer support their West European partners. After all, the US was becoming more of a Pacific power and more interested in its own hemisphere. Yet, despite the rise of Mr Gorbachev, the Soviet Union was still a power to be reckoned with. Some West Europeans – especially in the French government in the mid-1980s – wanted to consider the building of an alternative security base to that provided by NATO. This led to the revival of the WEU and pressure for the EC to develop a parallel process dealing with foreign and security questions. An alternative view was concerned that the US had too strong a defence presence in Europe and that Washington's New Cold War policies were adversely affecting the security of the continent. The only way for the West Europeans to emerge from the shadow cast by the Pentagon was for them to build up their own foreign and security policy within the WEU and European Political Cooperation. Furthermore, the creation of a single European market would strengthen the West European's ability not just to pay for their own defence but to uphold their commercial interests in trade negotiations should the United States decide to pressurize them in those forums.

The Realists, when viewing the Maastricht Treaty would place emphasis on it being an international agreement between the governments of the 12 member states. They would therefore see it as a compromise between those states' national interests with parts of the Treaty being inserted to satisfy particular governments. Thus the United Kingdom has opt-out clauses on EMU and on Social Policy. The Spanish and other 'Club Med' states obtained the Cohesion Fund. The French and the German governments wanted EMU and a common foreign and security policy. Furthermore, they would regard the European Union as being an instrument for the emerging hegemony of its strongest state – Germany.

A Realist view of the end of the Cold War places the emphasis on the triumph of the West's diplomacy and military dispositions. A relatively united NATO on the INF issue, increased Western defence expenditure in the early 1980s, together with the threat of President Reagan's Strategic Defence Initiative, saw off the Soviet threat, or at least brought the Soviet leaders to the negotiating table to accept Western terms (Risse-Kappen, 1991, 173).

Realist concerns after the end of the Cold War are quite different from that of the Liberal Institutionalists, and place international organizations in Europe in a different light. In Mearsheimer's view (written in 1990), 'if the present Soviet threat to Western Europe is removed, and American forces depart for home, relations among the EC states will be fundamentally altered. . . . Western European states will begin viewing each other with greater fear and suspicion, as they did for centuries before the onset of the Cold War' (1990, 47). Bipolarity, nuclear weapons and an equal military balance had kept the peace in Europe for 45 years. With an end to bipolarity and balance and a reduction in nuclear weapons, NATO will disappear and Europe would 'probably be substantially more prone to violence than the past 45 years' (op. cit., 6). Mearsheimer's answers to this new threat was that Britain, the US and the Soviet Union should balance-off rising German power, Germany should be allowed nuclear weapons, and hyper-nationalism shoul.' be kept at bay, especially in Eastern Europe (op. cit., 54–5).

All this would suggest that, from the Realist perspective, it would be worthwhile for the West Europeans to keep a United States presence in Europe 'because, so far, the twentieth century has not produced a model of European security that could stand without the United States' (Joffe, 1992, 47). At what price the US would be prepared to stay in Europe, and whether Europe would be prepared to pay that price remain open questions.

Prospects

The two sets of views outlined above – the Realist and the Pluralist – give both a different picture of the role of international organizations in Europe in the past and currently, and a variation in their importance in the 'New Europe'. Both have hard questions to ask about the future of international organizations in post-Cold War Europe. The Pluralists are concerned about which tasks particular institutions may adopt and how best to extend their membership. They have been debating the eventual form of the European society that they see developing and how it might fit in with the other political layers in Europe. The Realists, meanwhile, see NATO and the EC being substantially weakened – if not swept away – by the end of the Cold War, with a jump 'Back to the Future' (Mearsheimer, 1990, after Zemeckis), meaning the pre-Cold War period. Unless a power balance is restored in Europe then the continent will descend into the sort of internecine wars seen before 1914 and in the inter-war period.

Should then the emphasis be placed on institution-building or on balance-creating in Europe? The immediate response to the collapse of communism and the Soviet bloc might suggest the latter. It would seem that, without the Soviet threat and with a retracting United States, European institutions are apt to disintegrate. The problems with the Maastricht Treaty and with the European Economic Area, US–EC disputes within GATT and the inability of any of the institutions to deal with the disputes in ex-Yugoslavia seem to display the shortcomings of the Liberal Institutionalist approach. The supporters of institution-building might answer that the various organizations have scarcely been given a chance.

It may also be that the two viewpoints are asking the wrong questions. If European politics is seen in terms of inter-state power, then the diagnosis will be 'lack of balance' or 'too few nuclear weapons'. This ignores not only the massive changes in European society over the past 50 years that have altered certainly the western part of the continent from a collection of sovereign states to a Community, states, regions and localities with a variety of relations between them. It also ignores all that has been learnt from the Cold War period with its economic waste and its effect on statecraft (Gaddis, 1992, 38 and 43). It presumes that the Cold War changed nothing. If Europe's problems are seen in institutional terms, the danger is that emphasis will be placed on finding the right organizational form or constitution to the neglect of more deep-seated problems.

Perhaps reference should be made here to a more complex and thoughtful approach advanced in the works of Johan Galtung, especially in his book *The European Community: A Superpower in the Making* (1973). According to Galtung, the Europe of the EC works by using three aspects of structural power: exploitation, fragmentation and penetration.

Exploitation means that in any exchange relationship, one group gets more out of it than the other. For example, the free market of the EC might allow companies from Northern Europe to exploit cheap labour in Southern Europe and evade addressing the social problems of those areas. This is known as social dumping, and is an issue that the EC itself has tried to address through its Social Charter and Cohesion Fund.

Fragmentation is the old tactic of divide and rule. In this case, the centre (Brussels) is united in the form of the Commission negotiating on behalf of the whole of the Community, while the periphery is divided into a hierarchy of non-EC European and Third World states that wish to do business with the Communities.

Penetration means the way that the dominant area can enter into the dominated regions, such as by co-opting their élites and by an inequality in the distribution of inequality. This would lead to the totality of the rich areas seeing it in their interests to co-opt the rulers of the peripheral areas and exploit the population there in order to get, for example, cheap raw materials.

So these three factors – exploitation, fragmentation and penetration – have led to a structure of dominance and dependence. The centre – the EC in Brussels and the industry and commerce of Northern Europe – is dominant; whilst the periphery – the outer areas of the EC, the Third World and, increasingly, the East and Central European states – become dependent.

The dangers are then that the New Europe will become one divided by economic and social factors. The ethnic conflicts in the Balkans will be largely ignored and 'locked out' by the Western part of Europe by, for example, tighter immigration laws. A continuation of economic recession, or a new economic downturn in the future, will set region against region and worker against worker. Economic and monetary union could be paid for by the poorer regions. Wider environmental questions will go unsolved as the economic cost of action and the fear of lost markets increases.

As well as building a structure that may bring international peace to Europe, the political leadership of European countries has the task of building social peace. The institutions are in place for the construction of a European security community – NATO, NACC, WEU, the EC and the European Union, and CSCE. A more serious question is whether the European Union can contribute to the social peace.

References

Almond, G. and Powell, G.B. 1966: *Comparative Politics: A Developmental Approach.* Boston: Little, Brown.

Archer, C. 1992: *International Organization*, 2nd edn. London: Routledge.

Ashley, R.K. 1984: The Poverty of neorealism. *International Organization* 38:2, 226–86.

Bull, H. 1966: The Grotian conception of international society. In Butterfield, H. and Wight. M. (eds.), *Diplomatic Investigation* (London: Allen & Unwin).

Deutsch, K. 1957: *Political Community and the North Atlantic Area.* Princeton: Princeton University Press.

Duverger, M. 1972: *The Study of Politics.* London: Nelson.

Gaddis, J.L. 1992/3: International relations theory and the end of the Cold War. *International Security* 17:3, 5–58.

Galtung, J. 1973: *The European Community. A Superpower in the Making.* Oslo: Universitetsforlaget.

Gilpin, R.G. 1984: The richness of the tradition of political realism. *International Organization* 38:2, 287–304.

Joffe, J. 1992: Collective security and the future of Europe. *Survival* Spring, 36–50.

Keohane, R. and Hoffmann, S. 1990: Conclusions: Community politics and institutional change. In Wallace, W. (ed.), *The Dynamics of European Integration* (London: Pinter), 276–300.

Keohane, R. and Nye, J. 1974: Transgovermental relations and international organizations. *World Politics* XXVII, 39–62.

Lodgaard, S. 1992: Competing schemes for Europe: the CSCE, NATO and the European Union. *Security Dialogue* 23:3, 57–68.

Measheimer, J.J. 1990: Back to the future: instability in Europe after the Cold War. *International Security* 15:1, 5–56.

Mitrany, D. 1966 *A Working Peace System.* Chicago: Quadrangle Books.

Morgenthau, H.J. 1960: *Politics Among Nations. The Struggle for Power and Peace.* New York: Alfred A. Knopf.

Mortimer, E. 1992: *European Security after the Cold War.* London: Brasseys for IISS, Adelphi Paper 271.

Pinder, J. 1991: *The Building of a Union.* Oxford: Oxford University Press.

Risse-Kappen, T. 1991: Did 'peace through strength' end the Cold War? Lessons from INF. *International Security* 16:1, 162–88.

Taylor, P. 1990: Consociationalism and federalism as approaches to international integration. In Groom, A.J.R. and Taylor, P. (ed.), *Frameworks for International Cooperation* (London: Pinter), 172–84.

Waltz, K.N. 1979: *Theory of International Politics.* New York: Random House.

Index